SURFACE WATER

SURFACE WATER

ROBERT BOWEN
Ph.D., B.Sc.

Professor and Head, Department of Geology,
The University of Sierra Leone, Freetown, Sierra Leone

1807 1982

A WILEY–INTERSCIENCE PUBLICATION

JOHN WILEY & SONS
NEW YORK & TORONTO

Published in the U.S.A. and Canada by
Wiley–Interscience, a Division of
John Wiley & Sons, Inc.,
New York

British Library Cataloguing in Publication Data
Bowen, Robert
Surface water.
1. Water
I. Title
551.48   GB980

ISBN 0-471-87418-3

WITH 44 TABLES AND 32 ILLUSTRATIONS

©APPLIED SCIENCE PUBLISHERS LTD 1982

First published in 1982 in Great Britain by
Applied Science Publishers Ltd

Photoset in Malta by Interprint Limited
Printed in Great Britain by Galliard (Printers) Ltd, Great Yarmouth

Contents

Introduction

Next to air, water is the most essential of human requirements. The hydrosphere—the waters of the Earth, its oceans, rivers and lakes—is vital, constituting a feature unique in the solar system and one responsible for physical and climatic phenomena characteristic of the planet. Water moves through the hydrologic cycle and runs the heat engine of the Earth, approximately 97% of it occurring in the oceans. These contain vast natural resources including abundant plant and animal life and they assist in cleansing the atmosphere by becoming the final repository of air and land pollutants of which many are man-made. Unfortunately their ability to do this is diminishing because of rising pollution by toxicants such as DDT, nuclear by-products such as strontium-90 and oil spills. The oceans contain huge quantities of various substances mostly originating from the atmosphere, biological activity, river transport after rock weathering, groundwater, spreading zones along mid-oceanic ridges and crustal out-gassing. After hydrogen and oxygen, the commonest elements in them are Cl, Na, Mg, S, K, Ca, Br, C and B.

The atmosphere and the oceans together cooperate in an energy cycle important in controlling and equalising the Earth's surface temperature. Solar rays impinge upon the tropics most directly and at the poles least directly, areas between receiving them at intermediate angles. As these depart from 90°, the amount of reflected solar energy increases so that the quantity of heat retained by the planet's surface increases from the poles to the equator, tropical waters being warmer than polar ones. As the latter are heavier, they sink and initiate a slow deep ocean circulation compensated by polewards movement of surface waters to replace them. This pattern maintains polar climates at a higher temperature than otherwise would be the case. This interaction of air and oceans powered

1

by solar energy provides a reasonably favourable environment for life on Earth. Its importance may be inferred from the situation in Antarctica which, having practically no warm water circulation, is ice covered. Local variations in climate are caused by local variations in energy patterns of atmosphere and oceans. For instance, the differential heating of oceanic areas may release tremendous energy in tropical storms such as typhoons and hurricanes. Through evaporation and condensation processes, water is transferred from the oceans to the continents. Oceans lose more water in this way than they gain by precipitation and this is of crucial importance since the ensuing imbalance provides the relatively minute quantity of fresh water sustaining life on land. There water is very unevenly distributed and that flowing in river systems comprises the major life support and the bulk of the surface fresh water supply impounded in lakes. Deposition of precipitation on the ground represents the commencement of water circulation in the lithosphere. Its disposal is accomplished either by evaporation or evapotranspiration, by runoff or by percolation into the ground. Some water moving into the soil zone is retained, some penetrates the zone of aeration and some attains the zone of saturation thus adding to groundwater. Global detention on land of water as soil moisture, stream runoff and snow accumulation reaches a maximum during March–April and seasonal variation in this is paralleled by an inverse pattern of oceanic storage so that the oceans in October are estimated to have $7.5 \times 10^{18} \, cm^3$ more water than in the spring (although this is equivalent to a sea level change of only a centimetre or two). The residence time of water on land is short, about 10 to 100 days, as compared with that for the oceans of 40 000 years. This applies to the liquid phase because ice caps and glaciers have storage times which may be as much as 10 000 years.

Groundwater is a stable component of the hydrologic cycle of great importance to Man and most of it originates from precipitation which has percolated through the soil layers into the saturated region below. This has been discussed in detail by the author in a book on the subject published by Applied Science Publishers Ltd, London, in 1980.

The present volume is to some extent complementary to the earlier one and it is divided into five sections. The first deals with the hydrologic cycle, the second with the atmosphere, the third with rivers, the fourth with surface water bodies such as lakes and reservoirs, snow and ice, and the fifth with the oceans. It is intended to provide a useful survey of these topics and a general picture of surface water, a resource the importance of which cannot be exaggerated and one well described by Pindar as 'the best of all things'.

CHAPTER 1

The Hydrologic Cycle

1.1. SOME PRELIMINARY OBSERVATIONS ON WATER

Although most people think that England has a wet climate, the country actually receives only a moderate quantity of rainfall annually. However, this is spread out evenly throughout the year and does not prevent a severe drought arising at least once quinquennially. Many countries are much wetter and often have monsoonal rainfall whereas in other parts of the world extremely dry regimens are to be found. Of course rainfall is only one aspect of a dynamic water cycle operating on Earth and constitutes an end product of a process commencing with the heating of the surface water of seas and lakes by the sun which gives rise to evaporation. A humid mass of air is created above the water surface and, becoming further warmed by it, ascends into the atmosphere due to its being lighter than the overlying cold air. The study of water and its various modes of occurrence on and in the planet constitutes the science of hydrology.

Water is composed of oxygen and hydrogen, the common isotopic species being $^1H_2{}^{16}O$. Oxygen is Man's chief energy source and it is responsible for respiration and combustion processes. Hydrogen is unique among elements in that it possesses only a single electron and therefore is capable not simply of attaching itself thereby, i.e. through a valence bond, but can also link with another atom using one of the latter's electrons, i.e. through a hydrogen bond. In the water molecule, two hydrogen atoms are attached to each oxygen atom and the process can be repeated indefinitely. Essentially this phenomenon depends upon the fact that the hydrogen atomic shell has room for an additional electron and the oxygen atomic shell (in this case the outer of two) has room for two additional electrons.

The idea of species of water arose from the work of the Nobel Prize Winner Harold C. Urey (1894–1981) when in 1934 he discovered 'heavy water', i.e. water containing not hydrogen with an atomic weight of 1, but deuterium with an atomic weight of 2. This compound may be written either as $^2H_2^{16}O$ or as $D_2^{16}O$ or simply as D_2O. Later it was discovered that there is a third isotope of hydrogen, actually a radioactive one called tritium. It is now known that oxygen also has a series of isotopes, the significant ones being the common one ^{16}O, ^{17}O and ^{18}O. It may be seen from this that it is possible to prepare water containing six different isotopes and these may be combined in no less than eighteen different ways. Further it may be stated that if the various types of ions into which removal or addition of electrons may change atoms of water are taken into account, then a total of thirty-three species of this compound can be obtained. Naturally the species $^1H_2^{16}O$ is by far the most common. Deuterium occurs in amounts of about 200 ppm in natural waters while oxygen-18 is almost as rare, occurring at 1000 ppm. It is also important to note that the properties of heavy water differ somewhat from those of normal water, i.e. the familiar $^1H_2^{16}O$. For instance, D_2O has a slightly higher boiling point than the latter (101·4°C) and it freezes at a higher temperature (3·8°C). Finally, it is characterised by a higher viscosity than ordinary water. Perhaps the most surprising feature of deuterium is that it is inert so that plants will not grow in it and rats given it to drink will die of thirst, an indication that it is less reactive than ordinary hydrogen. Tritium will be discussed later in detail and here it is necessary only to mention that this radioisotope is formed in the highest layers of the atmosphere through cosmic ray bombardment and other processes, thereafter precipitating in rain or snow. Its half-life is 12·26 years and therefore after about 50 years it disappears from the environment. This characteristic can be used to 'date' groundwater and vadose water. Wines have also been dated by their tritium contents.

A. M. Buswell and W. H. Rodebush have summarised the isotopic species of water and their results may be stated thus:[1]

$^1H_2^{16}O, ^1H^2H^{16}O, ^2H^2H^{16}O$ (D_2O), $^3H^1H^{16}O, ^3H^2H^{16}O, ^3H^3H^{16}O,$
$^1H_2^{17}O, ^1H^2H^{17}O, ^2H^2H^{17}O, ^3H^1H^{17}O, ^3H^2H^{17}O, ^3H^3H^{17}O,$
$^1H_2^{18}O, ^1H^2H^{18}O, ^2H^2H^{18}O, ^3H^1H^{18}O, ^3H^2H^{18}O, ^3H^3H^{18}O, ^1H^+,$
$^2H^+, ^3H^+, ^1H^{16}O^-, ^2H^{16}O^-, ^3H^{16}O^-, ^1H^{17}O^-, ^2H^{17}O^-, ^3H^{17}O^-,$
$^1H^{18}O^-, ^2H^{18}O^-, ^3H^{18}O^-, -^{16}O^-, -^{17}O^-, -^{18}O^-$

This is the list of the thirty-three species of water referred to above.

Although water molecules exist in disorder in the liquid state, this is not the case with ice. Here the structure is crystalline and the arrangement of the oxygen and hydrogen atoms has been determined by X-ray diffraction, results showing that the two hydrogens are bonded to the oxygen roughly at right angles to each other (in fact at an angle of 105°) with the overall structure being hexagonal as in snowflakes. Every group has a centrally placed molecule surrounded by four others at the corner of a tetrahedron all of which are joined by hydrogen bonds. Interacting attractive forces produce an inwardly directed pressure and when the temperature reaches 0°C collapse occurs through thermal agitation of the molecules. Ice can melt at a lower temperature if external pressure is applied; this no doubt promotes earlier collapse. The average distance between the centre of an oxygen atom and the centre of the next one in an ice crystal is 2·72 Å (1 Ångstrom unit = 0·000 000 01 cm), but when melting occurs this increases to 2·9 Å.

In liquid water there is a random arrangement of molecules and this haphazard internal situation constantly changes so that the angle between two hydrogen atoms in a water molecule does not remain approximately a right angle but varies. Each atom of oxygen may attract not just two extra hydrogen atoms as in ice, but as many as five or six with each hydrogen atom being surrounded by as many as three oxygen atoms. Molecules flow by a rolling action and this is preceded by a breaking of at least one hydrogen bond, a fairly easy process which accounts for the relatively low viscosity of water.

Water is an excellent solvent for electrolytes such as sodium chloride and possesses a high dielectric constant, in fact the highest of any ordinary liquid. The reason for this is because of its molecular arrangement which means that in an agglomeration of molecules of water a hydrogen atom does not share its electron equally with the oxygen atom to which it is attached; in the situation that arises the electron lies closer to the oxygen. Consequently, the hydrogen atoms acquire a positive charge and the oxygen atoms a negative one. Hence when a substance is dissolved, the oxygen atoms are attracted to the positive ions and the hydrogens to the negative ones. In fact, water molecules which surround a positive ion take up an orientation with their oxygens next to the ion and vice versa. The water molecules thus separate and neutralise ions.

Contrary to common belief, water is a very good insulator if it is pure. The conductivity often observed is due to impurities in the water and not to the water itself. Water has a high specific heat and the strong bonding of its molecules results in the high melting and boiling points of the liquid which has a maximum density at 4°C of 1·000 g/ml.

1.2. HYDROLOGY

The Ad Hoc Panel of the Federal Council for Science and Technology in a report published in *Scientific Hydrology* in June 1962 defined hydrology as follows:

'Hydrology is the science that treats of waters of the Earth, their occurrence, circulation, distribution, their chemical and physical properties and their reaction with their environment, including their relation with living things. The domain of hydrology embraces the full life history of water on the Earth.'

To this definition, it may be added that the basis is the hydrologic cycle, i.e. the perpetual circulation of water and water vapour which penetrates three fundamental components of the planet, namely:

(i)   the atmosphere (that gaseous region overlying the hydrosphere and the lithosphere);
(ii)   the hydrosphere (water covering the Earth's surface);
(iii) the lithosphere (the outer part of the crust of the planet in which groundwater is located).

1.3. THE HYDROLOGIC CYCLE

Sometimes referred to as the water cycle, this is powered by solar energy and gravity. Water evaporates from oceans and continents (mostly from the former) and is carried into the atmosphere. It may drift for hundreds of kilometres before returning to the planetary surface as precipitation (rain, snow, hail or sleet). After falling, precipitation may undergo one of the following processes:

On land
(i)   interception by vegetation which prevents it reaching the ground;
(ii) collection on the Earth's surface where impermeable soils or rocks occur;

(iii) seepage into permeable soils or rocks;
(iv) contribution to streams which flow to lower ground and ultimately reach oceans;

On the oceans
(v) recombination with their surface waters.

When precipitation ceases, water in pools or on vegetation re-evaporates. Streams flow into river systems and the water eventually discharges into lakes or seas. Some water percolates into the earth and ultimately reaches the natural level of free groundwater, the water table. Deeper penetration is prevented by an aquiclude, a watertight geological stratum, hence groundwater tends to flow horizontally and may get to land at a lower altitude and reappear at the surface as a spring or enter a lake or river. Such an underground water reservoir below a water table constitutes an unconfined aquifer. An aquifer may be confined if the water-bearing stratum is trapped between two impervious layers. In such a case, the level to which the trapped water would rise if there were no overlying confining stratum, essentially an imaginary surface, is termed the piezometric surface. Completely confined aquifers are extremely rare because the impermeable confining layer (aquiclude) overlying them is usually faulted and thus can permit water to leak through. Additionally, if such aquifers have any outflow, no matter how small, water losses must be replaced if they are to continue in existence. Areas where infiltration is sufficient to make up for losses elsewhere are known as recharge areas. For confined aquifers the recharge area is usually located at a higher elevation where the aquifers are actually no longer confined. Fundamental aspects of aquifers and indeed groundwater generally have been examined by the author in his book on this subject published by Applied Science Publishers Ltd in 1980.[2]

The main processes involved in the hydrologic cycle are evaporation, precipitation, interception, infiltration, seepage, storage in various water bodies and two others now to be discussed, runoff and transpiration.

Where water falls on an impermeable land surface it flows away as runoff. In fact, the principal impact which Man makes upon the hydrologic cycle is found in his interference with natural surface runoff. For example, prior to the construction of the first Aswan Dam in Egypt most of the Nile's annual flow went to the sea and through evaporation into the atmosphere. Although the engineering works have not reduced loss by evaporation, the new Aswan High Dam diverts about four-fifths of the water from the original destination, the sea, to farm fields. A deleterious side effect is that the Nile no longer transports the fertile sediments of upland erosion into the fields it waters, as the new Aswan High Dam traps silt instead of letting it through with the water as did the old one. Transpiration occurs as a result of the drawing up of soil water through capillary action contributing, together with moisture from above, by means of roots and vegetable matter to leaves which return it, as water vapour, to the atmosphere. Where evaporation and transpiration occur in conjunction, they may be termed evapotranspiration.

That quantity of water going through the hydrologic cycle during any given period for a particular area can be evaluated by using the hydrologic or continuity equation

$$I - O = \pm \Delta S$$

where I refers to the total inflow of surface runoff, groundwater and total precipitation, O refers to the total outflow including evapotranspiration, sub-surface and surface runoff from the area and ΔS refers to the change in storage in the various forms of retention and interception. Figure 1.1 illustrates the hydrologic cycle.

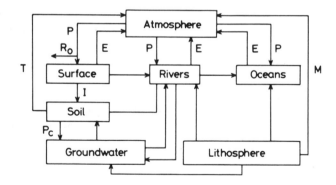

FIG. 1.1. The hydrologic cycle. P, precipitation; E, evaporation; T, transpiration; I, infiltration; P_c, percolation; R_o, runoff; M, magmatic or volcanic water.

Quantification is difficult because precise data are unavailable. However, it is believed that about $4 \times 10^5 \, \text{km}^3$ ($4 \times 10^{20} \, \text{g}$) of water are evaporated from the planetary surface annually, the oceans accounting for this and inland water bodies and wet soils contributing the residual 15·6%. The inland evaporation mainly takes place into relatively dry air masses, but a great deal of the water evaporated from the oceans is transported by maritime air masses (which are characterised by a much higher content of water vapour than continental air masses) to the continents where the total precipitation is thought to be approximately $100\,000\,km^3$ per year. Of this, perhaps more than a third returns to the seas as runoff and balances the excess of precipitation over evaporation inland.

It has been calculated that the mean annual precipitation for the Earth is 86·4 cm and this must be balanced by an equal amount of evaporation. Ninety-seven percent of all the planetary water, i.e. more than $1\cdot234 \times 10^{15}\,m^3$, is contained in the oceans. In 1964, V. T. Chow gave the distribution of fresh water on the Earth as follows:[3] polar ice, glaciers, 75%; groundwater between 762 and 3810 m, 14%; groundwater between the surface and 762 m, 11%; lakes, 0·3%; soil moisture, 0·08%; atmosphere, 0·035%; and streams, 0·03%. These are stationary estimates and it must be remembered that although the water content of the atmosphere is relatively small at any given instant, vast amounts of water actually pass through it.

The functioning of the hydrologic cycle depends upon solar energy which evaporates water and warms humid air. Of the two million terrawatts continuously impinging on the Earth, just over half actually reaches the surface, the rest being absorbed or reflected by clouds and the atmosphere. Of that arriving on the surface, about one-third is used continually in evaporation. If the atmosphere and the Earth are considered as separate entities, then the radiation and conduction fail to give balanced heat budgets because the planetary surface has a net gain and the free atmosphere a net loss. However, a link between gain and loss is provided by the hydrologic cycle. That portion of the heat absorbed by the Earth's surface which is expended in evaporation is thereby transferred to latent heat which is later released to the atmosphere when water vapour condenses to form clouds.

Evaporation is maximal where relatively cool air sweeps over warmer oceans and the highest evaporation values are found in the northern hemisphere in the Atlantic and Pacific trade wind belts south of 30°N. Additionally, high values occur over the Northwest Pacific and North Atlantic oceans in the winter when cold and dry continental air masses move over warmer waters.

The average life of water vapour molecules in the atmosphere is variable, ranging from an hour to several days. Latent heat is normally liberated far away from the regions where evaporation took place. This is especially the case in the trade wind belts supplying much of the water vapour eventually precipitating in middle and high latitudes. The circulation of water may be seen therefore to comprise a crucial part of heat transfer from low to high latitudes as well as from oceans to continents. As regards the latitudinal belts of the oceans, there is a rather uniform pattern of evaporation characterising them, but the return flow of water to the oceans through river systems is markedly imbalanced. This results from the concentration of major rivers draining into the Atlantic Ocean as compared with the relatively small number of major discharge outlets into the Pacific Ocean. Table 1.1 illustrates this and is based upon US Geological Survey data.

TABLE 1.1

ESTIMATED RUNOFF OF THE EARTH'S MAJOR RIVER SYSTEMS

River	m^3/sec (hundreds)
Discharging into the Atlantic Ocean	
Eastern North America	
Mississippi	175·5
St. Lawrence	141·5
S. Atlantic slope	92·0
N. Atlantic slope	59·4
Europe	
Danube	63·7
Rhine	21·5
Rhone	16·7
Dnieper	16·7
Elbe	6·8
Garonne	6·8
Don	6·8
South America	
Amazon	1 018·8
Orinoco	169·8
Parana	148·9
Uruguay	38·5
Africa	
Congo	452·8
Niger	92·3
Orange/Zambesi	99·6
Nile	28·3
Total: Atlantic	2 656·4

TABLE 1.1 (continued)

River	m^3/sec (hundreds)
Discharging into the Pacific Ocean	
Columbia	97·6
Colorado	6·5
Yukon	50·9
Australia	100·2
Japan/Korea	63·7
Middle latitude Asian rivers	638·8
Total: Pacific	957·7
Grand total: Atlantic and Pacific oceans	3 614·1

Additional and related relevant data are appended in Table 1.2.

TABLE 1.2
OCEANIC AND LAND DRAINAGE AREAS

Ocean	Area in km^2 (millions)	Land area drained in km^2 (millions)	% of total land area	% of area drained to ocean area
Atlantic	98	67	45·3	68·5
Indian	65·5	17	11·5	26·1
Antarctic	32	14	9·4	43·5
Pacific	165	18	12·1	10·8
Interior drainage	—	32	21·7	—
Total	360·5	148	100·0	

This demonstrates that the Atlantic not only drains the largest part of the land surface of the Earth, but also that it has the highest proportion of land area drained to oceanic area.

1.4. SOME BASIC PRINCIPLES OF HYDROLOGY

The science is a well-established one and was initiated in modern times in the eighteenth century. Thereafter, continuous attempts have been made in order to refine the understanding of every distinct phase of the hydrologic cycle as well as interrelationships between the various phases. Perhaps the most significant aspects may be summarised as follows:

(i) Groundwater movement.

Groundwater occurs below the planetary surface in the zone of saturation (see Fig. 1.2). It is recognised that groundwater moves from high pressure points to low pressure points, i.e. down gradient. Such gradients are frequently (but not invariably) due to the types of rock involved and their structure.

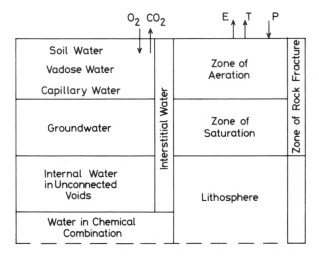

FIG. 1.2. Zone of saturation and contained groundwater in relation to the subsurface water profile. E, evaporation; T, transpiration; P, precipitation.

(ii) Velocity of flowing water.

It is recognised that either on the surface of the Earth or underground the velocity of flowing water is governed by differences in pressure head or slope as well as by the resistance of the confining channel or aquifer.

(iii) Water as a solvent.

It is known that water can dissolve and transport large quantities of mineral matter which undergo compositional changes if the water contacts various types of potential solutes. Major modification of landforms may result.

(iv) Water is not simply the isotopic species $^1H_2^{16}O$ as seen above and the variants are useful in tracing water through the hydrologic cycle.

(v) Water as a depositional agent.

As noted above, water can transport, sometimes removing and later depositing, huge amounts of solid rock waste some of which may be produced through its action as a promoter of subterranean chemical alteration.

(vi) Water in storage.

Natural subterranean or artificial surface storage of water modifies the regimen of water in an area by changing the time of flow.

As well as the above listed aspects, other factors might be mentioned. However, those cited are sufficient to indicate that practitioners of hydrology (who include geologists, geographers, geomorphologists and engineers) apply it to diverse activities which may be regarded as aiming to obtain as complete an understanding as possible of water in all of its properties and cycles. One invaluable benefit is the consequent inventorying of water resources on an areal and regional basis. Also, it is feasible to determine the quantity of water in storage, assess rates and volumes of precipitation, recharge and discharge, evaluate the quantitative availability and suitability of water for utilisation and forecast with some accuracy the effects of depletion, floods and droughts. This latter work facilitates the devising of appropriate flood control measures and alleviation of droughts (a period of 15 days or more without rain constituting an officially recognised drought).

1.5. TERRAIN HYDROLOGY

A variety of terrains occur throughout the planet and of course these are characterised by different features. A summary of the most significant terrains together with their relevant features is given below.

1.5.1. Arid and Semi-Arid Terrains

Semi-arid areas of the world are found in transitional zones between sub-humid belts and arid deserts. In many places, they are expanding by a process called desertification, the causes of which are not properly understood. The landscape in semi-arid regions is moulded by water movement acting upon pre-existing topography and it is greatly influenced by geology. A number of other factors are involved and these include aeolian effects such as wind erosion, solar energy in insolation and temperature change, etc., all of which contribute to mechanical weathering and landform alteration. In fact, arid and semi-arid terrains may be defined on the basis of three parameters: humidity, precipitation season and temperature regimen. Maximum aridity is encountered where at least one month annually is entirely devoid of rainfall. In such a region, evaporation exceeds precipitation for much of the time. A semi-arid region may be regarded as one in which precipitation occurs in a cold winter, the coldest month averaging between 0°C and 10°C with the hottest month falling into the range 20°C to 30°C. Actually, such conditions typify the Mediterranean semi-arid climate found, for instance, in Morocco and Lebanon, but such a regimen is also found in northern Iran and on the west coast of the USA at about 35° latitude. Together, semi-arid and arid areas comprise more than a third of the total land surface of the Earth as compared with cultivated land which comprises a mere 10% of the total. The main arid–semi-arid belt extends across North Africa (the Sahara) through Arabia (the 'Empty Quarter' or Rub al Khali) into the Salt Desert of Iran and the Takla Makan of central Asia. A lesser component is the Great American Desert of North America.

In the semi-arid regions, precipitation is restricted because moisture-bearing winds cannot penetrate into them or cool down in them as a result of the existence of high pressure zones. When precipitation here and in arid regions does take place, it is almost invariably in the form of rain. Despite the high evaporation potential, some precipitation may penetrate the groundwater system. This is demonstrated by the isotope investigations of E. Mazor and his associates in 1974.[4] Environmental isotope data from Kalahari groundwater showed that recent rain recharge had occurred within the preceding two decades or so in the northern and sometimes in the southern parts of this desert.

The major hydrological characteristics of semi-arid and arid zones where these are to any degree vegetated are high evapotranspiration rates—a result of the abundant heat energy available. Surface waters cannot maintain themselves against evaporation and so basins of inland drainage form over the longer term. Of course where incoming surface waters originating in non-arid regions contribute and exceed evaporative losses, basins are kept open as is the case with the Nile, the Euphrates–Tigris and the Colorado.

Precipitation is impure in that it contains salts and gases in solution. The salts are dissociated into cations (mainly calcium, magnesium, sodium and potassium) and anions (bicarbonate, chloride and sulphate), carbon dioxide being the principal dissolved gas. Such elements may originate from either a marine or a terrestrial source. It is estimated that the annual precipitation of sea salts for the dry steppe regions south of the Sahara amounts to about 3 kg per hectare. In the Kalahari the figure is 2 kg per hectare and in Iran about 1 kg per hectare. The process of surface runoff may concentrate such salts in central evaporating pans of closed drainage basins and infiltration to aquifers will contribute impure waters to these. As an example, D. J. Burdon and S. Mazloum in 1959 reported that the recharge waters to aquifers in Syria can contain from 50 to 200 ppm of total soluble salts.[5] In aquifers such as the Fars formation of Iraq–Syria (which is a lagoonal facies) soluble salts are very abundant. However, in other Middle East aquifers such as the continental arkositic sandstones of the Arabian area, soluble minerals do not occur. This may be a consequence of large quantities of groundwater flushing the aquifer by their movement. Normally amounts and rates of movement of groundwater tend to be small in the semi-arid zones so that mineralisation of them through dissolution of the aquifer rocks tends to be an important factor. Where aquifers discharge in springs or marshy ground, perennial rivers may carry off water and an oasis may arise. The Ghouta of Damascus is an instance of this and there the source is the 'heavenly' Barada river which flows mainly from Ain Figeh. Where discharge is small, a saline marsh may form such as the Qatara Depression in Egypt which probably derives its water from the sandstone aquifer of the Western Desert so famous during the Second World War. D. J. Burdon has indicated the following approaches as desirable in order to improve hydrological conditions in semi-arid zones:[6]

(i)   surface management involving the utilisation of water prior to evaporative loss;
(ii) controlled storage of surface runoff, for instance by spreading water over large areas through diversion from a stream bed or wadi behind earth banks in such a manner that flow velocity is never sufficient to cause erosion of the retaining structures;
(iii) controlled exploitation of aquifers to avoid overdraft;
(iv) weather modification, for instance by cloud seeding or by constructing dams to permit impounded water to be located upwind of the relevant semi-arid area;
(v)   desalination of brackish waters.

1.5.2. Limestone Terrains
Carbonate rocks are soluble and this leads to the formation of subterranean caverns, pipes and channels, i.e. features resulting from chemi-

cal weathering. A landscape showing a pattern of denudation in lime-stone and dolomitic rocks similar to that of a so-named region in Yugoslavia is termed karstic, denudation referring to processes which cause a general lowering of the land surface. Limestone terrains may be defined as regions where carbonate rocks extend from near the surface to below the water table. In them, chemical weathering by water may produce a residual deposit after removal of calcium carbonate in solution and this constitutes terra rossa, a red and clay-like soil which is insoluble. Such material may act as an impermeable cover screening underlying limestone from further solutional effects and the precipitation will pass off as runoff. Of course, later erosion of such a cover will lead to infiltration being resumed. Carbonate region hydrology is variable, ranging from the karst situation to one in which low permeability limestone may even act as an aquiclude, a very low permeability stratum. Clearly permeability in carbonate rocks is highly variable as a function of factors such as purity, calcium/magnesium ratio (introduction of dolomite) and structure. In a karst area the water table fluctuates in rapid response to precipitation input and outflow of water through solution cavities to places of discharge. Owing to the frequent occurrence of perched water storage in limestone terrains, it is permissible to query the validity of the water table concept in them.

1.5.3. Coastal Terrains
Here fresh water migrates down grade to the sea and, as a consequence of having a different density, does not usually mix with it except where subjected to dynamic factors such as tides, waves and currents. In fact, in aquifers in coastal regions lower density fresh water floats on higher density water. Since the ratio of the specific gravity of fresh water to sea water is 40:41, for every metre that fresh water stands above mean sea level, the surface of the salt water is to be found about 40 metres below this datum. Saline water in aquifers may be derived by the encroachment of sea water as well as a number of other causes such as entry of sea water in past geologic time, salt from salt domes or man-made saline wastes.

Saline water pollutes groundwater in many parts of the world, for instance the USA, Europe, Israel and Japan, and it is relevant to discuss the relation between fresh and saline waters further. Salt water was found to occur underground not at sea level, but at a depth 40 times the height of fresh water above sea level by J. Drabbe and W. Badon Ghyben in 1888–89 and B. Herzberg in 1901.[7,8] This was put down to a hydrostatic equilibrium existing between the two fluids of differing densities and an equation presented to explain it is known as the Ghyben–Herzberg relation. Figure 1.3 represents the balance between fresh and saline

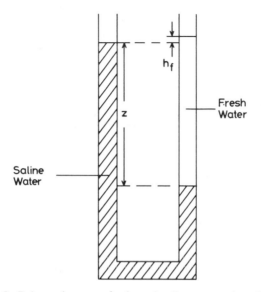

FIG. 1.3. Balance between fresh and saline waters in a U-tube.

waters in a U-tube. The pressures for each side must be equal so that

$$\rho_s g h_s = \rho_f g (z - h_f)$$

where ρ_s is the density of the saline water, ρ_f is the density of the fresh water, g is the acceleration due to gravity and z and h_f are as illustrated in Fig. 1.3. Solving for z

$$z = \frac{\rho_f}{\rho_s - \rho_f} h_f$$

which is the Ghyben–Herzberg relation. Under typical sea water conditions ρ_s may be taken as $1\cdot025\,\text{g/cm}^3$ and ρ_f as $1\cdot000\,\text{g/cm}^3$ and hence $z = 40\,h_f$. If the examination is transferred to a coastal situation, the quantity h_f becomes the elevation of the water table above sea level and z becomes the depth to the fresh water–salt water interface below sea level. As fresh water is flowing towards the sea, this is a hydrodynamic rather than a hydrostatic balance. Even if there were no flow, density considerations alone would result in the development of a horizontal interface separating overlying fresh water from underlying saline water. In fact, where the flow is almost horizontal, the Ghyben–Herzberg relation yields satisfactory results, but near the shore where vertical flow components become significant errors in the position of the interface arise. Unconfined aquifers have been discussed above but the argument applies equally well to confined ones in which the water table is replaced by the piezometric surface. Both water table and piezometric surfaces must lie above sea level and slope down towards the sea if fresh water–salt water equilibrium is to be attained. This results from the Ghyben–Herzberg relation. In situations where the underlying saline water is in motion with heads above or below sea level, the relation has been generalised by N. J. Lusczynski and W. V. Swarzenski.[9] The result for non-equilibrium conditions is in the form

$$z = \frac{\rho_f}{\rho_s - \rho_f} h_f - \frac{\rho_f}{\rho_s - \rho_f} h_s$$

where h_f is the altitude of the water level in a well filled with fresh water of density ρ_f and terminated at depth z and h_s is the altitude of the water level in a saline well with water of density ρ_s, also terminating at depth z. Where $h_s = 0$ the saline water is in equilibrium with the sea so that the above equation reduces to its predecessor.

Potential flow theory has been used by S. Charmonman and others to take account of approximations implicit in the Ghyben–Herzberg relation and provide more accurate solutions for the shape of the fresh water–salt water interface alluded to earlier.[10] One result is in the form

$$z^2 = \frac{2qx}{\Delta\rho K} + \left(\frac{q}{\Delta\rho K}\right)^2$$

Figure 1.4 shows z and x, $\Delta\rho = \rho_s - \rho_f$, K is the hydraulic conductivity of the aquifer and q is the fresh water flow per unit length of shoreline. The corresponding shape for the water table is given by

$$h_f = \left(\frac{2\Delta\rho qx}{K}\right)^{\frac{1}{2}}$$

The width (x_0) of that submarine zone through which fresh water discharges into the sea is obtainable for $z = 0$ to give

$$x_0 = -\frac{q}{2\Delta\rho K}$$

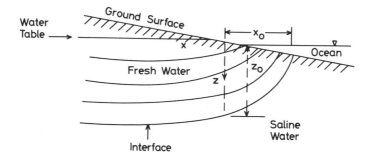

FIG. 1.4. Flow pattern of fresh water in an underground coastal aquifer.

and the depth of the interface beneath the shoreline z_0 occurs where $x = 0$ so that

$$z_0 = \frac{q}{\Delta \rho K}$$

As regards the shape of the fresh water salt water interface, some observations are pertinent. Naturally in the field there is no sharp interface, but rather a brackish transitional region up to several metres thick and developing as a result of dispersion by flow of the fresh water together with effects due to such factors as tides, recharge and the pumping of wells. Usually the maximal thicknesses of such transitional zones occur in very permeable coastal aquifers which are subject to heavy pumping. In one case in Honolulu, concentrated pumping has caused a localised transition zone over 300 m thick to arise.[11] One consequence of the transitional zone is that its seawardly directed flow transports saline water in that direction, this of course originating from underlying saline water. From considerations of continuity, a small landwardly directed flow in the saline water region must exist. In the transition zone itself, the salinity of the groundwater increases progressively with depth from that of the fresh water to that of the saline water and relative salinity S_r may be calculated from

$$S_r = 100 \left(\frac{c - c_f}{c_s - c_f} \right)$$

where c is the salinity at a particular depth within the transition zone and c_f and c_s are the salinities of the fresh and saline waters respectively.

   Much research has been done on unsteady movements of the transition zone, for instance by G. F. Pinder and H. H. Cooper Jr in 1970.[12] If an aquifer contains an underlying layer of saline water and is being pumped by a well which penetrates only the upper fresh water part of the aquifer, then a local rise of the interface below the well takes place, a phenomenon termed upconing. The interface will rise with continued pumping and may ultimately reach the well. The result of that will be that the well will have to be shut down, after which the denser saline water will settle down to its original position. Criteria for taking fresh water from such wells from above saline water have been proposed as a result of investigations by, among others, N. L. Ackermann and Y. Y. Chang in 1971.[13] Referring again to limestone terrains in this connection, it is germane to point out that coastal aquifers in karst create special difficulties as regards sea water intrusion because the many fissures facilitate the entry of saline water in unique configurations, see for instance the work of V. T. Stringfield and H. E. LeGrand in 1971.[14] One result is the emergence of brackish springs and the creation of solution channels in Mediterranean peripheral countries which discharge fresh water as submarine springs. Pumping of such channels to prevent the wasting of fresh water which might otherwise occur can cause saline water to be received in a matter of hours through sea water entry.

Control of saline water intrusion may be effected using one or more of the following techniques:

(i) Modifying the pattern of pumping, for instance by changing the locations of the pumping wells.

(ii) Artificially recharging the groundwater system either by means of surface water spreading or recharge wells for confined aquifers.

(iii) Maintaining a continuous pumping trough with a line of wells adjacent to the sea so that sea water flows inland from the latter to the trough while fresh water within the basin flows in a seaward direction towards the trough. Such an extraction barrier yields brackish pumped water which normally is discharged into the sea.

(iv) Creating an injection barrier by maintaining a pressure ridge along the coast using a line of recharge wells, high quality water being necessary for recharge into the latter.

(v) Installing an impermeable sub-surface barrier parallel to the coast throughout the vertical extent of the aquifer and using appropriate materials such as sheet piling, clay, emulsified asphalt, cement grout, bentonite, silica gel, plastics or calcium acrylate (see also the author's book *Grouting in Engineering Practice*, the second edition of which was published by Applied Science Publishers Ltd in 1981[15]).

As populations have increased and associated water demands have grown, saline intrusion has become ever more common, for instance in the Netherlands, Italy, Germany and Japan as well as along the coasts of the USA.[11] In Israel an interesting case of faults probably acting as conduits for the active contamination of an aquifer by saline water has been described by A. Arad et al.[16] They referred to the Na'aman catchment area where the water in the Judea Group aquifer varies from fresh to saline. An irregular distribution of high salinities along the major east–west trending faults indicates this.

It may be appropriate here to cite the classification of water based upon the total dissolved solids concentration of the US Geological Survey (Table 1.3).

TABLE 1.3
CLASSIFICATION OF WATER

Type	Concentration of dissolved solids (total) ppm
Fresh	0–1000
Brackish	1000–10 000
Salty	10 000–100 000
Brine	More than 100 000

To summarise it may be stated that as long as salinity is immobile it does not constitute a problem. Difficulties arise when saline waters encroach upon or mix with fresh water. They may develop in situations where coastal aquifers contact the ocean and increasing demand for water from the former reverse normally seawardly directed flow thereby causing sea water to penetrate inland (saline intrusion). Although control measures as outlined above may be applied, in some cases filtered salt water may be utilised, for instance in the fish processing industry. In this particular example a saline well which has become contaminated by salt water encroachment may be used between a fresh water well zone and the coast as has been pointed out by A. Vanderberg.[17]

1.6. CHANGE IN THE HYDROLOGIC CYCLE

Naturally occurring fluctuations of measurable variables in the hydrologic cycle such as evaporation, transpiration, precipitation, stream flow, the water table, etc. take place all the time locally, but it is believed that these do not interfere with a basic trend towards an ultimate state of dynamic equilibrium, a condition which may be anticipated since the primary energiser of the cycle, heat energy from the sun, remains constant throughout the life span of the human race. Two factors are responsible for promoting the final attainment of the state of dynamic equilibrium and these are:

(i)   erosion-initiated alterations to the planet's topography, itself resulting mostly from the action of water within the hydrologic cycle;

(ii) biological consequences of erosion, for instance silt deposition in lakes fostering acquisition of nutrients by the diminishing quantity of water and the thriving and multiplying of microorganisms which later form a biological sediment on which vegetation also thrives.

These two factors have operated throughout much of the history of the Earth, but a new component has been introduced by the activities of Man. As was seen in the case of the Nile this can be deleterious and another instance is afforded by the Hoover Dam in the USA, the reservoir of which has collected so much silt originally conveyed to the sea that it has lost half of its initial capacity for water-borne sediments. However, possibly the worst effects of human interference with the hydrologic cycle are to be found in the field of irrigation. This activity has ruined vast areas of fertile cropland because natural water (especially groundwater) employed in hot, dry areas becomes progressively enriched in mineral salts (a small proportion of which it contains to begin with) as a result of high rates of evaporation. Eventually the salt content in the unevaporated water has become so great that the concentration of salts in the transition zone from which crops obtain water exceeds their tolerance. The sole solution is to leach out such accumulated salts by additional irrigation which carries them, in solution, deep underground. Excess irrigation of this type raises the water table so that the practice can result in water-logging of the land. In the case of Pakistan huge areas suffer because they are irrigated by river barrages and associated canals so that every year approximately 40 000 hectares of food-producing land are being lost to cultivation.

Other damaging activities include excessive groundwater pumping which may cause overdraft, lowering of the water table or in a confined aquifer lowering of the hydrostatic pressure so causing diminution or drying up of rivers and springs. Excess pumping from a confined aquifer can also cause elastic deformation of the water-bearing strata. Urbanisation affects the hydrologic cycle because extensive paving and road construction promotes runoff and may deprive an aquifer of its recharge area. If such an aquifer is the source of supply for the city concerned, the larger the latter grows the less water will be available to it.

From these considerations it can be seen that the activities of Man are more often than not to a greater or lesser degree adverse. Some proposed projects can be viewed therefore as inherently undesirable. One such is the suggested dam on the Ob river in the USSR. This river flows north and the scheme is intended to divert its waters through a system of canals into the Aral and Caspian Seas thus making fresh water formerly running into the Arctic Ocean available for irrigation in the region of western Siberia and Kazakhstan which is arid.

In the Third World the demand upon the hydrologic cycle is much lower than in the technologically developed countries. While inhabitants of the former manage on amounts of water which can be as low as 12 litres daily, in England normal usage exceeds this by a factor of twelve while in the USA the figure rises to as much as 250 litres per capita every 24 h. Additionally, as there are so many more facilities needing water in the developed countries, they also impose demands upon water supply. The unremitting expansion of population, especially in the Third World, is another factor in the ever-rising need for water, a need which could become critical in the near future. This assertion is believed to be justified although realistic estimates of current world consumption of water are almost impossible to arrive at because of the inadequacy of available statistics. In a modern city in the Western World average daily consumption may reach 2000 litres per head (including personal, commercial and industrial usage). However, perhaps a norm may exist around 500 litres or so per head per day. The rate of increase in urban water consumption is assessed at approximately 1% per head annually. If this concept is applied to the USA with its existing population growth rate, then over a decade a total increase of around 30% in water consumption may be expected. In regard to this, it must be remembered that to satisfy this increased demand it is necessary not merely to increase the primary supply but also to improve the capacity of supply mains, add to the number of purification plants, widen storage and

distribution systems, enlarge sewage systems and their associated treatment plants, etc., all very daunting and expensive tasks indeed. Of course
urban demand is but a small fraction of the requirements of Man, many
of which are connected with the provision of foodstuffs and here natural
rainfall provides the bulk of the water. In many parts of the world, such
as India and Egypt, the availability of water for crop production is a
vital factor for life itself. In Egypt it has been noted that the increasing
amount of water from the Nile brought under control since 1900
correlates with the rising population curve. Bearing in mind that the
average man of, say, 75 kg weight requires ten times that weight of water
annually and that growing, say, 75 kg of wheat requires more than
100 000 kg of water, the vast scale of agricultural water consumption
becomes explicable. About one-tenth of the world's total area of land is
cultivated and of this about 10% is under artificial irrigation, the bulk
of the remainder receiving water from natural sources such as rainfall
and subterranean seepage. The irrigated 1% of the planet's total land surface uses approximately 1·5 million m^3 water each year. However, industrial utilisation is continually increasing and while it takes 1000 kg of water
to produce an egg, it also takes 300 kg of water for every kg of steel
manufactured, 250 kg of water for every kg of paper produced and 600 kg
of water for every kg of nitrate fertiliser produced. Owing to its high
specific heat, water is used in industry to convey heat and one important
application is in nuclear reactors where it is employed as the medium
transferring heat from the core to heat exchangers in which steam for
driving generators is produced. Water is also used as a moderator in
water cooled reactors, i.e. it acts to slow down neutrons to the velocity at
which they can effect fission in a uranium atom. This latter process
suffers from the drawback that water absorbs a large percentage of
neutrons and can be effective therefore only with enriched uranium. A
better moderator is afforded by that isotopic species of water incorporating deuterium, namely $^1H^2H^{16}O$ (or HDO as it is frequently written)
and constituting the famous 'heavy water'. Heavy water is an excellent
moderator and does not absorb many neutrons, but it is expensive.

1.7. WASTAGE IN THE HYDROLOGIC CYCLE

Natural wastage occurs through evaporation from the soil surface and
this can be reduced if the soil is covered by compost. Evaporation also

takes place from large water bodies and in the case of reservoirs it has been reduced by application in hot countries of a thin layer of cetyl alcohol to their surfaces. This is a non-toxic compound, the presence of which does not impede the passage of oxygen, sunlight or rain. Artificial wastage results from the thoughtlessness of human beings, particularly in agriculture. It has been stated that half of the water provided for irrigation is lost before getting to the area of use and of that water which does arrive only about 50% is actually employed by the crops. There is no doubt that wastage could be reduced in agriculture, the most damaging manifestation of this phenomenon. For instance, loss of water through seepage in channels can be obviated by lining these structures. As regards urban wastage, a survey has shown that the introduction of water meters for individual consumers minimises domestic losses. Unless control measures are more widely and stringently applied, it is probable that the coming water crisis will be accelerated. This is a strange state of affairs because in point of fact there is sufficient water available for Man's needs and if his habits improve the problem could be overcome rapidly.

Natural evaporation from the oceans exceeds precipitation into them by approximately 9%. The precipitation falls on the land areas and is mostly being returned to potential usage as fresh water through river systems. This quantity of water actually exceeds human requirements and it does not include the considerable reserves of groundwater. Part of the trouble stems from the unfortunate fact that Man is accustomed to obtain water freely or at minimal cost; a fact which has prevented sufficient effort being put into its distribution as compared with, say, oil or natural gas from which huge returns on investment can be obtained. Insofar as water is common in Europe and most of the USA, an uneconomic price is being charged for it—only a few cents per cubic metre in America for instance although prices are rising in the United Kingdom. In parts of the world where water is at a premium, the use of expensive and sophisticated technology such as desalination has pushed up the price of water so that, for example, in Kuwait when the first such plant was installed the resultant water cost no less than US$1·25 per cubic metre. Later development of the flash distillation process has lowered this to 25 cents or less per cubic metre—still far more than in the USA. A psychological resistance to higher prices may mean that the public generally prefers inadequate, low priced water supplies to plentiful, economically priced water.

1.8. THE INTERNATIONAL HYDROLOGIC DECADE

This constituted work essential to forward planning and resulted from a resolution tabled before the Executive Board of UNESCO in November 1961 which recommended an international ten year programme. This was approved at the General Conference three years later and implemented as the International Hydrologic Decade in January 1965. There were 60 participating countries and the objectives were defined as:

(i)   assessment of existing knowledge coupled with identification of gaps in it;
(ii) standardisation of techniques, instrumentation and terminology utilised in hydrology throughout the world;
(iii) creation of a worldwide system for collection of hydrologic data;
(iv) institution of research work and promotion of training activities;
(v)   organisation of systematic international exchange of hydrologic information.

Many of these endeavours proved more or less successful. On the research side special studies were aimed at integrating and interpreting measurements in selected water basins throughout the world. A single instance may be cited as an illustration. This is the study of precipitation–runoff relations effected in a small ($2 \cdot 6\,km^2$) basin called Modry Dul in northern Czechoslovakia by T. Dincer et al.[18] Clearly the runoff at a basin outlet comprises several components such as direct surface runoff, interflow and groundwater discharge which are interrelated and separable by hydrograph analysis. The assumption is made that a basin consists of a series of linear reservoirs where outflow is directly proportional to the amount of water in storage, i.e. $S = KQ$, and this leads to exponential recession curves of the form

$$Q_t = Q_0 \exp(-t/K)$$

where Q_t and Q_0 are the discharges at time t and $t = 0$ respectively and K is the storage coefficient. In 1940, B. S. Barnes gave another flow recession equation:

$$Q_t = Q_0 K_r^t$$

where K_r is the recession constant.[17] Analysis of the hydrograph is effected by plotting logarithms of the discharge against time and identifying and separating different components of the stream flow in the order of their recession constants. Identification of the different components of the total runoff may be made using environmental isotopes and this obviates the necessity of assuming that the relevant hydrological systems are linear reservoirs, i.e. that the flow recession curves are exponential. Tritium concentrations in groundwater contributions to stream flow will differ from those in surface runoff. Also, for a particular snow melt or storm period, runoff resulting through such phenomena has a characteristic tritium label. On the other hand the tritium content of the groundwater contribution does not change for long periods of time. Hence it is feasible to utilise an equation of the following type:

$$rc_s + (1-r)c_g = c_r$$

where r and $(1-r)$ are the relative contributions of surface and groundwater to the stream flow and c_s, c_g and c_r are the concentrations of tritium in surface runoff, groundwater and stream flow respectively. The term r can be calculated for any given day from the preceding equation. The actual number of samples necessary is not high because of the small variation which exists for a single melting season or storm. At Modry Dul the tritium content of the base flow was found to be constant at 730 TU (tritium units) during the winter 1965–66. By contrast the snow cover in the basin had concentrations ranging from 200 to 300 TU with an average value of 250 TU. During the snow melt season the tritium concentration did not approach the tritium concentration of the snow-pack. A relation was found to exist between the sub-surface flow and the total discharge and this has been used to separate the sub-surface flow component (assumed to have a constant tritium concentration of 730 TU) from the direct snow melt water reaching the stream channel.

Some basins were selected because they represented typical climatic, geological or topographic conditions, others because they included an international frontier and hence offered the possibility of assembling coordinated data.

Among subsidiary aims of the IHD (International Hydrologic Decade) were those of producing publications on the most modern technology and drawing the attention of the general public to the importance of water in modern life.

1.9. THE UNITED NATIONS INTERNATIONAL DRINKING WATER SUPPLY AND SANITATION DECADE

On November 10, 1980 a new worldwide project was launched called the UN International Drinking Water Supply and Sanitation Decade scheduled to run through the period 1981–90. It originated in the context of obtaining clean water for all by 1990 proposed by the UN Conference on Human Settlements (Habitat) in Vancouver in 1976. Subsequently, cost estimates were drawn up by the World Bank and the World Health Organisation in readiness for the 1977 UN Water Conference in Mar del Plata where the plan for an International Drinking Water Supply and Sanitation Decade was approved unanimously. Facts listed in Table 1.4 emphasise the importance of the venture.

TABLE 1.4

NUMBER OF PEOPLE IN DEVELOPING COUNTRIES (OUTSIDE CHINA) WITHOUT CLEAN WATER AND SANITATION IN 1980 (ESTIMATED ON THE BASIS OF GOVERNMENTAL DATA SUPPLIED TO THE WHO)

Sector	Population (millions)	Population without clean water (millions)	Population without adequate sanitation (millions)
Urban	703	177 (25%)	331 (47%)
Rural	1612	1143 (71%)	1399 (87%)
Total	2315	1320 (57%)	1730 (75%)

Also relevant are the data given in Table 1.5 taken from *World Water*.[19]

Peter Bourne, the UNDPs Water Decade Coordinator believes that the endeavour will offer the possibility of achieving as great a change in the quality of human life in the world as any programme ever launched by the United Nations. Despite its reluctance to interfere in national governmental strategic planning and priority setting, the UN has declared the Decade to be a cooperative matter and a section of WHOs Environmental Health Division, the Geneva based GWS unit, has produced a Donor Catalogue listing promises made by, to date, about 30 multilateral and bilateral funding agencies. In February 1981 *World Water* and WHO produced a Water Decade Directory giving details of the current status of water supply and sanitation as well as Decade plans of various governments. Technological transfer within and between countries is being organised by the Netherlands based International Reference Centre for Community Water Supply (IRC). International cooperation is coordinated from New York where UNDP Deputy Administrator G. Arthur Brown chairs the interagency steering committee with representatives from UNDP, WHO, UNICEF, FAO, ILO, the World Bank, the UN Department for Technical Cooperation for Development and UNESCO.

TABLE 1.5

NUMBER OF PEOPLE IN DEVELOPING COUNTRIES IN MILLIONS TO BE REACHED
WITH CLEAN WATER AND SANITATION BY 1990 IF THE DECADE'S TARGETS ARE 100%
ACHIEVED (WHO FIGURES AGAIN BASED UPON INFORMATION SUPPLIED BY
GOVERNMENTS)

UN region	Water			Sanitation		
	urban	rural	total	urban	rural	total
Asia and the Pacific (ESCAP: west to Iran)	203	925	1128	355	1136	1491
Latin America (ECLA: inc. Caribbean)	108	110	218	212	120	332
Africa (ECA: inc. N. Africa)	104	310	414	130	342	472
West Asia (ECWA: Arab world outside Africa)	16	22	38	20	25	45
Europe (ECE: e.g. Cyprus, Portugal)	14	21	35	30	30	60
Totals	445	1388	1833	747	1653	2400

The financing of the endeavour is a complex matter. In 1979, approximately US$2·4 billion were committed to water supply and sanitation
aid and this represented almost 40% of the total assistance. The origins
were as follows: 43% from the World Bank; 23% in bilateral aid from
national and agencies of western governments; 17% from various multilateral development banks; 7% from OPEC agencies; 6% from UN agencies (primarily UNDP and UNICEF); and 4% from non-governmental
(i.e. voluntary) organisations. The amount derived from the World Bank
(US$900 million) was almost three times the average during the past five
years and reflects the fact that 1979 was a very active year for the Bank
in the fields of water supply and sanitation. In the period 1979–83, the
Bank is expected to make an average commitment of US$700 million
annually to water supply and sanitation projects together with an
additional amount for the water and waste disposal components of
projects in other sectors. Apropos other donors, their attitudes are
determined by aversion to interfering in the planning policies of the
developing countries as well as the current adverse economic situation.
Other problems arise from the increasing tendency of bilateral donors to

offer 'tied' aid, i.e. assistance involving the purchase of equipment or services from the donor country. This can cause unnecessary difficulties in operation and maintenance as well as forcing countries away from appropriate technology with its simpler solutions more suited to available skills. The World Bank believes that US$12 000 annually is the reasonable spending level to be achieved during the Water Decade. This is double the current level, but nevertheless the best result can only be to maintain the number of unserved people in the Third World at 1500 million by 1990, i.e. exactly the same number as in 1975. Improving on this would entail changing priorities in the developing countries both towards water and sanitation and within them. Past neglect of rural projects accompanied by migration to towns have created great problems in the peripheral areas of the latter. It is reassuring therefore that many donors are now adopting a basic need approach to aid and technical assistance which gives greater emphasis on deprived rural areas. As an additional step, the UN is encouraging agencies and governments to include water supply and irrigation components in related projects, especially those in the field of general irrigation and agricultural development. The major remaining preliminary task for the Decade appears to be the devising of an adequate accounting mechanism which should not prove too difficult in view of the expertise represented by the World Bank, WHO, ILO and the other UN agencies involved. In this connection Ernst Becher of the WHO/World Bank Cooperative Programme in Geneva has recorded his own views proposing employment of a set of critical indicators to plan and monitor progress towards the aims of the Decade. These are based upon a survey effected in cooperation with the Algerian authorities and the basic requirements are listed by Becher as follows:[20]

(i)   they should be brief and to the point;
(ii)   they should be relatively simple to determine;
(iii) they should be factual;
(iv)   they should be dynamic and monitor trends rather than providing static descriptive material.

Financial indicators suggested for water and sanitation may also be given:

(i)   present value of installations per person served;
(ii)   current rate of investment by project and per person served;
(iii) income, expenditure and operating net for the last three years, per

person served and compared with the standard costs in systems of a similar type;

(iv) average cost price per m³ of water produced and/or billed;

(v) planned investment per person to be served during the National Development Plan;

(vi) expenditure for water/sanitation per family/household as a percentage of its revenue (with particular reference to the lowest income group).

It may be useful also to add some details regarding the social, technical and managerial efficiency indicators proposed.

(i) Social indicators include local rate of infant mortality per 1000 aged 0 to 1 year, number of reported cases of water-borne diseases over those of 1979, service coverage of water supply, rate of connections in water supply, rate of needs satisfaction in water supply, rate of service coverage in sanitation, rate of connections to sewage systems.

(ii) Technical indicators include rate of operation of the service (average number of hours of operation per 24 h day), conditions of systems and metering (volume of water distributed and volume of water produced), rate of potable water use in litres per head daily (maximum, average minimum), rate of backlog demand for house connections, rate of backlog demand for sewage connections.

(iii) Management efficiency indicators include meeting operating costs (= operating costs and revenue from the sale of water), utilisation of fixed assets (= present value of fixed assets and revenue from the sale of water), number of technical personnel per 1000 inhabitants.

These indicators can be applied also to the sanitation sub-sector by selecting the corresponding variables.

Finally, WHO has stated through its Director-General Halfdan Mahler that the number of water taps per 1000 population will be more meaningful as a health indicator than the number of hospital beds per 1000 population. The former Secretary-General of the UN, Kurt Waldheim, regards the goal of clean water and sanitation for all by 1990 as eminently achievable and it is to be hoped that this view proves to be correct.

1.10. DROUGHT, A DISRUPTION IN THE HYDROLOGIC CYCLE

The huge planetary-wide hydrologic cycle is frequently interrupted by droughts which were particularly prevalent in 1977. Earlier in the 1970s, drought was widespread, especially in the Sahel belt of West Africa, a region of aridity always subject to the phenomenon, but the devastation of 1977 was on an unusually large scale and entailed the deaths of tens of thousands of people and millions of livestock. In addition the physical environment was severely damaged and sociopolitical institutions suffered. The most affected region included the Sahelian Six, namely Mauritania, Senegal, Mali, Upper Volta, Niger and Chad covering an area 56·5% of that of the USA and representing approximately 19% of the total area of Africa. Except for Senegal and Mauritania, these are landlocked countries. The word 'sahel' means 'shore' in Arabic and refers to a rather narrow belt of semi-arid climate and vegetation running along the northern and southern edges of the Sahara which the great drought affected. However, it was not confined here. The Gambia and Northern Nigeria were also badly hit and lesser effects were experienced in the form of much reduced harvests in Egypt, Kenya, Somalia, Zaire and Tanzania. Ethiopia was involved too. Of course, like the Sahel, Africa is generally very drought-prone, probably more so than any land area in the world. In the Maghreb (Morocco, Algeria and Tunisia), Libya and Botswana periodic droughts occur. To illustrate the point that the great drought was only the worst of many in recent years, Nino Bertoni in 1980 reported that an internationally assisted water relief effort is urgently required in a country in the Horn of Africa, namely Djibouti.[21] This is a land which is normally arid or semi-arid and the rainfall is confined to a wet season extending over a mere month or so. There is a very small population of around 300 000 people to which has been added perhaps 30 000 or more Somalian refugees from Ethiopia, hence the need for water has been exacerbated. As a result of its low level of development, Djibouti is unable to aid itself. There are no technical personnel available for this and it appears that broken water drilling equipment is to be seen in many places, equipment unprotected from the weather, saturated with salt and of course irreparable due to lack of spare parts and technicians. There are no deep well pumping units and six completed deep well holes are non-exploitable as a result of the unavailability of pumps. The previous (French) administration left a couple of rigs in Djibouti, but these have been so over-used that they are practically non-functional. Three new machines donated by the Arab states are both too large and too sophisticated to be employed and in any case would need foreign technicians to operate them. Bertoni commented that vehicles in general are in a deplorable state of disrepair in the country. Consequently, the rural inhabitants have been compelled to resort to semi-nomadic life patterns in an attempt to locate water supplies and in fact are so depressed by the situation that the merest rumour of any of this precious commodity being available elsewhere can trigger an almost total and rapid abandonment of a village with resulting disruption to ordinary life. UNICEF which sponsored Bertoni's visit is concerned that groundwater cannot be used in existing circumstances and it may be noted that the affair has become so tragic that children in one area became rationed to a single drink daily with adults (except for the sick and expectant mothers) restricted to a drink every second day. The effects in a normal daily temperature rising to around 40°C at noon can be imagined.

The frequent droughts in Africa alluded to above makes it clear why the continent includes approximately one-third of the planet's arid lands, also why the lack of water constitutes the primary brake on economic development in more than half of it, as for instance in the Sahel. Here, rainfall at best amounts to only about 650 mm annually and in the Sahara it falls to as little as 250 mm per year. During the great drought, the hydrology of the entire region was very much affected. The River Niger ran at its lowest level within memory and could be forded at Niamay while for the first time in history the River Kano stopped its flow and Lake Chad was reduced to a third of its normal size. Water table levels fell drastically due to lack of recharge and as a result many wells dried up. Naturally as supplies diminished in an area herds concentrated around better wells and so the surrounding pasture became exhausted. Possibly the Sahara is expanding by desertification, a process which can result from a breakdown in the dynamic equilibrium which ought to exist between livestock and natural grazing resources leading to rapid devegetation, increased wind and water erosion and consequent reduction in the human and livestock carrying capacity of the region. Fires (grass burning), overcropping and tree felling are equally important factors in desertification through devegetation; the latter manifests itself in the flora which changes from desirable perennial grasses to less desirable fire resistant annual species. Control measures include seeding to establish an appropriate grass cover, sand dune fixation, afforestation and conservation, etc. These will begin near towns because desertification usually commences on the fringes of these or water centres due to sedentary and nomadic livestock concentrations, small plot farming and the cutting of trees and uprooting of shrubs for fuel and construction purposes. Land degradation continues to expand and eventually vast areas become transformed into desert, hence the Saharan expansion. The United Nations Sudano-Sahelian Office with a branch in New York is particularly concerned in investigating and planning with regard to desertification problems. Large scale irrigation schemes have been proposed in various parts of West Africa. For instance, the Manantali Dam on the Bafing tributary of the Senegal River in Mali permits coverage of over three-quarters of a million acres with an associated 100 000 kW hydroelectric power station. A US$42 million barrage about 20 km above St Louis in Senegal is aimed at prevention of sea water incursion and facilitating year-round navigation of the river up to Kayes in Mali. Guinea would require several dams, but construction has been impeded by the country's withdrawal from OMVS, the Organisation of Senegal River States. Construction of the Selingue Dam on the Sankarini tributary envisaged the irrigation of 100 000 acres and support of a 40 000 kW hydroelectric power station. Other proposals include a US$17 million Tiga Dam in Kano state, Nigeria, to irrigate 180 000 acres, a US$167 million scheme in the Rima Basin, North West Nigeria (the Bakolori project) to control 75 000 acres and a plan for Lake Chad.

Drought in Africa is a very serious problem, therefore, but one that also occurs in many other parts of the world. Some instances may be given, starting with a recent and catastrophic event in the Hebei province in China which was without appreciable rainfall from July 1979 until summer 1981. In fact, this was the worst drought to affect northern China for four decades and its consequences were so dire that outside assistance was requested for the first time since the Communist Government came to power in 1949. The corner of Hebei province involved lies about 300 km south of Peking and local officials there are quoted by Michael Weisskopf as stating that about one-third of the population, approximately 14 million people, were subsisting on insufficient grain rations.[22] Two million children were suffering from serious malnutrition and concomitant diseases such as anaemia, hepatitis and rickets. Half of the wells in the area are dry and groundwater levels have fallen by more than 10 m in places. Additionally, rivers are at less than half their normal levels. Of course a huge number of livestock have died, over 165 000 acres of saplings have perished and the total cost of the drought exceeds US$1 billion in agricultural losses. At Gang Nan reservoir, usually the major supplier of water in south east Hebei, the water level is only 25% of normal so that peasants have been forced to fish from sand bars which have surfaced. The valves were closed in April 1981 leaving only one operational reservoir in the south east. It is clear that a great proportion of the enormous Hebei plain, once China's grain basket, is a near desert covered with withered corn stalks, cotton plants and wheat. Since the whole province has a population almost equal to that of France, the scale of the disaster can be appreciated and it is not surprising that the need for US$1 billion in aid has driven the Government to ask the UN for help. Of this sum, US$40 million is earmarked for medical care and the United Nations Children's Emergency Fund has already supplied 35 million vitamin pills for distribution in Hebei and Hubei provinces. In the latter, violent flooding in 1980 rendered millions homeless and they had not been rehoused by spring 1981. Indeed 20 million people were living on government-issued rations thereafter hence their involvement in UNICEFs activities. One of the worst aspects of the Hebei drought is that no planting could be undertaken in spring 1981 because the villagers had enough to do just trying to stop petrifying of the earth. Perhaps the worst hit area in Hebei is Hengshu district where the food ration fell to a mere pound or so of corn meal daily amounting to only 1500 calories, i.e. half the daily minimum requirement. Malnutrition is common, most of the children being pallid, listless and underweight. The vagaries of nature are well illustrated by the fact that in Szechuan province during July 1981, flooding killed thousands and left hundreds of thousands homeless when the Yangtze River suffered its highest waters for 85 years and, among other things, smashed into a newly completed dam, the Gezhouba Dam, fortunately without appreciably damaging the structure. Although around the same time Jaipur in the predominantly desert state of Rajasthan in India was cut off by floods with almost two metres of water flowing through its streets and numerous people killed, India is often affected by drought and, as in China, the effects can be more horrendous than in the much more sparsely populated continent of Africa. As agriculture is vital to the lives of hundreds of millions, lack of water or for that matter flooding are highly significant. The interesting part of the situation is that northern India and also Pakistan are endowed with a massive regional mountain terrain with a great deal of water, the Indus River for instance being one of the world's largest natural sources of fresh water carrying—with its 5 tributaries from which Punjab derives its name (panj = five)—over twice as much as the average annual flow of the

Nile each year. Unfortunately the regimen is monsoonal and so the heavy rains that arise destroy vast areas of summer food crops and inadequate conservation entails loss of water on a massive scale. Remedial measures are undertaken, for instance the Kandi Watershed Project in Punjab with which the author was involved in 1980, but they are usually insufficiently financed to really solve the problem. Even summer reduction of water flow to a trickle in places should really pose no difficulty because under the Indus Basin there is a huge subterranean reservoir distributed in a series of aquifers which could and should be exploited. Despite all this, drought and accompanying famine are regular concomitants of life especially in eastern India where the enormous quantities of water conveyed by the Ganges River and the Brahmaputra River into the Bay of Bengal every year ought to obviate or at least extensively alleviate them.

In the USA there was a very severe drought in the east during 1980 and this even led to essentially meaningless symbolic gestures such as banning the placing of glasses of water for diners on restaurant tables in Washington, DC and elsewhere.

In the United Kingdom a very serious drought occurred in 1976 and the situation became so bad that in areas with very low supplies it was proposed to work a three day week for industry, a direct result of delay in implementing sufficient storage capacity coupled with a freak weather pattern. This latter also affected France and other European countries very badly, except perhaps for the wines of that vintage.

Droughts are diagnosed if a dry period extends through 15 or more rainless days. This can be done by examining the condition of the soil. Soil is composed of humus and mineral particles derived from rock weathering and the irregular shapes and sizes of the latter produce a variety of soil types. Spaces are left between the particles and enable large quantities of water to be taken up. Generally, soils with a uniform consistency conduct water more rapidly than those in which there are layers of different aggregate forms of different degrees of compaction. Of special significance is the physical condition of the soil surface. If this becomes compacted it can decrease the infiltration rate and in heavy rains, water impinging upon such a surface may actually flow over the top of the soil and constitute runoff (particularly on slopes). Obviously this can be accompanied by extensive erosion in areas subject to very heavy rain storms, but even in temperate regions compaction problems may arise and may manifest themselves, for instance, in the form of water-logged fields. Ever heavier farm machinery contributes to making compaction even more of a nuisance.

In such conditions where soil is water-charged, even when no rain falls for the 15 day period officially constituting a drought, a true drought does not exist. Also seasonal factors enter into the matter because 15 days without rain in summer have quite different consequences from a similar rainless period in winter.

1.11. ISOTOPES IN THE HYDROLOGIC CYCLE

The stable environmental isotopes utilised in hydrological studies are primarily those of hydrogen ^1H and ^2H (deuterium, D) and of oxygen ^{16}O and ^{18}O, but to a lesser extent those of carbon ^{12}C and ^{13}C and of sulphur ^{32}S and ^{34}S are frequently employed and other radioactive environmental isotopes have found important applications in hydrology. The most important of these latter are tritium, the radioactive isotope of hydrogen, ^3H, often designated T and ^{14}C, radiocarbon. However, others have been used even though much more rarely and these include the radioactive isotope of the noble gas radon, ^{222}Rn, and the radioisotope of silicon, ^{32}Si.

Tritium and radiocarbon are naturally produced by the interaction of cosmic radiation with the atmosphere through the reactions $^{14}N(n,T)^{12}C$ and $^{14}N(n,p)^{14}C$ respectively, also from the sun and by artificial pulses produced in thermonuclear explosions. The man-made isotopes have become dispersed throughout the planetary atmosphere and their participation in the hydrologic cycle is now regulated by natural processes. Of course isotopes of hydrogen and oxygen are almost perfect tracers of water because they constitute parts of the chemical elements of the water molecule and their concentrations are usually unaffected by interactions with aquifer materials when in the groundwater component of the cycle. However, in geothermal regions such interactions assume a much greater significance for oxygen isotopes. In Table 1.6 relevant information regarding these is listed.

As regards the stable isotopes of hydrogen and oxygen, they show compositional variations in natural waters as a result of natural processes such as evaporation during which the light molecules of water $(H_2^{16}O)$ are more volatile than those which contain a heavy isotope, i.e. $HD^{16}O$ or $H_2^{18}O$. As a result of this fact water vapour evaporated from the oceans is depleted by approximately 12 to $15\%_0$ (parts per mil, i.e. parts per thousand) in ^{18}O and by approximately 80 to $120\%_0$ in deuterium in relation to the oceanic water. When this atmospheric water vapour undergoes successive cooling and condensation with the pro-

TABLE 1.6

ENVIRONMENTAL ISOTOPES OF LIGHT ELEMENTS UTILISED IN HYDROLOGY

Isotope	Relative abundance in nature (%)	Decay	Half-life	Maximum energy (keV)
^{1}H	99·985	Stable		
^{2}H (D)	0·015	Stable		
^{3}H (T)	10^{-15}–10^{-12}	—	12·26 years	18·1
^{12}C	98·89	Stable		
^{13}C	1·11	Stable		
^{14}C	$1·2 \times 10^{-10}$	—	5 730 years	156
^{16}O	99·76	Stable		
^{17}O	0·04	Stable		
^{18}O	0·20	Stable		
^{32}S	95·00	Stable		
^{33}S	0·76	Stable		
^{34}S	4·22	Stable		

The values given for the tritium content of precipitation refer to the pre-1952 period (lower value) and the thermonuclear era year 1963, northern hemisphere (higher value), and the radiocarbon value is that in modern carbon before 1950.

duction of clouds and precipitation, the less volatile heavy molecules condense preferentially and leave a residual water vapour which is more and more depleted in deuterium and oxygen-18. Consequently, successive precipitations derived from the same initial water vapour mass become progressively depleted in heavy isotopes. W. Dansgaard in 1964 has indicated that because the degree of condensation of a water vapour mass depends upon the temperature a relationship between isotopic composition of precipitation and its temperature of formation is to be expected.[23] As the temperature of formation decreases, the δ-values of the precipitation also decrease (this expression is explained below). The temperature dependency produces seasonal isotope variations of precipitation (winter precipitation being depleted in heavy isotopes with respect to summer precipitation), latitudinal variations (high latitude precipitation is depleted with respect to low latitude precipitation) and altitude variations (the heavy isotope content of precipitation decreases with increasing altitude); see for instance H. Moser and W. Stichler who, in 1970, discussed deuterium measurements in snow samples from the Alps.[24] This last effect, the altitude effect, is very important in regional hydrological studies and can facilitate groundwaters originating from recharge areas at different elevations. In general the effect is about 0·3‰ decrease in ^{18}O content and 2·5‰ decrease in D content per 100 m increase in elevation.

Variations in the deuterium and oxygen-18 contents in precipitation are linearly correlated. H. Craig in 1961 gave a relationship which best fits points representing the isotopic compositions of precipitation samples from all over the world.[25] It is

$$\delta D\%_{oo} = 8\delta^{18}O\%_{oo} - 10$$

and is valid at least for values of $\delta^{18}O$ lower than zero with respect to SMOW (standard mean ocean water).† The $\delta\%_{oo}$ represents the difference in parts per mil of the isotopic ratio of a sample with respect to that of

---

† Harold C. Urey and his group originally used PDB-1 Chicago standard for δ measurements in palaeotemperature analyses and on the SMOW scale the value for this is $+0.22\%_{oo}$. 'Average ocean water' was defined in 1953 utilising samples from Atlantic, Pacific and Indian Ocean sources and standard mean ocean water in 1961 in terms of NBS isotope reference sample number one, the first almost coinciding with the second. It is thought appropriate because the oceans constitute the initial and end points of any important hydrological circuit and contain c. 97% of the water present on the planetary crust. SMOW has $\delta^{18}O$ and δD both equal to zero, mandatory in an ultimate standard.

In September 1976 in Vienna during the Consultants Meeting on Stable Isotope Standards and Intercalibration in Hydrology and Geochemistry, however, it was decided that for practical reasons the Vienna–SMOW standard (V–SMOW) should be employed and original SMOW has the following isotopic composition with respect to it:

$$\delta D = +0.2\%_{oo} \text{ and } \delta^{18}O = +0.04\%_{oo}$$

These minor variations do not affect the arguments used above and later. The D/H absolute ratio of V–SMOW has been determined by R. Hagemmann et al. in 1970 (*Tellus*, **22**, 712) as

$$D/H \text{ (V–SMOW)} = (155.76 \pm 0.05) \times 10^{-6}$$

The $^{18}O/^{16}O$ absolute ratio has been determined by P. Baertschi in 1976 (*Earth Planet. Sci. Letts*, **31**, 314) as

$$^{18}O/^{16}O \text{ (V–SMOW)} = (2005.20 \pm 0.45) \times 10^{-6}$$

According to R. Gonfiantini in 1978 (Standards for stable isotope measurements in natural compounds, *Nature*, **271**, 534–6), V–SMOW was obtained by mixing distilled ocean water with small amounts of other waters in order to bring its isotopic composition as close as possible to the defined SMOW. A further standard has been proposed and may be mentioned. This is SLAP (standard light Antarctic precipitation) which has the following values relative to V–SMOW:

$$^{18}O \text{ (SLAP)} = -55.5\%_{oo} \text{ and } D \text{ (SLAP)} = -428\%_{oo}$$

mean ocean water

$$\delta\%_{oo} = \left[\frac{R_{sample}}{R_{SMOW}} - 1\right] \times 1000$$

where R is the isotope ratio D/H or $^{18}O/^{16}O$.

In some parts of the world the penultimate equation possesses a different intercept on the δD axis, but a slope of 8 is usual. Precipitation subject to significant evaporation during its fall does not obey the equation. Evaporation enriches both heavy isotopes in water but not in the relative proportion indicated in it. It is interesting to note that when precipitation infiltrates, the mixing in the unsaturated zone irons out isotopic variations and the resultant water reaching the saturated zone has a composition which corresponds to the mean isotopic composition of infiltration in the region. This is normally slightly different from the mean isotopic composition of the precipitation in the same region because not all of the latter during the year infiltrates in the same proportion. In temperate continental locations spring and summer precipitation partly or wholly re-evaporates from the soil before infiltration has an opportunity to take place. In the aquifer the isotopic composition usually remains unchanged unless exchange occurs with the oxygen of the strata or, as may happen in arid zones, evaporation takes place from the water table. Exchange does not take place to any significant degree at the water temperatures usually found in aquifers, but may do so in the case of thermal waters in geothermal regions. Clearly, therefore, the isotopic composition of a groundwater will relate to precipitation in the recharge area at the time when recharge occurred. This is important because groundwater may be tens of thousands of years old and the climatic conditions of the area may have altered considerably since recharge.

As regards tritium, this is produced naturally in the upper atmosphere by the interaction of cosmic radiation with it at a rate of about 0·25 atoms/cm^2/sec according to D. Lal and H. E. Suess.[26] During 1953 and thereafter until 1962, a series of injections of man-made tritium entered the atmosphere through thermonuclear testing and small quantities are released continuously by industrial nuclear activities. Most of the tritium produced in the atmosphere is rapidly oxidised to HTO and incorporated in the hydrologic cycle. In view of its half-life, it then constitutes a very valuable label for water that has been in the atmosphere within the past two decades. Of course the dilution by H_2O results in a very low tritium concentration so that an enrichment treatment is required before it can be measured. The tritium content of natural waters is expressed in tritium units (TU), one tritium unit corresponding to a concentration of 1 tritium atom per 10^{18} hydrogen atoms, effectively the lowest limit of detection in the majority of laboratories. Before 1953, cosmic radiation-produced atmospheric tritium showed a concentration of around 10 TU in temperature zone continental meteoric waters. After 1953, a great increase measurable in orders of magnitude occurred as a result of thermonuclear testing as was indicated by R. M. Brown in 1961.[27] Values as high as 10 000 TU were attained in the northern hemisphere in 1963 following the extensive testing of 1961–62; see L. L. Thatcher and B. R. Payne.[28] Subsequently, a decrease in the tritium concentration of precipitation occurred until 1968 because of the moratorium on the explosion of thermonuclear devices in the atmosphere. After 1968 the tritium decrease has lessened considerably so that existing tritium concentrations in precipitation remain well above pre-1953 values. The International Atomic Energy Agency in Vienna publishes data regarding the concentrations of tritium in precipitation sampled at many stations throughout the world and from these tritium deposition at any particular location can be estimated. Of course in groundwater studies tritium measurements provide information on the time of recharge to the system in confined aquifers. Unfortunately, in unconfined aquifers unrepresentatively low tritium contents may be present due to only slight infiltration in arid and semi-arid regions or long percolation time where the water table is very deep or even age stratification in water in the saturated zone. If groundwater has a concentration of less than about 3 TU, no water younger than 25 years can be present while tritium contents between 2 and 20 TU indicate that a small quantity of thermonuclear tritium is present and probably indicates the presence of water from the first bomb test period from 1954 to 1961. Tritium contents in excess of 20 TU demonstrate that such water is of recent origin. If variations occur throughout the year and are related to variations in precipitation over the area of recharge, the throughput is both direct and rapid and the transit time may be estimated from the time lag in appearance of the annual peaks. The variability may result from a seasonal change in the source of the water or the relative proportions of water from different sources. In the latter case young, high tritium content water may mix with tritium dead water of deeper circulational origin. The foregoing argument is based upon the assumption that dispersivity is negligible, i.e. that the groundwater remains discretely segregated according to age during transit. This will not be so in nature and consequently tritium peaks and valleys become smoothed out thus only revealing periods and not specific years of recharge. Sometimes waters with tritium contents running to hundreds of tritium units may occur and no fluctuations can be observed. This probably represents young water which has become very well mixed with older water in the aquifer. The dimensions of the groundwater reservoir dampens the fluctuations occurring in the recharge water and the system constitutes a 'well mixed reservoir' illustrating exponential discharge and a mean residence time of water within it can be estimated following the approaches of A. Nir in 1964[29] and T. Dincer and G. H. Davis in 1967.[30] In 1974 K. Przewlocki and Y. Yurtsever devised more complex conceptual mathematical models and digital simulation approaches in interpreting tritium tracer variations in hydrologic systems.[31] Radiocarbon has also been utilised in residence time studies where these exceed the 50 year span of tritium. This is because its half-life is so much longer that it extends the age range from several hundred to about 50 000 years. Each of the radioisotopes has its own unique rate of decay described by the half-life, the time required for one-half of the radioactive atoms to decay. The decay law is expressed thus:

$$N = N_0 e^{-\lambda t}$$

where N is the number of radioactive atoms present at time t, N_0 the number present initially and λ the decay constant in reciprocal time. Clearly the time needed for half the original activity to decay is independent of the number of atoms at the beginning and inserting this time, the half-life designated $t_{1/2}$, into the preceding equation, the following is derived:

$$\tfrac{1}{2}N_0 = N_0 e^{-\lambda t_{1/2}}$$

from which is derived

$$\lambda t_{1/2} = \ln 2 = 0 \cdot 693$$

The decay law is the basis of radioactive dating and with reference to groundwater

$$A = A_0 e^{-\lambda t}$$

where A is the observed radioactivity, A_0 is the activity at the time the water entered the aquifer and the other symbols have the meanings already ascribed to them.

As regards radiocarbon, the ratio $^{14}C:^{12}C$ is constant in living material using carbon dioxide in its life cycle and in substances like water which react with CO_2. This is the 'modern ^{14}C content' alluded to earlier in Table 1.6 and related to the situation up to 1950. Subsequently, excess radiocarbon has been added to the atmosphere as a result of thermonuclear testing so that present levels are larger than 'modern' levels. The 'modern' ^{14}C remains constant so long as equilibrium with the atmospheric reservoir is maintained, but when removal from this occurs, e.g. when water leaves the aerated zone to enter the groundwater system, then the quantity of radiocarbon decreases according to the law of radioactive decay. In practice this 'dating' tool is difficult to employ because the different chemical forms of carbon present in groundwater must be considered together with possible interactions.

As regards radon-222, this has a half-life of 3·8 days and most groundwater contains traces of the gas produced by continuous decay of ^{226}Rn in rocks. Some may escape to the atmosphere and concentrations of it in rain have been utilised to distinguish the source of moisture in monsoonal precipitation in India.

Silicon-32 has a half-life around 600 years[†] and could fill the gap

---

[†] As regards the half-life of ^{32}Si, this is not precisely known and the value assigned to it is an approximate mean of the highest given in the literature which include the following:

(i)   60 years (Turkevich, A., Samuels, A., 1954. Evidence for ^{32}Si, a long lived beta emitter. *Phys. Rev.*, **94**, 364).

(ii)   276 ± 32 years (Demaster, D. J., 1980. The half-life of ^{32}Si determined from a varved Gulf of California sediment core. *Earth Planet. Sci. Letts*, **48**, 209–17).

(iii)   280 years (Jantsch, K., 1967. Kernreaktionen mit Tritonen beim ^{30}Si. Bestimmung der Halbwertzeit von ^{32}Si. *Kernenergie*, **10**, 89).

(iv)   330 years (Clausen, H. B., 1973. Dating of polar ice by ^{32}Si. *J. Glaciol.*, **12**, 411).

(v)   500 years (Honda, M., Lal, D., 1964. Spallation cross sections for long lived radionuclides in iron and light nuclei. *Nuc. Phys.*, **51**, 363).

(vi)   650 years (Geithoff, D., 1962. Über die Herstellung von ^{32}Si durch einen (t,p)-Prozess. *Radiochim. Acta Bd 1*, **Ht 1**, 3).

(vii)   710 years (Lindner, M., 1953. New nuclides produced in chlorine spallation reactions. *Phys. Rev.*, **91**, 642).

The effective 'dating' range will be four half-lives, so clearly this will range from 250 to almost 3000 years according to which value is adopted, but in any event the radioisotope always fills part of the gap between tritium and radiocarbon.

between tritium and radiocarbon in hydrological dating work. It is a radioactive isotope produced by the cosmic ray-induced spallation of argon. It rapidly oxidises to $^{32}SiO_2$ which is scavenged from the atmosphere by precipitation. The total annual production is extremely small, only a few grams in fact, but more was produced artificially during the thermonuclear bomb test series of 1961 to 1962.

1.12. THE GLOBAL WATER BALANCE

Studies of this have been made by a number of workers, but only first approximations are possible at present. With regard to individual oceans their water balances involve precipitation, evaporation and runoff as well as water exchange between them and may be expressed thus

$$P + r = E \pm \Delta W$$

where P is precipitation, E is evaporation, r is runoff and ΔW is the water exchange factor. Table 1.7 is an attempt at quantification.

TABLE 1.7
WATER BALANCE OF THE OCEANS IN CM/YEAR

	Precipitation	Runoff from adjacent land areas	Evaporation	Water exchange with other oceans
Atlantic	78	20	104	−6
Arctic	24	23	12	35
Indian	101	7	138	−30
Pacific	121	6	124	13

For continents the water balance equation reduces to

$$P = E + r$$

and Table 1.8 is an attempt at quantification.

For the entire planet, it appears that precipitation and evaporation are of the order of 100 cm and the data may be represented as below in Table 1.9.

Additional important information is contained in Table 1.10.

Water is a global resource and the oceans, ice caps, glaciers, lakes, rivers, streams, soils and the planetary atmosphere contain almost

TABLE 1.8

WATER BALANCE OF THE CONTINENTS IN CM/YEAR

	Precipitation	Evaporation	Runoff
Africa	67	51	16
Europe	60	36	24
Asia	61	39	22
North America	67	40	27
South America	135	86	49
Australia	47	41	6

TABLE 1.9

THE GLOBAL WATER BALANCE (CM/YEAR)[32]

	Precipitation	Evaporation	Runoff
Oceans	112	125	− 13
Continents	72	41	31
Earth	100	100	0

$1\frac{1}{2}$ million cubic kilometres of it, nearly all in the salt waters of the seas which cover three-quarters of the Earth's surface. Of the residual 28% or so, some three-quarters is contained in polar ice caps and glaciers. Most of what is left comprises primarily deep lying groundwater. That minute fraction still unaccounted for is continually recycling and precipitation equals evaporation at an overall world rate of approximately 1000 mm annually as stated in Table 1.9 above. The imbalance entailed by the fact that the oceans lose more water by evaporation than they gain from precipitation is vitally important for life on land, the tiny proportion of fresh water thus gained being sufficient to sustain it.

On a regional basis, water is very unevenly distributed. That flowing in river systems, while a very small quantity of total water, is the major life support as it provides for the bulk of the surficial fresh water supply impounded in lakes.

In the West people are fortunate in that water can usually be drunk directly from the tap without fear. That this is not the case elsewhere was one of the motivating factors behind the organisation of the International Drinking Water Supply and Sanitation Decade programme of the United Nations and its specialised agencies. Whether this can achieve results paralleling the situation for instance in the United Kingdom where about 2 tonnes of water are supplied to each household weekly is unlikely to be known until the end of the decade, but it appears

TABLE 1.10

DISTRIBUTION AND RESIDENCE TIME OF VARIOUS CONSTITUENTS OF THE PLANETARY WATER BALANCE[33,34]

Item	Volume (km^3)	Percentage of total	Residence time (years)
Supply			
Oceans	1.37×10^9	97·2	40 000
Icecaps, glaciers	29.2×10^6	2·13	10 000
Groundwater down to 4 000 m	8.35×10^6	0·59	5 000
Fresh water lakes	125×10^3	0·0089	100
Saline lakes and inland seas	104×10^3	0·0074	100
Soil moisture and vadose water	67×10^3	0·00475	1
Atmosphere	13×10^3	0·00092	0·1
Rivers (average instantaneous volume)	1.25×10^3	0·00009	1
Total	1.41×10^9	100	
Budget			
Annual evaporation from oceans	350×10^3	0·026	
Annual evaporation from land	70×10^3	0·005	
Total annual evaporation	420×10^3	0·031	
Annual precipitation on oceans	320×10^3	0·024	
Annual precipitation on land	100×10^3	0·007	
Total annual precipitation	420×10^3	0·031	
Annual runoff to oceans	32×10^3	0·003	
Annual groundwater outflow to oceans	1.6×10^3	0·0001	
Total annual runoff and outflow	33.6×10^3	0·0031	

to be rather improbable although some amelioration will be effected. The attainment of such results would bring its own problems as in the United Kingdom—all water supplied must be removed after usage. Hence the sewerage system must become more extensive as Celia Kirby pointed out in 1979.[35] In fact the provision of sewers in developed countries is also a problem; for example in the UK there is a vast underground network that has been in existence since the island's cities and towns expanded in the last half of the nineteenth century; this has been neglected and hence extensive renovation and replacement are urgently required. Assuming an average life expectancy of a century for pipes and conduits and with a constant rate of installation, the United Kingdom's commitment to replacement alone ought to be around 1% of the total annual expenditure on water resources and could amount to a very large sum probably exceeding £300 million (US$600 million or so).

When extremely large and very old cities such as London are considered, the problems are compounded and according to Celia Kirby £15 to £20 million should be spent there immediately. One of the difficulties in executing remedial work in such areas is that maps of sewers installed a long time ago are often unobtainable. As in the UK there are some 234 000 km of regional water authority sewers together with 200 000 km of buried pipes of highway authorities, no easy solutions are available and the case of a Public Health Inspector may be mentioned—he referred to futile efforts to trace the path of some disused sewers utilising tracer dyes and not a drop of the chemical used ever reappeared.

Water circulation in the atmosphere and oceans is closely related to the global energy budget. The annual input of solar radiation into the system and the net loss of terrestrial radiation produce a positive energy budget in low latitudes and a negative energy budget in middle and high latitudes, the budget being balanced at about 35° latitude for annual averages. As a result of this heat, transport in a polar direction is essential if the high latitude zones are not to become progressively colder and the low latitude zones progressively hotter. Such transport occurs through atmospheric transport of sensible and latent heat in the form of water vapour which later condenses as well as through the transport of warm water by oceanic currents. Approximately 80% of polar directed heat transport occurs in the atmosphere where latent heat transport reflects the pattern of the global wind belts on either side of sub-tropical high pressure zones and at about 10°N and 10°S the flux is equatorially directed consequent upon the transport of moisture into the equatorial low pressure trough by the trade winds. Most of the atmospheric heat transport is by warm air masses, however, i.e. sensible heat transport. As regards oceanic currents, the principal ones are the Gulf Stream and Kuro Shio in the northern hemisphere and the Brazil Current and the poleward branches of the Equatorial Currents in the south west Pacific and south west Indian Oceans in the southern hemisphere. They are most important at about 35° to 40° latitude. Obviously the interdependence of the various parts of the hydrologic cycle means that a change in any of the various climatic parameters can produce extensive repercussions, e.g. a 1% increase in evaporation from the tropical oceans would cool a 200 m layer by 3°C in half a century according to J. S. Malkus in 1962.[36] Of course such climatic changes occurred in the past and can be detected by a number of techniques, among them palaeotemperature analysis using oxygen isotope ratios. This investigative tool was devised by Harold C. Urey and utilised by many workers including the author.[37,38] Research shows that during the Quaternary glacial maximum ice affected an area three times greater than the present ice cover and the mass of ice on the planet exceeded that of today by a factor of about five. A concomitant lowering of sea level occurred and this reached as much as 160 m. This probably caused a decrease in precipitation and evaporation because of the exposure of a greater land area. Conversely, a rise in sea level promotes higher precipitation and evaporation. The quantification of these assertions is difficult although 20% would seem a reasonable estimate, at least during the full glacial stages. At the end of these when the climate commenced to ameliorate, increased runoff from the melting ice caps caused an eustatic rise in sea level probably beginning around 18 000 years BP (before the present) at a time when the datum lay perhaps 100 to 120 m below that of today and proceeded steadily and practically into historic times.

It is clear that other information would be required to improve knowledge of the global water balance, especially in its localised aspects, because this would facilitate water planning. Of course future demand will always be difficult to estimate but extra data acquisition is going on all the time. Water studies oriented towards weather forecasting could be very significant. Sophisticated computer modelling already exists for global air circulation, but will not be sufficiently specific for small areas to aid water planners for some time yet. Demand projections may be made despite the difficulty in forecasting alluded to above—this is enforced by the long period required to implement new supplies which may extend over two decades or more. Finally, there remains the freak weather pattern and whether these can ever be predicted in enough time to counteract their often disastrous impact is questionable. One can only hope that continued and continuous effort will enable tragedies such as the great drought in the Sahel either to be averted or ameliorated, concomitantly obviating or at least reducing their economic, sociopolitical and ecological consequences which are often so horrendous that they are unmeasurable.

REFERENCES

1. BUSWELL, A. M. and RODEBUSH, W. H., 1956. Water. *Scientific American*, **194**, 4, 76–89.
2. BOWEN, R., 1980. *Ground Water*. Applied Science Publishers Ltd, London and Halsted Press, New York.

3. CHOW, V. T., 1964. Hydrology and its development. in: *Handbook of Applied Hydrology*. McGraw-Hill Book Company, New York.
4. MAZOR, E., VERHAGEN, B. T., SELLSCHOP, J. P. F., ROBBINS, N. S. and HUTTON, L. G., 1974. Kalahari groundwaters: their hydrogen, carbon and oxygen isotopes. in: *Isotopic Techniques in Groundwater Hydrology*. IAEA, Vienna, 203–25.
5. BURDON, D. J. and MAZLOUM, S., 1959. Some chemical types of groundwater from Syria in salinity problems in the arid zones. *UNESCO-Arid Zone Research*, **XIV**, 73–90.
6. BURDON, D. J., 1974. Data on water resources for the agricultural development of Tokar Delta and Red Sea Hills, Sudan ME. FAO.
7. DRABBE, J., BADON GHYBEN, W., 1888–89. Nota in verband met de voorgenomen putboring nabij Amsterdam. Tijdschrift van het Koninklijk Instituut van Ingenieurs, The Hague, Netherlands, 8–22.
8. HERZBERG, B., 1901. Die Wasserversorgung einiger Nordseebader. *J. Gasbeleuchtung und Wasserversorgung*, **44**, 815–9 and 842–4.
9. LUSCZYNSKI, N. J. and SWARZENSKI, W. V., 1966. Salt water encroachment in southern Nassau and southeastern Queens Counties, Long Island, New York, USA. US Geol. Surv. Water Supply Paper 1613-F.
10. CHARMONMAN, S., 1965. A solution of the pattern of fresh water flow in an unconfined coastal aquifer. *J. Geophys. Res.*, **70**, 2813–9.
11. TODD, D. K., 1980. *Groundwater Hydrology*. John Wiley and Sons, New York.
12. PINDER, G. F. and COOPER, H. H., 1970. A numerical technique for calculating the transient position of the salt water front. *Water Resources Res.*, **6**, 875–82.
13. ACKERMANN, N. L. and CHANG, Y. Y., 1971. Salt water interface during groundwater pumping. *J. Hydraulics Division., Am. Soc. Civil Eng.*, **97**, HY2, 223–32.
14. STRINGFIELD, V. T. and LEGRAND, H. E., 1971. Effects of karst features on circulation of water in carbonate rocks in coastal areas. *J. Hydrology*, **14**, 139–57.
15. BOWEN, R., 1981. *Grouting in Engineering Practice*, 2nd edn. Applied Science Publishers Ltd, London and Halsted Press, New York.
16. ARAD, A., KAFRI, U. and FLEISHER, E., 1975. The Na'aman springs, northern Israel: salination mechanism of an irregular fresh water–sea water interface. *J. Hydrology*, **25**, 259–74.
17. VANDERBERG, A., 1975. Simultaneous pumping of fresh and salt water from a coastal aquifer. *J. Hydrology*, **24**, 37–43.
18. DINCER, T., PAYNE, B. R., MARTINEC, J., TONGIORGI, E. and FLORKOWSKI, T., 1968. An environmental isotope study of the snowmelt-runoff in a representative basin. IAEA, Tech. Repts Ser. 91, 190.
19. WORLD WATER, 1980. D-Day for the Water Decade. Special reprint of articles from the journal in November and December 1980 produced for UNICEF and UNDP, 8–10.
20. BECHER, E., 1980. Measuring the Decade's success in D-Day for the Water Decade. Ibid., 8–10.
21. BERTONI, N., 1980. Djibouti needs water. *New York Times*, 4 September.

22. WEISSKOPF, M., 1981. Devastating drought forces China to seek foreign help. *The Washington Post* reprinted in the *Guardian Weekly*, April 19.
23. DANSGAARD, W., 1964. Stable isotopes in precipitation. *Tellus*, **19**, 435–63.
24. MOSER, H. and STICHLER, W., 1970. Deuterium measurements in snow samples from the Alps. in: *Isotope Hydrology*. IAEA, Vienna, 43–57.
25. CRAIG, H., 1961. Standard for reporting concentrations of deuterium and oxygen-18 in natural waters. *Science*, **133**, 1833.
26. LAL, D. and SUESS, H. E., 1968. The radioactivity of the atmosphere and hydrosphere. *Ann. Rev. Nucl. Sci.*, **18**, 407–35.
27. BROWN, R. M., 1961. Hydrology of tritium in the Ottawa Valley. *Geochim. Cosmochim. Acta*, **21**, 199–216.
28. THATCHER, L. L. and PAYNE, B. R., 1965. The distribution of tritium in precipitation over continents and its significance to groundwater dating. *6th Int. Conf. Radiocarbon and Tritium Dating*, Pullman, Washington, 603–29.
29. NIR, A., 1964. On the interpretation of tritium 'age' measurements of groundwater. *J. Geophys. Res.*, **69**, 2589–95.
30. DINCER, T. and DAVIS, G. H., 1967. Some considerations on tritium dating and the estimates of tritium input function. *Proc. 8th Cong. Int. Ass. Hydrogeol.*, Istanbul, 276–85.
31. PRZEWLOCKI, K. and YURTSEVER, Y., 1974. Some conceptual mathematical models and digital simulation approach in the use of tracers in hydrological systems. in: *Isotope Techniques in Groundwater Hydrology*, 2, IAEA, Vienna, 425–50.
32. BUDYKO, M. L., 1962. The heat balance of the surface of the Earth. *Soviet Geog.*, **3**, 5, 3–16.
33. NACE, R. L., 1967. Water resources: a global problem with local roots. *Environmental Sci. Tech.*, **1**, 550–60.
34. MENARD, H. W. and SMITH, S. M., 1966. Hypsometry of ocean basin provinces. *J. Geophys. Res.*, **71**, 18, 4305–25.
35. KIRBY, CELIA, 1979. *Water in Great Britain*, Penguin Books, Harmondsworth.
36. MALKUS, J. S., 1962. Interchange of properties between sea and air. in: *The Sea*, Vol. 1, 88–294.
37. UREY, H. C., LOWENSTAM, H. A., EPSTEIN, S. and MCKINNERY, C. R., 1951. Measurements of paleotemperatures and temperatures of the Upper Cretaceous of England, Denmark and the southeastern US. *Bull. Geol. Soc. Am.*, **62**, 399–416.
38. BOWEN, R., 1966. *Paleotemperature Analysis*. Elsevier, Amsterdam.

CHAPTER 2

The Atmosphere

2.1. ENERGY IN THE ATMOSPHERE

The air is a mechanical mixture of gases and so highly compressible that its lower layers are much denser than overlying ones. It constitutes the atmosphere which is probably unique in the solar system because it contains water vapour, most of this being near its saturation point as a result of which cloudless conditions can change rapidly to obscure ones. Atmospheric water amounts to only 0.1% of the total quantity of water on the planetary surface but it is very significant in determining surficial conditions on the Earth. This is because of its effect upon impinging solar radiation and outgoing infrared radiation. About 84.4% of atmospheric moisture is derived from oceanic evaporation. The energy of the atmosphere appears to remain constant and only derives in part from the sun, another source being terrestrial heat escaping from the planetary interior. As regards the former (termed insolation), 28% is reflected and lost at once and while some of the remainder is intercepted by water vapour, ozone and dust in the atmosphere, 48% is absorbed by the Earth. It is apparent that the atmosphere is mainly heated from below because the Earth absorbs more of the insolation than the atmosphere. The component absorbed by the Earth is ultimately returned to space, but only after a complex transfer process. Convection currents carry sensible heat and evaporated water vapour upwards to the troposphere (defined below); the latter contains latent heat abstracted from the evaporating surface. Long wave radiant heat is also radiated by the planet but, unlike solar radiation, this is quickly absorbed by water and water vapour so that very little escapes through the atmosphere and only a minute

51

fraction reaches space directly. The bulk is absorbed by water vapour or clouds and reradiated, nearly all of this returning to Earth where it is absorbed, converted back to heat and again radiated. Thus a heat exchange process is maintained between the planet and its atmosphere. That large quantity of heat retained in the lower atmosphere is a consequence of this greenhouse effect. Of course there is a considerable variation of the heat budget with latitude. Over the Earth as a whole the poles receive less heat from the sun than the equatorial belt, hence the difference in temperature between the two regions. It has been found that the polar caps (embracing the areas between 35°N and 35°S to the poles) have an annual heat deficit, about half of the planetary surface together with most densely settled areas suffer a net radiative loss of heat over the year but the equatorial belt (35°N to 35°S) shows a net gain (insolation exceeding loss by radiation). Atmospheric circulation prevents the poles from getting progressively cooler and the equator from getting progressively warmer. There is also a variation of temperature with altitude.

In the lower atmosphere, temperatures decrease with elevation and this phenomenon is termed the lapse rate of temperature. It varies from place to place, but a variation also occurs from moment to moment. Lapse rates involve a fall in temperature with increase in altitude so that this is represented positively. Where an inverted lapse rate occurs, i.e. temperature rises with height, a negative sign is utilised. Upper air soundings indicate that the region of the atmosphere with positive lapse rates is succeeded by a region in which temperatures show a slow rise with height. The former is termed the troposphere, the latter the stratosphere. The boundary between the two is termed the tropopause. Practically all water vapour occurs in the troposphere and so do clouds and storms, the stratosphere being clear, dry and almost invariably cloudless. The tropopause varies in altitude and is lower with low temperature, low pressure and in winter. In the UK the tropopause oscillates between 20 000 and 40 000 feet whereas the tropical tropopause is at about 55 000 feet with a temperature of approximately −80°C. The tropopause acts as a lid limiting convection and constitutes an inversion level or weather ceiling. The stratosphere extends upwards from it to about 50 km and contains most of the total atmospheric ozone which reaches a peak density around 22 km. However, the maximum temperatures associated with the absorption of the solar ultraviolet radiation by ozone do not occur until the more exposed upper levels are reached at the stratopause where they may rise to over 0°C. Marked seasonal temperature changes affect the stratosphere so that, for instance, the cold winter conditions may suddenly warm because of circulation changes and temperatures at about 25 km may rise from $-80°C$ to $-40°C$ in a couple of days. Above the relatively warm stratopause, temperatures decrease to a minimum of about $-90°C$ around 80 km where a layer termed the mesosphere is found (some authors extend the meaning of this term to cover a layer extending from 20 to 80 km). Above 80 km the temperatures rise with elevation, an inversion referred to as the meso-pause. Here noctilucent clouds may occur over high latitudes in summer. They probably arise from meteoric dust particles acting as nuclei for ice crystals when traces of water vapour are carried upwards by high level convection caused by the vertical decrease of temperature in the mesosphere. Pressure is extremely low in the mesosphere, decreas-ing from approximately 1 mb at 50 km to 0·01 mb at 90 km. Above the mesosphere the atmospheric densities are very low indeed and the region of the thermosphere in its lower part comprises nitrogen (N_2) and oxygen (both molecular and atomic, i.e. as O_2 and O). Above 200 km atomic oxygen predominates. Temperatures rise with elevation as a result of the absorption of ultraviolet radiation by atomic oxygen. Above 100 km the atmosphere is increasingly affected by solar X-rays and ultraviolet radiation which cause ionisation. Penetration of ionising particles from 300 km to 80 km, especially in zones about 20° to 25° latitude from the Earth's magnetic poles, produces the Aurora Borealis and the Aurora Australis. Sometimes these phenomena occur at altitudes up to 1000 km and this demonstrates that a rarefied atmosphere extends to a much greater extent than is commonly supposed. The layers above 80 km are sometimes termed the ionosphere, but occasionally it is a term applied only for regions of high electron density between about 100 and 300 km. The mesosphere is followed by the exosphere and magneto-sphere. The exosphere has a base between 500 and 750 km and here the atmospheric constituents are atoms of oxygen, hydrogen and helium (about 1% of these being ionised). The last two have low atomic weights and can escape into space because the chance of molecular collisions deflecting them downwards diminishes with increasing altitude. Hydrogen is replaced as a result of the breakdown of water vapour and methane near the mesopause. Helium is produced by the action of cosmic radiation on nitrogen and also by the decay of radioactive elements in the crust of the Earth. Ionised particles increase in frequency through the exosphere and beyond about 2000 km in the magnetosphere there are only electrons and protons, charged particles which are concentrated into two bands at approximately 4000 and 20 000 km known as the Van Allen 'radiation' belts, presumably as the result of the trapping of ionised particles from the sun, the solar wind, and also perhaps cosmic radiation by the terrestrial magnetic field. It is possible that at 80 000 km or so the atmosphere of the Earth merges with that of the sun.

As regards the composition of the atmosphere, air is made up of the gases listed in Table 2.1.

TABLE 2.1
CONSTITUENTS OF THE ATMOSPHERE EXPRESSED AS
PERCENTAGES OF THE TOTAL MASS OF DRY AIR

Gas or vapour		Mass % of dry air
Fixed gases	Nitrogen	75·51
	Oxygen	23·15
	Argon etc.	1·28
	Other gases	Trace
Variable gases	Carbon dioxide	<0·03
	Water vapour	<3
	Ozone	<0·0005

The term fixed gases used in Table 2.1 means those which do not vary in their relative proportions except at very great altitudes. The variable gases with which water vapour is included show rapid and wide variability. Despite its minute amount, ozone is significant because it dominates the thermal behaviour of the stratosphere.

Water vapour is that stage of the hydrologic cycle from which precipitation derives and serves as an important store house of heat. Large quantities of heat are added to the oceanic surface to produce evaporation and the resultant water vapour carries away latent heat which can be transported through great distances and later released as warmth when condensation takes place. Water vapour differs from most gases in that it can acquire part of the impinging solar energy and so warm up the air and also in being capable of intercepting outgoing terrestrial radiation so that a considerable amount of heat is retained in the lower atmosphere.

2.2. ATMOSPHERIC MOISTURE

Relevant data are given in Table 2.2.

TABLE 2.2
MEAN WATER CONTENT OF THE ATMOSPHERE IN cm OF RAINFALL
EQUIVALENT

Month	Northern hemisphere	Southern hemisphere	World
January	1·9	2·5	2·2
July	3·4	2·0	2·7

The average storage of water in the atmosphere is about 2·5 cm and this only suffices for approximately 10 days supply of rainfall over the planet as a whole. However, there may be intense horizontal influx of moisture into the air over any given region and this permits short-term rainfall totals greatly in excess of 2·5 cm. The atmosphere acquires moisture by evaporation from oceans, lakes, rivers and soils as well as by transpiration from plants, i.e. through evapotranspiration.

Evaporation takes place whenever energy is transported to an evaporating surface if the vapour pressure in the air is less than the saturated value. The saturation vapour pressure increases with temperature. Energy is expended to overcome intermolecular attraction whenever liquid changes state and becomes vapour, this energy being obtained by the removal of heat from the environment causing an apparent heat loss (latent heat) and thus a diminution in temperature. The latent heat of vaporisation to evaporate 1 g of water at 0°C is 600 calories whereas at 100°C it is 540 calories. Conversely, the process of condensation releases this heat so that the temperature of the air mass in which it occurs rises as the water vapour reverts to the liquid state. Daily temperature range is moderated by moist air conditions when evaporation takes place during the day and condensation takes place at night. Evaporation also involves an addition of kinetic energy to the individual water molecules. As their velocity rises so does the possibility that they may escape into the atmosphere, the most rapid ones being the first to do so. A concomitant of this is that the residual liquid will lose energy and temperature. Thus evaporation will diminish the temperature of this residual liquid by a quantity proportional to the latent heat of the process.

Evaporation rate depends in part upon the difference between saturation vapour pressure (pressure exerted by a vapour in a saturated atmosphere) at the water surface and the vapour pressure of the air as well as in part upon the availability of a continual energy supply to the surface. Wind velocity is extremely important because wind usually imports unsaturated air to an area and this can absorb the available moisture.

Transpiration occurs when the vapour pressure in leaf cells exceeds the atmospheric vapour pressure and it is controlled by those atmospheric factors determining evaporation as well as by plant factors such as stage of growth, leaf area and temperature and quantity of soil moisture. It takes place mostly during the daylight hours when the leaf pores or stomata are open. It varies with season as does evaporation. It is difficult to separate water evaporated from soil, intercepted moisture which remains on vegetational surfaces after precipitation and later evaporated and transpiration. Losses from natural surfaces through evapotranspiration can only be measured indirectly, sometimes by using the moisture balance equation:

Precipitation = Runoff + Evapotranspiration + Soil moisture storage change

The appropriate instrument is a lysimeter which facilitates measurement of percolation through an enclosed soil block with a vegetational cover after recorded precipitation. Regular weighing is effected so that weight changes not due to rainfall or runoff are ascribed to evapotranspiration. Where the soil block is regularly watered, the vegetable cover always gives the maximum possible evapotranspiration and the corresponding water loss is termed the potential evapotranspiration, PE (water loss related to available energy), and it forms the basis for a system of climate classification derived by C. W. Thornthwaite. Theoretical approaches to the problem of assessing evaporation rates follow several lines. One relates average monthly evaporation from large water bodies to the mean wind velocity and the mean vapour pressure difference between the water surface and the air in the form

$$E = Ru(e_w - e_a)$$

where E is evaporation, R an empirical constant, u the wind velocity and e_w and e_a the vapour pressures involved. This is an aerodynamic solution taking into account the factors which remove vapour from the surface of the water. A second is based upon the energy budget. The net balance of solar and terrestrial radiation at the surface (Rn) is utilised for evaporation (E) and the conduction of heat to the atmosphere (Ht) so that

$$Rn = EL + Ht$$

where L is the latent heat of evaporation. While the net radiation can be measured Ht can be estimated as a proportion of E and not measured. The relation Ht/EL is termed Bowen's ratio and it is proportional to the ratio of the vertical gradients of temperature and vapour pressure between the surface and the level of instrumental measurements in the air. The utilisation of Bowen's ratio depends upon the assumption that vertical transfers of heat and water vapour by turbulence occur with equal efficiency and evaporation is determinable thus

$$E = \frac{Rn}{L(1-\beta)}$$

where β is Bowen's ratio as defined above. H. L. Penman has combined both of the above lines and so managed to eliminate some of the unmeasurable quantities. He expressed evaporation losses in terms of four meteorological elements which are usually regularly measured. These are:

(i)   sunshine duration which clearly relates to amounts of radiation;
(ii)   mean air temperature;
(iii) mean air humidity;
(iv)   mean wind velocity (this limits losses of heat and vapour from the surface).

Penman's formula has been used to calculate annual evaporation over the United Kingdom and gives a range from 38 cm in Scotland to 50 cm in parts of south and southeast England. Thornthwaite's method gives results for annual potential evapotranspiration in southeast England as 64 cm.

Turning to humidity, the moisture content of the atmosphere is measurable by determining the total mass of water in any given volume of air, i.e. the density of the water vapour, and thereby the absolute humidity is derived (g/m^3). The mass mixing ratio may also be used, i.e. the mass of water vapour in grams per kilogram of dry air. For most purposes the specific humidity is identical as it is the mass of vapour per kilogram of air including its moisture. Most of the atmospheric moisture content occurs below 550 mb pressure level, i.e. below 5574 m, and below about 700 mb there is a marked seasonal effect, diminution taking place in the winter season. Another significant measure is relative humidity, the actual moisture content of a sample of air compared with that contained in the same volume of saturated air at the same temperature. Lastly, the dew point temperature may be mentioned. It is the temperature at which saturation occurs if air is cooled at constant pressure without either the addition or removal of vapour. Where air temperature and dew point are equal the relative humidity is 100%. The atmosphere transports moisture horizontally as well as vertically and the amounts which have to be moved meridionally so that the required moisture balance at a given latitude may be maintained are indicated in Fig. 2.1. Where this is

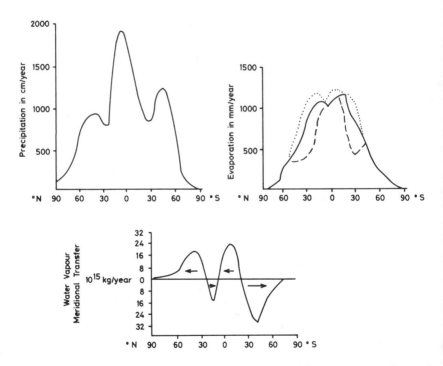

FIG. 2.1. Average yearly latitudinal distribution of precipitation, evaporation and meridional transfer of water vapour.

achieved, precipitation − evaporation = net horizontal moisture transport into the air column. It may be noted that there is equatorwards transport in low latitudes and polewards in middle latitudes. It may also be noted that usually local evaporation is not the main source of local precipitation, the bulk being transported into an area by advection.

Environmental isotopes have been used in studies of the source of atmospheric moisture and its transport. Radiosondea and other instruments have provided much information on quantities of moisture present and also the relevant horizontal flux. Divergences in this latter may arise as a result of precipitation (a negative divergence, a convergence of moisture flux) or evapotranspiration (a positive divergence). Of course the amount of moisture which is transported by the atmosphere across a region is far greater than any removed by precipitation or added by evapotranspiration. V. Starr and J. P. Peixoto in 1964 gave some interesting implications for the mechanics of the general circulation based on the hemispheric flux of water vapour.[1] If enough stations are present in an area it would be feasible from divergence computations to derive detailed data regarding the level of evapotranspiration within a region. Even so no extra knowledge would arise from these as regards the actual origin of the bulk of atmospheric moisture. For that, environmental isotopes may be helpful and will be. considered under the sections of stable and unstable (radioactive) isotopes.

2.2.1. Stable Isotopes

The stable isotopes in question are deuterium and oxygen-18. There is a global collection system sampling precipitation on a monthly basis, the World Precipitation Network which submits samples for analysis to the International Atomic Energy Agency and the World Meteorological Organisation of the United Nations. The spatial and time distribution of the stable isotopes are derived and the data published from time to time in the *Technical Reports* series of the IAEA (see, for instance, No. 96 (1969) covering the period 1953–63 and No. 117 (1970) covering the period 1964–5).[2,3] Some of the conclusions which have been drawn by E. Eriksson and others may be given.[4] Usually δD and $\delta^{18}O$ are highest over tropical regions and decrease towards the poles as well as towards continental interiors. However, there is a seasonal variation increasing the parameters in summer and decreasing them in winter. Also, they decrease with altitude as noted in Chapter 1. Most of the transport is of the eddy diffusion type comprising random drifting of air masses having different moisture contents and consequently there is a good deal of variation with time of the isotopic composition of water vapour. Nevertheless atmospheric moisture at any spot location must be characterised by its source (place of origin on the planetary surface) and by its history during transportation (reflecting all processes which have influenced the isotopic composition since leaving the source). Such processes influencing the isotopic composition include not only condensation but also atmospheric mixing. Of course this extends the possible source area and makes it very difficult to determine. The problem is complicated by the fact that a set of combinations can be imagined all of which could give rise to a moisture package having the same isotopic composition. In short only rather wide origin groups and histories can be associated with certain isotopic compositions of atmospheric moisture and these may be summarised as follows:

(i)   High values of δD and $\delta^{18}O$ occur in moisture which probably originated in warm oceanic regions or in coastal areas in warm climates.

(ii) Low values of δD and $\delta^{18}O$ are probably associated with atmospheric moisture of polar origin. In this case it may be assumed that if the actual origin was in a warm oceanic area removal of most of the moisture occurred during transportation. Hence such a moisture package could have either source according to its subsequent history.

2.2.2. Unstable Isotopes

The unstable isotopes include tritium and radon. Tritium is useful in tracing atmospheric moisture and, as noted earlier, is added to the troposphere by inflow from the stratosphere where it is produced by the interaction of cosmic high energy radiation with atmospheric components thus: $^{14}N(n, T)^{12}C$ and artificially through thermonuclear explosions. There is also a small solar-produced content. The naturally produced tritium level in precipitation is about 10 TU, but this has been vastly exceeded by injections of 'bomb' tritium from time to time since 1952. These have labelled precipitation with quantities of the radioisotope which can be measured relatively easily. Actually, the rather low specific tritium activities in all types of water in nature makes it necessary to enrich tritium in most samples to be measured. This is done by electrolysis of the water sample until only a very small fraction of the original containing a large quantity of the original tritium remains. The electrolysis can be performed in an alkaline solution and a 250 ml sample is treated in a cell until a final volume of 2·5 ml or less is obtained. This is sufficient in view of the improved characteristics of counting systems which can handle very low energy beta emitters. Both single photomultiplier and coincidence liquid scintillation counting systems were employed twenty years ago by, for example, I. S. Boyce and J. F. Cameron.[5] Continuous improvements have been made subsequently.

Present concentrations of tritium in precipitation at any one place vary with season, maxima occurring in the late spring and summer both in the northern and southern hemispheres. Concentrations are lower in the latter. A decade or so ago the levels were higher than now but even today they remain above the natural (pre-1952) levels. Investigations in the late 1960s showed that there existed a latitude-dependence so that concentrations increased towards the poles over both oceans and continents, but the concentration gradient with latitude was found to be greater over continents and in the northern hemisphere. The influence of continental and maritime masses of air is very apparent in Europe and North America where penetrating polar air conveys higher concent-rations of tritium to mix with lower tritium maritime air brought over continents by westerly winds.

High tritium concentration gradients were very marked at interfaces between circulation systems, the steepest being on the western continental coasts. Tritium maxima in the northern hemisphere occurred in 1963 and in the southern hemisphere in 1964–65, but there is evidence that northern hemisphere air can penetrate into the southern hemisphere. Radon and other radioisotopes will be discussed later.

Condensation is intimately linked with precipitation, indeed it is the direct cause of the latter, and occurs under varying conditions associated with changes in factors such as temperature, pressure and humidity. Thus it can take place when air temperature falls with the volume remaining constant and cooling reaches dew point, or alternatively when air volume increases without addition of heat. Cooling can result from adiabatic expansion. It may take place by contact when warm and moist air passes over a cold land surface. Obviously the process is most difficult in clean air because moisture requires a surface upon which to condense. Hygroscopic nuclei may be provided by particles of dust, smoke, sulphur dioxide, salts such as sodium chloride or similar substances which can be wetted. The size range involved is from $0.001\,\mu m$ to as much as $10\,\mu m$. Once formed, water droplets grow by a complex process which is usually slow. There is also a considerable size difference between cloud droplets and raindrops. This suggests that the rate of formation of the latter is not wholly dependent upon condensation. Falling raindrops are subject to evaporation in that air zone below cloud base which is unsaturated so that a droplet of $0.1\,mm$ radius will evaporate after a fall of only $150\,m$ at a temperature of $5°C$ and 90% relative humidity. There is a great variety of cloud types and they are classified on the basis of shape and vertical extent as well as altitude. A general taxonomy is shown in Table 2.3.

TABLE 2.3
CLOUD TYPES BASED ON ALTITUDES

Type	Tropics	Middle latitudes	High latitudes
High	>6 000 m	>5 000 m	>3 000 m
Medium	2 000–7 500 m	2 000–7 000 m	2 000–4 000 m
Low	<2 000 m	<2 000 m	<2 000 m

Ten groups of cloud types exist. High cirriform cloud comprises ice crystals while stratiform clouds are layered, cumuliform ones having a heaped appearance. Medium level clouds carry the prefix alto- while low clouds carry nimbo-. A broad genetic grouping may also be made on the basis of vertical motion mechanisms which produce condensation and four possible categories are:

(a) gradual uplift of air covering a wide area in connection with a low pressure system;
(b) thermal convection on the local cumulus scale;
(c) uplift as a result of mechanical turbulence (forced convection);
(d) ascent over an orographic barrier.

As regards the formation of precipitation, as noted earlier condensation alone cannot explain this. Two theories attempt to and may be noted here.

(1) Collision, coalescence and sweeping may generate drop growth. If the cloud top lies above freezing level ice crystals will be present and these may fall and coalesce. Coalescence is a slow process, but nevertheless a drop can reach 200 m radius within an hour. However, droplets must exceed 19 μm in size before they can coalesce with other droplets so that droplets smaller than this in radius are simply swept aside without colliding at all. Turbulence may encourage collisions especially in cumuliform clouds and the resultant coalescence permits a much more rapid growth than condensation alone could instigate.

(2) The Bergeron–Findeisen theory is based upon the fact that the relative humidity of air is greater with respect to an ice surface than it is with respect to a water one. As the air temperature falls below 0°C the atmospheric vapour pressure diminishes more rapidly over an ice surface than over water and this results in the saturation vapour pressure over water becoming greater than over

ice, particularly between $-5°C$ and $-25°C$ where the difference exceeds 0·2 mb. Where ice crystals and supercooled water droplets coexist in a cloud the latter tend to evaporate so that direct deposition occurs from the vapour on to the crystals of ice. Parallel with the need for condensation nuclei for water droplets to form, freezing nuclei are required before ice particles can form. Actually small water droplets can be supercooled to $-40°C$ before spontaneous freezing takes place. It is found that there are far less freezing nuclei than condensation nuclei. The origin of the former may be very fine soil particles or meteoric dust; however, there is no real evidence that rainfall is related to meteorite showers.

This theory is the basis of practical rain-making by seeding. Silver iodide or dry ice (CO_2) are used to seed supercooled (water) clouds between $-5°C$ and $-15°C$ and promote the formation of ice crystals as well as encourage precipitation. Premature release of the latter can destroy updrafts and the cloud may dissipate so that rainfall may decrease rather than increase.

Of course rainfall is not the only form of precipitation. Snow falls when the freezing level is so near the ground that aggregations of ice crystals have insufficient time to melt before reaching it. To achieve this the freezing level must be at an altitude less than 300 m. It cannot fall when the air temperature attains $4°C$ or more and if this reaches $1·5°C$ at the surface mixed snow and rain is likely.

Hail (ice with enclosed air) occurs when the Bergeron–Findeisen process takes place in a cloud with a small liquid water content, ice particles accreting by the deposition of water vapour. Concentric layers of opaque and clear ice usually occur and the nucleus is a raindrop elevated in an updraft and frozen.

Adiabatic expansion was alluded to above and in this process there is neither addition nor subtraction of heat. Near the planetary surface changes are usually diabatic, i.e. air mixes and modifies its characteristics as a result of lateral motion and turbulence. Considering what happens when a package of air rises and a pressure decrease accompanies a volume increase and temperature decrease, the rate of the latter is termed the adiabatic lapse rate. Saturated air cools more slowly than dry air so that a saturated adiabatic lapse rate may be distinguished from a dry one. The former is of the order of $9·8°C/km$, the latter $9°C/km$ at $-40°C$ and only $4°C/km$ at high temperatures. The properties of moving air packages are plotted as path curves on graphs termed tephigrams which have several features of importance such as isotherms (lines of constant temperature), isobars (lines of constant pressure), etc. as well as adiabatic charts.

In the temperate regions the most marked manifestations of moisture changes are the great energy releases in thunderstorms motivated by massive upward and downward air movements occurring in one of the following forms:

(i)   rising cells of over-heated moist air;

(ii) along a squall line parallel with an air mass discontinuity such as a cold front;

(iii) in association with an initiation of instability through uplift over mountains of a moist air mass or through excessive localised convergence.

Such storms usually endure for an hour or two and commence when an air package is either warmer than its environment or is undercut by incoming colder air. Raindrops develop quickly when the freezing stage is attained by the vertical build-up of a cell but are supported by updrafts and so do not immediately precipitate. Electrical charges are generated and lightning usually accompanies downwardly directed precipitational downpours of rain.

Finally, the characteristics of precipitation should be discussed. Precipitation is taken to refer to all liquid and frozen forms of water, and therefore includes rain, sleet, snow, hail, dew, hoar-frost, fog-drip and rime (accreted ice on objects as a result of the freezing on impact of supercooled fog droplets). However, only rain and snow are significant in terms of contribution to the precipitation total in a region. Important characteristics are as follows:

(i)   Rainfall intensity. Intensity = quantity/duration of rainfall during an individual storm as well as in shorter periods and it is a factor the significance of which cannot be over-stressed as it has a great bearing on floods and flood control measures. Later, determination of transit time in a basin using radiotracers with special reference to the work of D. H. Pilgrim will be discussed.[6]

Chart records of the rate of rainfall, hyetograms, are essential to assess intensity which of course varies according to the time interval selected. Raindrop sizes vary with intensity so that with values of 0·1, 1·3 and 10·2 cm/h, the most frequent raindrop diameters are 0·1, 0·2 and 0·3 cm.

(ii) Areal extent of a rainstorm. Maximal 24 h rainfalls over areas of different extent in the USA may be cited (Table 2.4).

TABLE 2.4
DATA UP TO 1960

Area	Maximal 24 h rainfall (cm)
10 sq. miles (25·9 km^2)	98·3
10^2	89·4
10^3	76·7
10^4	30·7
10^5	10·9

Data of this type can provide information on the maximum rainfall to be anticipated for any given storm area.

(iii) Rainstorm frequency. The average time interval in which rainfall of a specified quantity or intensity can be anticipated constitutes the recurrence interval or return period. Data might indicate, for instance, that a 10 min fall of 2·5 cm is probable every two decades and perhaps a 24 h fall of 10 cm every thirty years but such average periods do not by any means imply that such falls necessarily occur in the twentieth and thirtieth years respectively of any selected period. Nevertheless similar estimates based on linear relationships are practically important for the design of flood control systems.

The various forms in which precipitation may manifest itself should be mentioned; these fall into three major categories according to the assumed mode of uplift of air, namely:

(i) Convective associated with cumulus and cumulo-nimbus clouds and having three sub-groups: (a) strong summer heating of the surface of the land will produce scattered convective cells and precipitation is of thunderstorm type and affects areas of the order of 20 to 50 km^2 in size producing individual heavy downpours usually lasting for $\frac{1}{2}$ to 1 h; (b) rain showers form in cold and moist air passing over a warm surface and conveying convective cells to produce an uneven distribution of precipitation parallel to the direction of the wind. Such cells may constitute a belt hundreds of kilometres in length and anything up to 100 km wide perpendicular to the air flow with cold fronts and line squalls; (c) in tropical cyclonic conditions cumulo-nimbus cells may become organised around the vortex in spiralling bands.

(ii) Cyclonic type precipitation varying in nature according to the type of low pressure system and its developmental stage, but essentially dependent upon an ascent of air through convergence of air streams in a low pressure area.

(iii) Orographic precipitation in which mountain barriers may trigger convective instability by initiating an upward movement or by differential heating of the mountain slopes. Also, they can increase cyclonic precipitation by retarding the rate of movement of the depression system as well as cause convergence and uplift through the funnel effect exerted by valleys upon air streams.

There are regional variations in the maximum altitude of precipitation and it is an observed fact that precipitation increases with height. In tropical areas the maximal precipitation occurs below the higher mountain summits from which altitude it diminishes upwards towards the crests. However, in the Olympic mountains of Washington precipitation increases up to the summits. It is believed that eddies at the crests may limit precipitation sampling and hence suggest—falsely—that quantities are lower than is actually the case.

If the worldwide pattern of precipitation is studied it becomes apparent that the distribution is more complex than, for instance, the distribution of mean temperature. The zonal pattern involves an equatorial maximum slightly displaced into the northern hemisphere like the thermal equator, very low totals in high latitudes and secondary minima in sub-tropical latitudes. Of course there are marked longitudinal variations superimposed on this. The distribution of the planetary land masses is significant because the southern hemisphere lacks the vast and arid mid-latitude continental interiors found in the northern one. Thus the oceanic expanses of the southern hemisphere permit mid-latitude storms to increase the regional precipitation average for 45°S by perhaps one-third as compared with that of the northern hemisphere for 50°N. A very significant feature not conforming to zonal distribution is the existence of monsoonal regimes, particularly in Asia.

2.3. ENVIRONMENTAL ISOTOPES IN HYDROMETEOROLOGY

The most important are those referred to earlier, namely the stable isotopes deuterium and oxygen-18 together with the radioactive isotope of hydrogen, tritium. The transportation aspect of the atmosphere is important because it conveys water vapour from the oceans to continents, hence these isotopes also. Clearly a non-steady state system is involved, but zonal characteristics have been recognised and may be summarised as follows:

(i) latitudinal motion with easterly winds in low latitudes and westerly winds in temperate latitudes in the lower part of the atmosphere;

(ii) stationary features such as high pressure cells over oceans in which air circulates;

(iii) random eddies transient in nature which travel in all directions and cause mixing by diffusion of air.

This latter is sometimes termed eddy diffusion or in German austausch. It can produce meridional transport as well, i.e. transport in a north–south direction. The eddy diffusion coefficient is believed to be approximately 10^5 times that of gases and for large scale horizontal eddy transport about 10^{10} times the molecular one for gases.[7]

These transport mechanisms are taken into account in formulating a model for the interpretation of environmental isotope data and evaporation should be considered as well. This is because it constitutes an interface phenomenon between the planetary surface and the atmosphere. Water surfaces continually lose and gain water as a result of the kinetic motion of water molecules in liquid and gas phases, i.e. an exchange process occurs and an imbalance in this produces either condensation or evaporation. If the case of tritium is examined, concentration of this radioisotope in the surface waters of the oceans is far lower than in precipitation and atmospheric moisture as a consequence of the enormous size of the former together with the efficiency of the mixing at least in the upper hundred metres. When exchange takes place between the atmosphere and the seas much more tritium enters the water surface than leaves it and even where evaporation is going on, a net transport of tritium into the seas from the atmosphere continues. Actually it appears that exchange of water between the atmosphere and the oceans exceeds evaporation by at least a factor of three and W. F. Libby computed that oceanic areas must have a precipitation rate of 2·7 m/year in order to balance the tritium influx from the atmosphere (assuming that precipitation is the sole removal mechanism for tritium).[8] If exchange is also taken into account and assumed to be twice as effective as precipitation, the precipitation figure becomes 0·9 m/year. Such exchange also operates over lakes and indeed all surface water bodies which have good internal mixing and even soil water may be influenced by the process if the air–water interface is sufficiently large. Of course groundwater is completely separated from such exchange processes.

As regards deuterium and oxygen-18 these occur as HDO^{16} and H_2O^{18} both of which have slightly lower saturation vapour pressures than the ordinary water molecule, H_2O^{16}. Obviously, therefore, there is a slight fractionation of the deuterium and oxygen-18 in all processes of evaporation and condensation, these heavier isotopes becoming enriched in the liquid phase and depleted in the vapour one. W. F. Dansgaard in his classic paper of 1964 demonstrated the relationship between oxygen-18 content and mean annual temperature for a number of North Atlantic stations and some of the data are shown in Fig. 2.2.[9] The relation is expressed as a straight line of slope 0·69‰/°C and this is in agreement with the isobaric cooling model for stations in the temperature range 0°C to 10°C when the initial temperature is 20°C. Of course the effects of

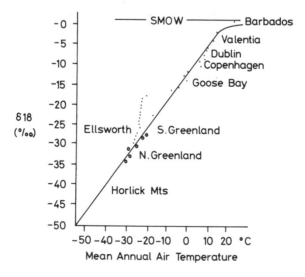

FIG. 2.2. Relationship between ^{18}O content of precipitation and mean annual air temperature.

eddy diffusion transport of water vapour may occur and produce a resulting fractionation effect only half of that calculated by Dansgaard.[10] A relation between the mean isotopic composition of precipitation and the mean quantity of precipitable water in the atmosphere was derived by E. Eriksson.[10] It is

$$\delta_{18} = 2{\cdot}3(\beta - 1) \log \overline{W} - \text{constant}$$

where $\overline{W}$ is the mean precipitable water in the atmosphere. β should take the value α, this being the fractionation coefficient for the isotope for purely advective transport of water vapour or $\sqrt{\alpha}$ for a pure eddy diffusion transport.

Eriksson utilised values of β of 1·0045 for the eddy diffusion case and $\beta = 1·009$ for the advective case.[10] An appreciable scatter in his results reflects the extremely complex character of fractionation in nature. Most of the data incline to the value $\beta = 1·0045$, however, rather than to the higher figure and this is consistent with the fact that large scale eddy diffusion is the sole means by which water vapour can be brought from source areas in low latitudes to sink regions in temperate and high latitudes.

The relation between deuterium and oxygen-18 in precipitation was examined by W. F. Dansgaard and his conclusions are summarised in Fig. 2.3.[9]

During evaporation the fractionation factors for the two stable isotopes increase and while the effect for deuterium is rather small, it is

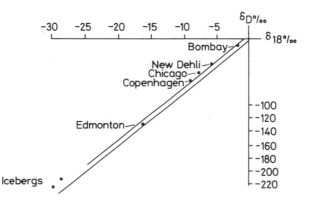

FIG. 2.3. Relationship between deuterium and oxygen-18 in precipitation. After Dansgaard.[9]

considerable for oxygen-18. Referring to Fig. 2.4 therefore, freshly evaporated water vapour should give a precipitation with a $\delta_D-\delta_{18}$ relation lying at some point on the line A_0-A_2 which has a slope of 5. As a result of further condensation the precipitation will change along the line C_1 if A_1 is the starting point of the condensation. The line C_1 has a

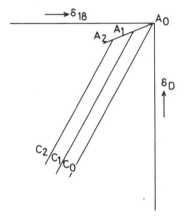

FIG. 2.4. Schematic diagram of $\delta_D-\delta_{18}$ relationships during rapid evaporation (A_0-A_2) and condensation (lines C_0C_1 and C_2). After Dansgaard.[9]

slope of about 8 and this can be expected if no kinetic effect operates during condensation. Should the original composition correspond to the point A_2 then the $\delta_D-\delta_{18}$ relation will follow line C_2. If there were to be no kinetic effect during evaporation then the $\delta_D-\delta_{18}$ relation would follow line C_0 during condensation and this must pass through the $\delta_D-\delta_{18}$ point of the original composition. Hence the relation by condensation is displaced relative to the C_0 line and the amount of this displacement depends upon the magnitude of the kinetic effect during evaporation.

Actually the displacement must be related to the evaporation rate of the relative humidity of near surficial air in source areas for water vapour and hence it may be possible to utilise it as an indicator of conditions in these areas. W. F. Dansgaard also noted a relation between isotopic composition and monthly rainfall and this he termed the amount effect.[9] Months characterised by heavy rainfall show lower isotope concentrations than months with low rainfall and the effect is especially pronounced in tropical regions. The reason for the phenomenon was discussed and it became apparent that there is no correlation between rain intensity and isotopic composition. However, the frequency of rain is higher in high rainfall months and this would entail higher relative humidity in sub-cloud air hence less evaporation from raindrops. In turn this would mean that the amount effect is explained since evaporation rate from raindrops determines the isotopic composition—the greater the evaporation, the higher the isotope concentration in the residual raindrop.

However, there are other possible explanations. Air masses have a tendency to converge in tropical regions and the region where this occurs must be one characterised by vertical instability leading to strong convection. Stability conditions are affected by the temperature and other properties of air at higher altitudes and comparatively cold air at such elevations facilitates the initiation of convection and thus more frequent precipitation. Much mixing between lower warm, moist air and upper cold air occurs during convection and so the isotopic composition of water vapour in the latter may be presumed to influence the isotopic composition of precipitation. The amount effect may reflect the average synoptic situation during different months.

Turning now to tritium, its circulation in nature differs from that of water (hence that of deuterium and oxygen-18 also) and as noted earlier the major source is the stratosphere with the major sink the oceans. Naturally the circulation pattern depends upon the motion of the atmosphere and eddy diffusion processes, but resolution of these is not completely possible because not much is known regarding the stratospheric distribution of the radioisotope. However, maximum concentrations in precipitation are found to take place in May and June in the northern hemisphere. Somehow the radioisotope is transferred from the stratosphere to the troposphere and here it becomes mixed with the water vapour of the moist layer of the lower part of the latter thereafter being brought down to the planetary surface in precipitation. Over oceanic areas the exchange of water vapour between the surface of the sea and the atmosphere is approximately twice as effective as precipitation in removing tritium from the atmosphere. As regards the continents the sole net removal of tritium in precipitation is that corresponding to continental runoff and this is approximately half that of precipitation. Hence the estimating of tritium removal from the atmosphere on the basis of the tritium concentration in precipitation yields a figure of approximately three times the removal by precipitation over oceans and perhaps 50% of precipitated tritium over continents.

Variation over continents is large and dependent upon the runoff. A constant influx from the stratosphere would suggest the same deposition of tritium over land and sea, but taking into account such factors as precipitation, exchange and evaporation it is to be expected that, as is indeed the case, there will in fact be much lower concentrations of tritium in precipitation over oceans than over land.

When air penetrates a continent from the ocean the tritium content is initially low but thereafter it increases rapidly to reach a much higher and stable level. The time of adjustment to stable values depends upon the rate of removal, but is in any case higher when continental air passes out over oceanic areas and the tritium decreases than when maritime air is brought into continental areas. Tritium has been proposed as a useful tool for determining the rate of evaporation from sea water in hurricane areas and G. Östlund in 1965 reported data qualitatively indicative that evaporation rates in such circumstances are significant in maintaining the energy of hurricanes.[11] As a matter of fact though, it is essential to determine the vertical flux of tritium in order to compute evaporation rates. Of course in hurricane areas it is extremely difficult to estimate such a vertical flux. Tritium has been used also as a tracer for snow accumulation on high altitude glaciers, but it is necessary that no snow melting should ever occur which is the case in Greenland for instance. Of lesser importance than tritium are radon-222 and silicon-32, both of which were mentioned in the preceding chapter. Radon-222 has been utilised in atmospheric studies apropos moisture source identification in monsoonal rains in India and may be investigated in surface waters and groundwater as well. Some of this work relates to the health hazard which the gas can constitute. Although its half-life is only 3·8 days it decays to a series of short lived daughter products which are radioactive and can be inhaled and retained in the lungs. Radiation may arise from the bedrock and uranium-238 can be present, give rise to radium and through the decay of this, radon. Radon may also arise from the decay of thorium-232 and then has a half-life of only 54·4 secs. In this case the daughter products are insignificant because there is insufficient time for them to emerge from rock or soil. Alum shales and uranium and thorium enriched granites are rocks of the type to produce the gas, the former containing uranium also, as well as uranium enriched pegmatites. Radon may emanate from the ground if factors such as soil porosity, groundwater table level and air pressure are suitable and its escape is facilitated by fracturation and weathering of the strata. After its emergence it passes into the atmosphere. Diffusion through soil is related to soil type; radon can penetrate much further through dry sands than through clays in unit time. Radon may emerge through groundwater seepage at the surface, springs, rivers or other water bodies. The hazardous nature of the gas has been discussed by a number of workers including R. J. Guimond and associates in 1979 and C. V. Åkerblom and Carole Wilson in 1981.[12,13] One of the findings mentioned by the last two authors is that groundwater with high concentrations of radon-222 may enter houses using it as household water and thereafter be released to the indoor atmosphere, the ratio between the radon content of the indoor atmosphere and the radon content of the water being about 1 to 10. Radon in groundwaters of dolomitic and calcareous aquifer in Apulia in Italy have been investigated by G. Magri and G. S. Tazioli in 1970.[14] The radon contents of the waters were ascertained by means of *in situ* measurements of gamma activity of the decay products fixed on activated carbon by filtering the water. This can be done fairly quickly and there is a precise relation which, for any given concentration of radon in the water, correlates the filtration time with the quantity of radon fixed. Radon fixation on activated carbon actually occurs in increments which decrease exponentially as a function of filtration time according to the formula

$$A_t = A_\infty (1 - e^{Ct})$$

where A_t is the activity relative to the amount of radon fixed in time t, A_∞ is the activity of the radon fixed at saturation and C is a constant for the particular filtering equipment utilised.

Turning now to silicon-32, its hydrology has been discussed by D. Lal *et al.*.[15] This radioisotope is produced as a result of nuclear interactions of cosmic ray particles with atmospheric argon nuclei as indicated earlier and it is a useful tracer in hydrology, glaciology and oceanography. Measurements have been effected in precipitation rivers and lakes and the technical preparation follows this procedure:

(i) scavenging of the dissolved silicon in water by a ferric hydroxide precipitation using very large amounts of water (5 tons or more) so that the activity is measurable;

(ii) extracting radiochemically pure silica from the ferric hydroxide scavenged slime;

(iii) allowing ^{32}P activity to wax in practically secular equilibrium with ^{32}Si decay by permitting the pure silica extract to stand over periods extending from one to three months;

(iv) milking a radiochemically pure sample of ^{32}P;

(v) counting the milked ^{32}P activity over periods of one to two months.

The most difficult part of the entire operation is connected with the very low net ^{32}P activities which at best run to only 5, 10 or 15 counts per hour. Consequently, counting statistics become a major problem. However, long lived contamination activities are insignificant because of the half-life of ^{32}P which is a mere 14·3 days. In Indian precipitation from five stations it was found that the mean annual weighted concentration of ^{32}Si is 0·3 disintegrations/min per 10^3 litres with a geographical and temporal variation of less than 0·1 disintegrations/min per 10^3 litres as of 1970. The radioisotope is a thermonuclear bomb test fallout product, but since there were no major detonations in the atmosphere after 1963 (the moratorium year) by the time of the above mentioned measurements, the atmospheric levels had probably returned to near-normal.

It is necessary to add that other radioisotopes may prove to be important in hydrology. These include ^{39}Ar which is produced naturally in the atmosphere by interactions between cosmic ray particles and atmospheric argon nuclei with a global average production rate of about 10^{-2} atoms/cm^2/sec compared with 3×10^{-3} atoms/cm^2/sec for ^{32}Si. It has a half-life of 270 years and because of this, coupled with the fact that 99% of exchangeable argon is in the atmosphere, the specific activity of ^{39}Ar (^{39}Ar/Ar) is believed to be independent of altitude, latitude and longitude. Also, dissolved argon is probably a tracer in groundwaters. Measurements again entail using large masses of water (5–10 tons), but can be employed in 'dating' groundwaters younger than 1000 years. Another potentially useful radioisotope is ^{85}Kr which was injected into the atmosphere as a result of thermonuclear detonations. It is a conservative tracer with a half-life of 10·4 years and could be applied to young groundwaters. Unlike tritium, which has a rather similar half-life but the atmospheric inventory of which has shown marked fluctuations in recent decades, ^{85}Kr has a well known atmospheric inventory which slowly increases with time. Another potentially useful tool for 'dating' old groundwaters, i.e. those with ages from 100 000 to 10^6 years, is total dissolved helium. This becomes dissolved after exchange with the atmosphere (around 4×10^{-5} ml/litre) or as a consequence of degassing from the planetary crust. The rate of degassing could be determined and applied in association with radiocarbon dates.

2.4. CIRCULATION IN THE ATMOSPHERE

Flow patterns fall into two main categories, namely:

(i) Anticyclones and depressions of relatively short duration. The anticyclone involves cyclic circulation with a life history and roughly circular shape associated with high pressure. In many instances tropospheric air is warmer in them than in depressions and they may be cold or warm. They constitute secondary circulation features.

(ii) Eddies of anticyclonic or cyclonic type remaining stationary for long periods and constituting primary circulation features.

Circulation is governed by great wind belts and these include the trade winds, the disturbed westerlies, polar easterlies and monsoons. Peter J. Webster has discussed monsoons in detail and noted that the largest occur in Asia, Australia and Africa together with the adjacent seas.[16] The fundamental causes of monsoonal phenomena are differential heating and cooling of land and ocean together with pressure differences in the atmosphere arising therefrom and becoming equalised by winds plus the change in direction of such winds consequent upon the rotation of the Earth. There is a third factor which is important as well and this relates to the triple point of water. The latter is the combination of temperature and pressure at which solid, liquid and gas can exist, namely $0.01°C$ and a pressure of 6.104 mb. Water molecules in an environment near to the triple point are freely interconvertible between the three states. The ability of water to evaporate and condense readily in the atmosphere is of tremendous significance in monsoonal circulation. In changing from a solid to a liquid, energy is necessary to break down the crystalline structure of ice to permit water molecules to move freely in the liquid state. Energy is also required to convert the liquid into the vapour, i.e. during the process of evaporation. Energy expended in the process is stored as kinetic energy of the molecules of the water vapour and when this condenses the energy is released. Consequently, while a phase change occurs, energy is added or subtracted without temperature change. The significance of moist processes is to be found in the fact that water evaporated at any stated time from the planetary oceans stores approximately one-sixth of the solar energy reaching the Earth's surface. When water condenses and falls as rain, energy stored in the vapour phase is released. In monsoonal circulation part of the vast reservoir of solar energy collected over the oceans can be released over land when the water in moist oceanic air condenses over the land. It is the release of this energy that produces the giant power and duration of the monsoonal rainy season. As noted above the basic driving mechanism of the circulation is that the atmosphere is heated differentially because land regions tend to be warmer than oceans in summer and cooler in winter.

Land and sea therefore are seen to respond differently to solar radiation and there are two reasons for this. One is that water has a higher capacity to store heat than land, in fact its specific heat exceeds that of dry land by a factor exceeding two. Inferentially the specific heat of land increases when it is wet. The second reason is that oceans have a high heat capacity because of intrinsic characteristics of water coupled with their ability to efficiently mix heat energy down to lower depths and thus distribute heat throughout a great mass of water. Wind activity at the surface will produce turbulent eddies which convey warmer surficial water to lower levels in summer; in winter heat accumulated during the summer is released by a reverse of this process. Since there is a diminution in the incident solar radiation the water surface cools and sinks, being replaced by warmer water rising from below. Because of the high specific heat of water and mixing the temperature of the oceanic surface varies much less than that of land and in fact the oceans act as a tremendous heat energy storage facility. As a result of the inertia of the system the cycle of maximum and minimum surface temperatures lags about two months behind the corresponding cycle of solar heating. In spring sensible heating occurs and the rate of heat transport from surface to atmosphere is proportional to the temperature differential between the two. Sensible heating initiates the first differential heating of the atmosphere over the land and the seas and generates potential energy which actually powers the monsoon system. Monsoonal winds are driven by conversion of part of the potential energy of the atmospheric system into kinetic energy. Moist processes play an important part in the annual circulation. During the summer monsoon, water vapour which is eva-porated from the oceans is carried along with air moving towards land. A package of air transporting moisture from the ocean is warmed by con-duction and by upwardly directed convective air currents over land and it begins to rise to higher altitudes with lower pressure. As the package ascends it cools adiabatically and water vapour condenses into raindrops. During condensation the solar energy which has maintained the water in the vapour phase is liberated and this latent heat is taken up by the air molecules and causes a diabatic temperature change in the air package.

Moist processes actually determine the time of onset of seasonal monsoons, also their maximum intensities as well as their retreats. The onset of the precipitation period occurs abruptly a few weeks prior to the summer solstice. However, the circulation only attains maximal intensity eight to ten weeks after the solstice. The delay results from the fact that the average precipitation on a land mass is directly related to the temperature of the ocean upwind from the land. The higher the surface temperature of the ocean is the higher the air temperature over the surface is and the more water vapour the air is able to transport. The more water vapour that is transported the greater the quantity of energy available for release when the water condenses over land. Thus the intensity of the monsoon circulation increases. The retreat of a monsoon is the gradual ceasing of precipitation sometime after the autumnal equinox. Differential heating between oceans and continents is then reduced and the energy injected into the system by water vapour transport is also reduced. The cooler air over oceans retains less water vapour and hence the latent heat released by precipitation over land areas gradually diminishes. A curious point is that there is no major monsoonal system in the Americas. The western hemisphere equatorial region is dominated by the Amazon Basin where an overlying air mass is subject both to sensible and latent heating for a great part of the year. In North America the winter radiative cooling produces considerable potential energy between the two hemispheres but interchange of air between them is blocked by the Andes. The Coriolis force makes cold North American air enter the Pacific Ocean as northeastern trade winds. If the Andes did not exist then differential surficial heating of the planet between the Amazon Basin and the Pacific Ocean would cause air to flow into the Amazon and this would leave a low pressure area over the South Pacific, this in turn causing trade winds to cross the equator. These northeast trades would then be turned by the Coriolis force towards the southeast and thus complete the path of interhemispheric flow. As the Andes do exist this does not happen and the cross-equatorial flow is weak in the eastern Pacific. The trade winds in fact continue across the Pacific to Indonesia. Also the eastern Pacific is dominated by cold water and so even if the Andes were non-existent the moisture content of the air would be too low to build up the high energy associated with Asiatic monsoons.[16] Air in circulation in the Amazon Basin is moistened by evaporation from the Atlantic Ocean.

Figure 2.5 shows changes of energy involving the Earth–atmosphere system and a tri-cellular model of northern hemispheric meridional

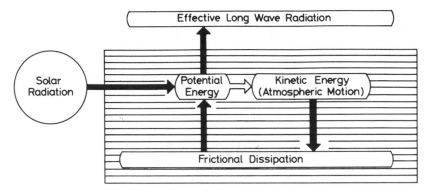

FIG. 2.5. Schematic energy changes involving the Earth–atmosphere system (lined).

circulation. The Coriolis force arises from the fact that the movement of masses over the planetary surface is usually referred to as a moving coordinate system (the latitude and longitude grid rotating with the Earth). It is a rotational deflective force involving apparent deflections of moving objects to the right of their line of motion in the northern hemisphere and to the left in the southern. The deflective force per unit mass is expressed as

$$-2\omega V \sin \phi$$

where ω = the angular velocity of spin (15°/h or 2/24 radians/h for the Earth = $7 \cdot 29 \times 10^{-5}$ radians/sec), ϕ = latitude and V = velocity of the mass. $2\omega \sin \phi$ is referred to as the Coriolis parameter (f). Some values of it are given below (Table 2.5).

TABLE 2.5
VALUES OF f

Latitude	0°	10°	20°	43°	90°
$f (10^{-4}/\text{sec})$	0	0·25	0·50	1·00	1·458

2.5. MEASUREMENT OF PRECIPITATION

Precipitation includes a variety of manifestations of water such as rain, snow, hail, sleet, etc., but mostly it arrives at the planetary surface as rain. Rain gauging is distinct from snow gauging and even more important. Rain gauges are very varied in their design and their usage differs quite considerably. Figure 2.6 illustrates the Hellman type, a

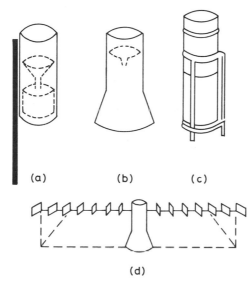

(a) (b) (c)

(d)

FIG. 2.6. Rain gauge types. (a) Hellman, (b) British standard, (c) US Weather Bureau, (d) ground surface level gauge.

British standard type, a US Weather Bureau type and a ground level rain gauge. However, there are literally hundreds of types. Some provide a continuous record of rainfall, but most of them require inspection at fixed times. Within most national rain gauge networks there is a considerable degree of uniformity accompanied by diversity between countries, compare the British standard gauge which is a brass cylinder one foot high and five inches in diameter with that of the USSR which is 2m high and is surrounded by a shield. Clearly this may raise difficulties apropos the comparability of results obtained from such divergent types and this is shown by the fact that tests made at the same site show differences from gauge to gauge as John C. Rodda has pointed out.[17] Actually the World Meteorological Organisation introduced an Interim Reference Precipitation Gauge in an attempt to obviate these difficulties but, due to the influence of wind variation, this also has a variable performance from site to site. In fact, wind is the most significant source of error in rain gauging. It can cause under-registration on the standard gauge and, of course, interacts with site characteristics and the gauge producing turbulence and eddies. The deleterious effects of wind can be minimised by installing the rain gauge so that its rim lies flush with the surface of the ground. Any splashing can be avoided by surrounding the rain gauge with a matting surface or alternatively by placing it into a shallow pit covered by a grid comprising narrow strips of metal or plastic. Even though rain gauges thus installed probably give data which most nearly represent the true rainfall, there is no absolute standard for this. That ground surface level gauges are better, however, is illustrated when the catch of rainwater in them is compared with the catch of conventional ones.

Actually the difference between ground surface level catches and those derived at standard height varies with gauge type and also with climatic factors. For instance, in the UK such differences could range from 3% to 10% for annual totals and in the case of single storms the ground surface level catch has been recorded as 40% higher. In tropical regions such as East Africa the effect is smaller because of the larger dimensions of rain drops and also the lower wind velocities.[17] In the case of snow gauging the errors which arise are higher because of the marked effects of wind on falling snow flakes. Since the errors implicit in measuring precipitation do not mean that additional water would be available at the ground surface if they did not exist, systematic mistakes are relatively unimportant in the application of rainfall data in water balance equations, particularly as even larger errors may arise in the determining of other relevant parameters such as evaporation and storage changes in groundwater aquifers. As well as problems arising from equipment, there are problems having their origins in the design of the instrument network and in the assessment of the mean from a set of point measurements. Random distribution of rain gauges has an advantage in that the results make it possible to derive statistically valid estimates for the mean rainfall. However, sometimes rain gauges are installed systematically in a region, e.g. at fixed distances with spacing controlled both vertically and horizontally. Of course if the objective is to obtain a useful flood warning system then the distribution determinants are different and a different arrangement will result. The conversion of point measurements of rainfall into an estimate of the mean for a region can be effected by constructing Thiessen polygons around each gauge (then each gauge's record is weighted according to the area of the polygon around it). This approach is objective as opposed to the isohyetal and isopercentile techniques. Another method is the utilisation of regression analysis but this succeeds only in regions where the topography controls rain distribution.

It may be added that Earl L. Neff has discussed the operation of rain gauges in an interesting paper in 1977 and come to the conclusion that, as mentioned above, optimal results are obtained where the gauge is inserted in a pit thus eliminating all wind effects.[18] An interesting instrument is a high accuracy recording pan-evaporimeter described together with some of its possibilities by G.W. Bloemen; it records pan-evaporation and rainfall both simultaneously and very accurately.[19]

2.6. MEASUREMENT OF EVAPORATION

As regards instrumentation there are four principal types of device used and these are:

(i) Atmometers, water-filled glass tubes which are open-ended and through this water evaporates from a filter paper (Piche variety) or a porous plate (Bellani variety). The tube supplying the water is graduated so as to read evaporation in mm but the latent evaporation so derived can be compared solely with another instrument's readings in a similar situation. As only the saturation deficit of the air is reflected by it the instrument provides data which may have little relation to actual evaporation from land or water surfaces.

(ii) Evaporation pans such as the Class A pan of the US Weather Bureau which is WMO approved and has the following dimensions: 122 cm diameter by 25 cm depth. The difficulties which may arise sometimes come from splashing, interference by birds or animals or fault installation. Results are very hard to relate to lake evaporation and the following relation has been found in the USA:

$$E_l/E_p = 0.6 \text{ to } 0.8$$

where E_l is lake evaporation and E_p is pan-evaporation.

(iii) Lysimeters, essentially enclosed soil blocks with a vegetational cover like that of the environment of location. Evapotranspiration is determined from

$$E = P + \Delta S - r$$

where P is precipitation, ΔS the weight change in a given time and r the percolation. A typical installation is illustrated in Fig. 2.7.

(iv) The evapotron is designed to attempt to measure the magnitude and direction of vertical eddies transferring water vapour upwards but it is extremely difficult to use this approach. Firstly, it must be possible to assess instantaneous changes of both vapour content and vertical velocity of air. Then a problem may arise from the effects of advection. Additionally, the subsequent determination of evaporation needs a computer to integrate the results.

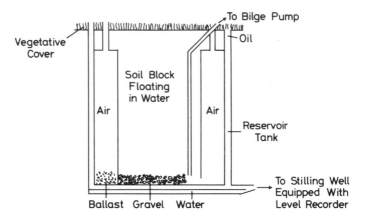

FIG. 2.7.   Lysimeter installation where instead of weighing the soil block, changes of water level are recorded.

As noted in (iii) above, evapotranspiration occurs in vegetated areas, i.e. moisture is being transferred from a vegetated surface and when the supply of this is unlimited the term potential evapotranspiration (PE) is employed. Although sometimes defined as the evaporation equivalent of the available net radiation ($PE = R_n/L$ where L is the latent heat of vaporisation with 59 cal/cm$^2 \approx 1$ mm evaporation) this may not always be the case.

Estimation of evaporation may be effected by the mass transfer approach which involves factors controlling the removal of vapour from the evaporating surface, namely the vertical gradient of humidity and the turbulence of the air flow. The expression

$$E = K u_z (e_w - e_z)$$

is relevant where K is an empirical constant, $(e_w - e_z)$ is the mean vapour pressure difference between the water surface and air at level z and the evaporation is related to the mean wind velocity at height $z(u_z)$. It is applicable to large water bodies such as oceans. Another means of estimating evaporation is the energy budget method based upon the fact that there is energy conservation so that the net total of long and short wave radiation received at the surface (R_n) is available to (a) transfer sensible heat, H, and (b) latent heat, LE, to the atmosphere and (c) sensible heat into the ground so that

$$R_n = H + LE + G$$

where G is transfer to the ground. As the fraction of R_n used in photosynthesis is negligible, evaporation may be determined by measuring the other terms:

$$E = \frac{R_n - H - G}{L}$$

R_n is measurable using a net radiometer and G can be calculated from data on the soil temperature profile or by directly measuring soil heat flux. H cannot be estimated easily but may be derived using Bowen's ratio $\beta = H/LE$. By substitution therefore:

$$E = \frac{R_n - G}{L(1 + \beta)}$$

Using Bowen's ratio assumes that the vertical transfer of heat and water vapour by turbulence occurs with equal efficiency.

Combined methods may be employed also, the most widely utilised perhaps being that presented by H. L. Penman in 1963.[20] He expressed PE as a function of available radiant energy R_n and a term E_α which combined saturation deficit and wind speed.

$$R_n = 0.75S - L_n$$

where $0.75S$ is the solar radiation absorbed by a grass surface and L_n the net long wave (terrestrial) radiation from the surface.

$$E_\alpha = f(u)(e_s - e)$$

where $f(u)$ is $0.35 (1 + 0.01u)$ for short grass and u is the wind speed at 2 m (miles/day), e_s is the saturation vapour pressure (mm Hg) at mean air temperature and e is the actual vapour pressure at mean air temperature and humidity.

The appropriate expression for short grass is given as

$$\text{PE (mm/day)} = \frac{\left(\dfrac{\Delta}{\gamma}\dfrac{R_n}{L} + E_\alpha\right)}{\dfrac{\Delta}{\gamma} - 1}$$

where $\dfrac{\Delta}{\gamma}$ = Bowen's ratio, γ being 0·27 (mm Hg/°F, the psychrometric constant) and $\Delta = \dfrac{de_s}{dt}$ (the change of saturation vapour pressure with mean air temperature (mm Hg/°F).

H. Olivier in 1961[21] proposed a simplified approach incorporating saturation deficit and radiation in which the relevant equation for PE in mm/day is

$$\text{PE} = (T - T_w)\frac{\bar{L}}{L^2}$$

where

$$L = \frac{S}{S_v} \text{ and } \bar{L} = \frac{\bar{S}}{\bar{S}_v}$$

S is the total solar radiation under clear sky conditions for the relevant station latitude for a given month, S_v being the vertical component of S, $\bar{S}$ is the average of the 12 monthly values of S, $\bar{S}_v$ is the average of the 12 monthly values of S_v, T is the mean monthly temperature in °C and T_w is the mean monthly wet–bulb temperature.

C. W. Thornthwaite in 1948 related data on consumptive utilisation of water in irrigated regions of the western USA to air temperatures (with adjustments for the length of days):[22]

$$\text{PE (mm/month)} = 16\left(\frac{10\,T}{I}\right)^a$$

where T is the mean monthly temperature in °C, a is an empirical function of I and

$$I = \sum_1^{12}\left(\frac{T}{5}\right)^{1·514}$$

Values can be calculated from nomograms or published tables and the method has been applied widely.

Finally, another approach depends upon the fact that if heat storage and sensible heat transfer are effectively zero then PE may be obtained approximately by:

$$\text{PE (mm/year)} \approx \frac{R_{NO}}{L} \approx 0 \cdot 18 \sum T$$

where R_{NO} is the net radiation budget of a wet ground surface and T is the sum of daily mean temperatures exceeding $10°C$.

A temperature formula for actual evaporation yielding annual quantities in mm for catchments is:

$$E = \frac{P}{\sqrt{0 \cdot 9 + \left(\dfrac{P}{I}\right)^2}}$$

where P is annual precipitation in mm, I is $300 + 25T + 0 \cdot 05T^3$ and T is the mean air temperature in $°C$.

Environmental isotopes may be applied to the problem of atmosphere–surface water evaporation from lakes and this is based upon the fact that lake and reservoir waters are enriched in deuterium and oxygen-18 with respect to regional precipitation owing to preferential removal of isotopically light $H_2{}^{16}O$ as water vapour. The actual degree of enrichment is closely linked with the water balance of the lake or reservoir.

In extreme cases the enrichment can be very high and J. C. Fontes and R. Gonfiantini have given a good instance of this from the Sahara in 1967.[23] Water of a small lake originating due to a flood in a wadi showed increasing D and ^{18}O contents during the period in which it was subjected to heavy evaporation. Near its disappearance the isotopic contents of the lake were higher than those of precipitation by 170‰ and 38‰ for deuterium and oxygen-18 respectively.

H. Craig et al. in 1963 demonstrated that in nature the heavy isotope enrichment is limited by molecular exchange with atmospheric water vapour and the rate and extent of this are dependent upon the relative humidity in the atmosphere with respect to the surface water temperature of the water body concerned.[24] High concentrations of dissolved salts lessen enrichment in heavy isotopes induced by evaporation and if the lake is drying up then the heavy isotope contents of the waters initially increase, attain a maximum and thereafter decrease, the effect being more marked for deuterium than for oxygen-18.

In Chapter 1, page 39, it was noted that the relationship

$$\delta D\%_{oo} = 8\delta^{18}O\%_{oo} - 10$$

derived by H. Craig best fits points representing the isotopic composition of precipitation samples from all over the world.[25] Of course variations do occur. For instance P. Fritz *et al.* in 1981 gave

$$\delta D\%_{oo} = 7 \cdot 8\delta^{18}O\%_{oo} - 10 \cdot 3$$

as the meteoric water line based upon spring and surface water together with precipitation studies in the High Andes, Chile.[26]

However, waters submitted to evaporation processes deviate systematically from this general sort of relation found in non-evaporated meteoric waters because in nature these occur under non-equilibrium conditions, i.e. when the atmosphere is not saturated with water vapour. By contrast the condensation of atmospheric water to produce precipitation takes place at the equilibrium point when the atmosphere is saturated with water vapour. The accompanying Fig. 2.8 shows

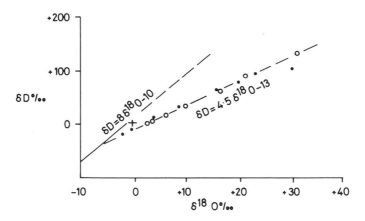

FIG. 2.8. D and ^{18}O variations in two drying Saharan Lakes.•, ○, saline lake samples showing effect of increasing salinity; +, SMOW.

precipitation line and evaporation line data from the drying Saharan Lakes alluded to above, one containing salt water and showing isotopic effects produced by increasing salinity. Consequently in $\delta^{18}O$–δD diagrams values for different stages of an evaporating body of water tend towards a straight line with a slope sharply different and lower than that of meteoric water.

The water balance of a lake is determined by the water input and the losses of water and if the two do not match then the volume must change thus:

$$dV = (J + P - O - E)dt$$

where dV is the change in volume of the lake in time dt, J is the rate of inflow (from rivers, groundwaters, etc.), P is the precipitation rate over the lake, O is the rate of outflow and E is the rate of evaporation. Of course it is difficult to actually determine some of these parameters, especially evaporation. Stable isotopes can be employed as follows: the stable isotope balance can be expressed

$$d(V\delta_1) = V d\delta_1 + \delta_1 dV = (J\delta_j + P\delta_p - O\delta_o - E\delta_E)dt$$

where δ_1 is the isotope content of the lake water and $d\delta_1$ its change during time dt. This approach was utilised by U. Zimmermann and D. H. Ehhalt in a study of Lake Neusiedl in Austria.[27] They eliminated total inflow because of the difficulty of assessing it and combined the last two equations to give the following:

$$E = \frac{P(\delta_P - \delta_J) + O(\delta_j - \delta_O) + dV(\delta_J - \delta_1) - V \times d\delta_1}{\delta_E - \delta_J}$$

This equation is stated to be valid only on a short time scale by Zimmermann and Ehhalt.

The isotopic composition of the evaporating moisture, δ_E, is determined by isotope separation effects during the evaporation process and also by isotope exchange and it can be calculated using an equation derived by D. H. Ehhalt and K. Knott[28] and also by H. Craig and L. I. Gordon.[29] This is:

$$\delta_E = \frac{\alpha^+ \delta_1 - h\delta_A - \epsilon^+ - \epsilon_K}{1 - h + \epsilon_K}$$

where α^+ is $1 - \epsilon^+ = R_v / R_L$, equilibrium isotope fractionation factor, R_v is the isotope ratio of the vapour, R_L that of the liquid, ϵ_K is the kinetic separation, h is the relative humidity with respect to the temperature of the lake and δ_A is the isotopic composition of the atmospheric water vapour. This equation was derived on the assumption that at the water surface the water vapour is in equilibrium with the water of the lake and also complete mixing has occurred, the isotopic composition and concentration of atmospheric water vapour being uninfluenced by the evaporation.

δ_E clearly depends upon the isotopic composition of the water vapour in the atmosphere (δ_A) and the relative humidity h. Accurate measurements of both of these parameters is necessary in order to obtain δ_E. In the case of deuterium the kinetic fractionation ϵ_K may be neglected and this makes it simpler to utilise this isotope.

Turning now to Lake Neusiedl there was a considerable practical difficulty in calculating δ because approximately 45% of the actual surface is covered by reeds. It is necessary therefore to make two calculations, one of evaporation from the unvegetated lake surface and the other of evapotranspiration from the reedy areas. The isotopic content, δ_E, of the total moisture produced by evapotranspiration from the lake, E, is given by the weighted mean:

$$\delta_E = \frac{E_F}{E}\delta_{E_F} + \frac{E_R}{E}\delta_{E_R} + \frac{T}{E}\delta_T$$

where $E = E_F + E_R + T$, E_F being evaporation rate of the free water surface, E_R the evaporation rate of the reed covered surface, T the transpiration rate of the reeds, δ_{E_F} = isotope content of evaporating moisture from the free water surface, δ_{E_R} = isotope content of evaporating moisture from the reed covered surface and δ_T = isotope content of the transpired water. Preliminary data on pan-evaporation for July and August 1968 were available and permitted estimation of the weighting factors as follows:

$$E_F/E = 0.5; \ E_R/E = 0.2: \ T/E = 0.3$$

Evapotranspiration from April to September 1968 was found to be $173 \times 10^6 \, m^3$ which is in good agreement with an estimate of $233 \times 10^6 \, m^3$ for a whole year obtained using conventional methods by F. Kopf.[30] However, Zimmermann and Ehhalt indicated that although their investigation was detailed and careful, the accuracy of their result for total evapotranspiration could not be regarded as better than 50%. It may be inferred from this that in temperate climates with usually high relative humidity the isotopic approach can be difficult in application.

An interesting investigation of Perch Lake evaporation was effected by P. J. Barry and W. F. Merritt in 1970.[31] However, this involved using tritiated water tracer and will be discussed in Chapter 4. As regards environmental tritium its concentration in atmospheric waters and hence its input in the balance equation have changed since the thermonuclear bomb testing commenced in 1952 as was noted earlier. No steady state tritium concentrations have been available subsequently so periodic balances are required. The tritium balance equation in a well mixed reservoir was given by J. R. Gat *et al.* in 1968 as follows:[32]

$$R_L \Delta V + V \Delta R_L = R_P P - (R_S I_S + R_G I_G - R_O O)\Delta t$$
$$- E \left[\frac{R_L}{K(1-h)} - \frac{hR_A}{K(1-h)} \right] \Delta t$$
$$- \lambda R_L V \Delta t$$

where O is the outflow, P is the precipitation, E is the mean evaporation rate, R_S is expressed in tritium units, I_S is the surface inflow, I_G the groundwater inflow, λ the decay constant for tritium ($\lambda = 0.055$/year) and K is a constant.

As it is very difficult to estimate isotopic fractionation effects, these may be neglected. The groundwater input may be neglected also in the case of tritium. The tritium balance equation may be simplified thereafter to:

$$R_L \Delta V + V \Delta R_L = R_P P - I_S R_S - E \left[\frac{R_L}{1-h} - \frac{hR_A}{1-h} \right] \Delta t$$
$$- R_O O \Delta t - \lambda R_L V \Delta t$$

The following parameters are known or measurable: P, I_S, R_P, V and R_L as well as t. h can be estimated if atmospheric humidity and lake temperature measurements are effected and, in continental climates, $R_P \approx R_A$.

In association with the mass–balance equation and the balance equations of other stable isotopes, the tritium balance equation is applicable to solving water balance problems in both natural lakes and artificial reservoirs. However, the assumption that $R_P \approx R_A$ may not be valid in arid regions. R_A, the isotopic ratio of the atmospheric water vapour may then be measured by observing the change in tritium concentration in standard evaporation pans located near to the water body. Alternatively, or as a control, it can be measured directly by sampling the water vapour.

As regards transpiration it may be noted that water in the leaves of plants becomes enriched in oxygen-18 and deuterium and the determination of D/H and $^{18}O/^{16}O$ ratios has demonstrated that the removal of water vapour from leaves is a non-equilibrium process. The actual degree of enrichment depends upon the relative humidity of the atmosphere as well as upon latitude. Daily variations in relative humidity correlate with variations in the isotopic composition of water in plants, cf. for instance the work of R. Gonfiantini *et al.* in 1965.[33]

As regards sampling of waters for analysis, 5 ml samples are usually sufficient both for deuterium and oxygen-18, but 20 ml samples may be taken if duplicating results is considered advisable and also if later chemical analyses are to be carried out. Such samples are stored in polythene bottles if to be used soon, otherwise in well stoppered glass bottles. If water vapour is to be collected, this is done by pumping air through a glass trap at the temperature of dry ice. The exit of this is fitted with a sintered filter to prevent escape of ice crystals from the trap during pumping. The rate of pumping is kept low (only a few litres of air per minute) in order to ensure that the condensation of the water vapour is complete. Generally it is necessary to pump for several hours to ensure that a sufficient quantity of water becomes available for evaluation on the basis of relative humidity to be effected.

2.7. GAUGING OF SNOW

Although snow is a form of precipitation and indeed together with ice constitutes about 80% of all water in the land regions of the Earth according to J. Martinec and A. I. Danilin in 1968, its measurement is effected so differently from, say, rainfall that a separate discussion of it becomes necessary.[34] Assessment of snow cover in a systematic manner is essential in deriving the global water balance and also in solving various hydrologic problems. Snow depth measurements are simply effected, but are insufficient to provide the required data because of the fact that snow density shows great variation in nature. Direct measurement of the snow water content has been effected using nuclear instrumentation based upon the principle that gamma radiation penetrating a snow pack is absorbed in relation to the total snow water equivalent. Suitable instruments have been devised and can be equipped with telemetering systems so that they can be utilised in inaccessible and remote mountainous regions having heavy snow cover. Gamma radiation is attenuated in passing through a snow pack according to the following:

$$I = I_0 e^{-\mu x}$$

where I_0 is the intensity of the incident radiation, I the reduced intensity after attentuation, μ the linear absorption coefficient for water (per cm) and x is the water equivalent of the snow pack (cm). Employing this approach it is feasible to determine the snow water equivalent by measurement of the reduced intensity of gamma radiation. The type of instrument which may be used is illustrated in Fig. 2.9. A source of gamma radiation may be ^{60}Co which is encased in a lead shield and then installed in the ground and is flush with it. The radiation intensity

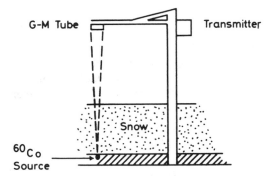

FIG. 2.9. Source–detector spatial arrangement in one type of snow gauge using nuclear instrumentation.

can be measured using a Geiger–Müller (GM) counter fixed at an appropriate distance above the source in the centre of a collimated radiation beam (this can be 4 or 5 m elevation). A scintillation detector may also be employed and has been by the US Army Corps of Engineers as L. J. Smith and D. W. Willen have pointed out.[35] In these and other variations the radioactive source is at soil level with a detector above it, but it is perfectly possible to use the alternative arrangement, namely to have the detector under the soil surface and the source elevated. This has been done in a number of countries, see for instance the work of V. Fischmeister in 1956 or D. L. Duncan and C. C. Warnick in 1963.[36, 37] The advantage of this plan is that the effects of considerable variations in temperature on the detector can be eliminated or at least reduced. A. I. Danilin has described a portable type of radioactive snow gauge utilised in the USSR which has a graduated metal rod with a gamma source located at its lower end and a detector at its upper end.[38] When this is inserted into snow the water equivalent of the layer between the source and the detector can be read off. In air-borne radiometric snow gauges the gamma sources are installed at the soil surface and the gamma ray intensity attenuated by snow is measured by an aeroplane flying at a fixed height of 30 to 90 m. The International Atomic Energy Agency together with Argentine investigators developed a method using X-ray film fixed above a radioactive source which is irradiated during a predetermined time interval by a collimated beam of gamma rays.[39] The optical density of the exposed film is a function of the radiation intensity and the film can be moved ahead automatically every 24 h so that a radiographic record of exposures results at the termination of the winter season.

The maximum snow water content which can be measured is dependent upon the strength of the radioactive source and a suitable one is ^{60}Co which emits gamma radiation of 1·2 and 1·3 MeV which is sufficient to penetrate deep snow packs. Calibration experiments have demonstrated that 30 to 80 mCi of this radioisotope are enough for snow gauges equipped with a GM tube. For X-ray instrumentation a much stronger source is necessary and here 0·5 Ci of ^{60}Co has been utilised. Air-borne radiometric snow gauging requires installation of 20 Ci of ^{60}Co. Efficient collimation is necessary in all cases so that the effects of different types of snow structure on scattering can be eliminated. Calibration is optimally effected using actual water columns and measured depths may be introduced into a tank installed between the radioisotope and the GM tube. Some workers have submerged radioactive sources in a swimming pool[37] or even in a natural lake[36] and in this manner have approximated an absorber of infinite size and the conditions of a continuous snow pack. An additional radioactive source is required in order to check the long-term stability of the GM tube and for this purpose and because of its long half-life ^{90}Sr ($T_{\frac{1}{2}} = 28$ years) is usually employed as a 'standard'. It is particularly important with X-ray film because calibration optical densities may be obtained using it. Daily images are analysed by means of an optical densitometer and the snow water equivalent determined according to the relationship between both readings in conjunction with a calibration curve. The accuracy of results depends not only on effective collimation and a sufficiency of strength in the source but also upon the duration of measurements. This is because the measurement error increases as the counting time decreases due to statistical fluctuations of the radiation. In a French type of instrument the requisite time for obtaining a predetermined number of counts is measured and with this fixed at 10 000 an accuracy of ±3 mm water is ensured for a range of measured snow water equivalents from 0 to 1200 mm.[34] As regards snow gauges with X-ray film the accuracy of optical readings affects the results which are stated as attaining a level of ±5%. In the case of air-borne radiometric snow gauges the results differed from the mean by 3% to 5% and from the check measurements by the standard method by 7%. Clearly radiotelemetry is useful and frequently utilised. It facilitates the acquisition of data at any time during the winter. Work on snow gauging is actively proceeding and M. Kodama *et al.* in 1979 gave details of an application of cosmic ray neutron measurements to the determination of the snow water equivalent.[40] Application of the water absorption character of cosmic ray neutrons to the determination of the water equivalent depth of a snow cover is discussed using a cosmic ray snow gauge. Attenuation curves set under or in snow or water are exponentially obtained. Continuous observation in the field over four snow seasons showed effectiveness even where the snow cover exceeded 1 m water equivalent.

Of course wherever a radioactive snow gauge is installed and operated the relevant safety precautions should be observed following regulations strictly, especially those pertaining to the shielding of the source. Gauges of this type are used in areas of fairly deep to deep snow and their employment in shallow snow sites is not justifiable. This is because in such conditions the snow water content can be measured using a weighing snow sampler. A suitable one for British conditions was described by E. A. Waring and J. A. A. Jones in 1980.[41] Aimed at shallow snow of short duration this identifies and measures snow cover by a hydraulic weighing system. Snow melt and rainfall are measured through a central draining system. An interesting natural radioisotope approach was proposed by G. O. Endrestøl in 1980.[42] This involves the measurement of snow water equivalent by the detection of natural gamma radiation.

2.8. ATMOSPHERIC WATER IN SOIL EROSION

Erosion of soil by water from the atmosphere, i.e. precipitation, may be considered as involving two sequential processes of which only the first concerns this chapter. They are raindrop erosion, namely the detaching of particles from the soil by impact and their removal by splashing, and runoff erosion which entails the transportation of loose material by the turbulent water flowing in sheets. Two concepts arise. One is the erosive power of raindrops and the other is the susceptibility to erosion by water of the soil. The quantity of soil in runoff is related to raindrop energy and in fact the prevention of raindrop impact reduces soil erosion. The importance of this is a consequence of the fact that in certain situations

90% of soil erosion on agricultural land is ascribable to this process. The median dimensions of raindrops increase with the intensity of rainfall (for low and moderate intensity falls) in the relation:

$$D_{50} = aI^b$$

where D_{50} is the median dimensions of raindrops in mm, I is the intensity in mm per hour and a, b are constants. In the case of high intensity rainfall it has been recorded that the drop dimensions diminish and the maximal sizes of drops are of the order of 5 to 6 mm diameter. The actual drop dimensions influence the velocity of impact. A drop of rain which is in free fall will accelerate under gravity until its force becomes equal to the frictional resistance of air. At this point the drop of rain attains its terminal velocity. As a consequence of the fact that fall distances to maximal velocity are short most drops will hit the ground at terminal velocity.

Rainfall intensities can be obtained from recording rain gauge data. The relationship between rainfall and soil loosening, separation and transportation is of great interest and the following equation is relevant:

$$G = KDV^{1 \cdot 4}$$

in which G is the weight of soil splashed (g), K is a constant for the particular soil type concerned, D is the diameter of the raindrops (mm) and V is the impact velocity (m/sec). A compound parameter known as the EI_{30} index has been derived in order to explain optimally soil losses in terms of rainfall. This is the product of kinetic energy E (in foot tons per acre inch) and intensity I (in inches per hour) where I_{30} specifically relates to the 30 min intensity, i.e. the maximum average intensity in any half hour period during a storm. Spatial patterns of this index in the eastern USA indicate that the potential hazard danger of an accelerated erosion is higher in the Gulf Coast region than in the western and northern areas of the country.

Splashing of soil shows great variability and it is much less significant where a vegetative cover exists and acts as a shield. Slope has a profound influence because where the soil is horizontal splash erosion can break up and move particles but no loss will occur. On an incline, however, such loss will occur and it has been shown that on a 10% (6°) slope 75% of soil splash is down the slope. Soil splash attacked surfaces can be damaged in a multitude of ways. For instance, debris may be transported to cause soil loss and elutriation occurs, i.e. nutrients such as humus may be removed. Also, the impact of raindrops can disperse surficial clay particles and promote the formation of surface runoff accompanied by runoff erosion. Runoff is believed not to arise immediately rain falls on to a bare surface of soil, water infiltrating into the ground if this is unsaturated and such infiltration taking place at a rate determined by a number of parameters such as vegetational cover, type, structure and texture of the soil, soil moisture content and the condition of the surface. Infiltration capacity is the maximum sustained rate at which a particular soil can transmit water and it varies with conditions—during a rain storm it can at first be rapid, but later it declines to a constant value. This decline results from rain packing, the in-washing of fine material, swelling of colloids and breakdown of the surficial soil structure. Here minimum infiltration capacity is displayed. If rain goes on for time t then

$$f_p = f_c - (f_0 - f_c)e^{-kt}$$

where f_p is the infiltration capacity, f_0 this parameter at maximum, f_c the parameter after decline to a constant value, k a constant and $e = 2\cdot71828$, the base of Naperian logarithms. As f_p diminishes with time during a rainstorm, runoff increases.

2.9. WIND AND PRESSURE

The air is a fluid exerting a sea level pressure of $c.$ 15 lb./in.^{2} on exposed surfaces. Atmospheric pressure is practically an exact measure of the weight of the atmosphere above an observation point. Pressure is force per unit area and considering an air column of unit cross-section its change with altitude is given by:

$$\Delta P = -g\rho\Delta Z$$

where P is pressure, g the constant acceleration due to gravity (981 cm/sec^2), Z the altitude and ρ the density.

The fundamental unit of pressure is the millibar, one thousandth of a bar. A bar is almost equal to the normal pressure of the atmosphere and is defined as 1×10^6 dynes per cm^2 (1 dyne is the force required to accelerate 1 g of mass 1 cm/sec).

It may be added that 1000 millibars (mb) are equal to $750\cdot1$ mm of mercury ($29\cdot53$ inches of mercury). Pressures vary in the atmosphere, both periodically and non-periodically. The best known periodic variations are diurnal and semi-diurnal. These have periods of 24 and 12 h respectively. The semi-diurnal variation is an oscillation of the atmosphere which encircles the Earth. Eliminating all other factors the barograph traces at all stations show two maxima and two minima during the day, the former taking place at 10 a.m. and 10 p.m., the latter at 4 a.m. and 4 p.m. The effect is most pronounced at equatorial stations where pressure at the maxima is over 4 mb higher than it is at the minima. This semi-diurnal variation is thought to be a resonance wave triggered by the regular travel of the heating effect of insolation around the planet and it has been suggested that it is proportional to the cube of the cosine of the latitude (which accounts for its large size at the equator). The diurnal variation is less regular than the semi-diurnal pressure wave because it depends upon solar heating more directly and also the kind of area involved. Over land areas pressure falls to a minimum during the warm afternoon hours, thereafter rising to a maximum in the early hours before the dawn. At sea the diurnal variation is much less marked than on land, pressure tending to rise by day and fall by night (the reverse of the situation over land). Periodic variations are often concealed in middle and high latitudes by the effects of non-periodic variations due to the passage of depressions and anticyclones.

Pressure varies with altitude and time and also horizontally. Hence, gradients exist as well and become apparent when isobars are plotted— they are significant in determining the behaviour of the wind. At 450 m to 900 m elevation outside the equatorial belt the wind blows mostly parallel to the isobars with a steady velocity proportional to the pressure gradient. Nearer the surface of the Earth the velocity drops and the wind blows across the isobars towards the low pressure at angles varying from 20° to 50°. The sense in which the wind blows depends upon the hemisphere. North of the equator the wind blows so that an observer with his or her back to it finds the low pressure to the left and vice versa. Of course these factors depend upon a balance of the forces acting on air in motion. One of these is the Coriolis force alluded to earlier; see page 78 and Fig. 2.5. Others include the pressure gradient force; the pressure gradient exerts a force which is proportional to its own magnitude acting at right angles to the isobars towards the lower pressure and tending to give to air an acceleration down the pressure gradient. Another force is centrifugal which acts radially outwards from the centre of curvature of the curved path of air movement on the planetary surface and it is proportional to the radius of curvature. Finally, friction may be mentioned; this retards movement when air moves over ground. Additionally there is an internal friction within the air itself. Frictional forces act in opposition to the wind direction.

That equilibrium of forces which exists when steady winds blow across the Earth's surface is termed the strophic balance of which the most significant is the geostrophic wind resulting from a balance between the pressure gradient and the deflectional force of the planetary rotation, i.e. a geostrophic wind results when these two forces are equal and opposite and this state of affairs may be expressed thus:

$$2\,\omega \sin \phi V_{\mathrm{g}} = \frac{1}{\rho} \times \text{pressure gradient}$$

where ω is the rate of spin of the Earth, ϕ the latitude, V_{g} the appropriate wind. The expression $2\omega \sin \phi$ constitutes the Coriolis parameter; see page 78. V_{g}, the velocity of the geostrophic wind, is the wind parallel to the isobars and at right angles to the pressure gradient. That term to the left in the above equation represents the deflectional force of the rotation of the Earth and the term to the right is the pressure gradient force per unit mass. ρ is of course the density of the air. This equation is one of the most important in meteorology.

Turning again to the effects of friction this is effective *vis-à-vis* the bottom layers of the atmosphere and it slows down the movement of air to a much greater extent over land than over the sea. Thus in the former case the wind at ground level may be reduced to only half the geostrophic wind or, in nature, the gradient wind. This distinction is made between the theoretical geostrophic wind and an actual gradient one. Both can coincide where air flow is horizontal and straight with no pressure changes in progress. Where different conditions prevail, however, the actual wind departs from the geostrophic value and this may arise where the air particles move along curved paths. As a result a new balanced condition arises in which the wind again becomes steady but has a velocity different from that of the geostrophic condition. This new balanced condition causes the gradient wind which blows when the pressure gradient is balanced jointly by the centrifugal force and by the deflecting force of the rotation of the Earth.

The circulation of the atmosphere is mainly horizontal, but as noted earlier precipitation results from upwards movements of large bodies of moist air. It has been demonstrated (by Stokes) that the motion of a small fluid element can be resolved into four component motions, namely:

(i)   a bodily transfer with no change either of shape or volume;
(ii) a spin about an axis passing through the fluid element;

(iii) a shear, i.e. a change in shape without any change in volume;
(iv) an expansion or contraction without any change in shape.

This analysis is actually basic to comprehension of the atmospheric circulation and clearly the first component predominates but the second (vorticity) is also important with the third (shear) not being very significant climatologically. The final component (divergence) is negligible in the atmosphere and meteorologists have restricted it to fit a two-dimensional framework and use the work to describe a purely horizontal divergence analogous to the expansion or contraction of a circle. Radial circulation of this type is most uncommon in the atmosphere and even then is found in equatorial latitudes only. However, divergence may occur frequently superimposed on transfer. Zones of divergence and convergence in air streams are normally zones of marked subsidence and uplift respectively. Divergent motion tends to produce clear and settled weather whereas if the air is sufficiently damp convergence will create clouds and rainfall.

It may be appropriate here to list the various types of air masses which may be found in the atmosphere together with some of their characteristics; this is done in Table 2.6.

TABLE 2.6
AIR MASSES, CLASSIFICATION AND CHARACTERISTICS AND MOISTURE CONTENTS

Major	Minor	Source areas	Properties at source
Polar	Maritime polar	Oceans north or south of approximately 50°N	Cool, moist and unstable
	Continental polar	Continents near the Arctic circle and Antarctica	Cold and dry, stable
Tropical	Maritime tropical	Trade wind belt and sub-tropical waters of the great oceans	Warm, moist and of variable stability (stable on the east sides of the great oceans, somewhat unstable on the west sides)
Tropical	Continental tropical	Low latitude deserts (mainly the Sahara and the Australian desert)	Hot, extremely dry and unstable

2.10. THE EARTH AND ITS ATMOSPHERE

The planetary mantle, the ultimate source of plate movements, was also the source of the water of the oceans which was at one time volcanic steam. The atmosphere, now four parts of nitrogen to one of oxygen, was once probably ammonia, methane and carbon dioxide emitted by volcanoes in the early Pre-cambrian period. Volcanic gases are predominantly hydrides i.e. molecules of a rather narrow variety of chemical elements (nitrogen, carbon and oxygen) combined with hydrogen. Consequently, the present day atmosphere arose as a result of the photochemical decomposition of ammonia and water vapour by ultraviolet radiation originating in the sun. Light hydrogen atoms and molecules escaped into deep space and left behind heavier oxygen and nitrogen ensnared by the planet's gravitational field. Methane also was decomposed and left carbon to combine with oxygen to form carbon dioxide. Since the production rate of oxygen from water vapour by UV radiation is too slow to convert all the carbon monoxide entering the atmosphere through geologic time to CO_2, all free oxygen in the atmosphere ought to have been taken up in forming carbon dioxide. Clearly there is free oxygen in the atmosphere and this results from plants which release it during photosynthesis. The Earth's atmosphere and oceans function as a vast heat engine powered by the sun and conditioning climate and weather, ocean waves and currents. The horse-power of it has been estimated as 2000×10^{12} and its working fluid is water vapour. As the Earth must radiate intercepted solar energy back into space at the same rate that it receives it so that terrestrial temperatures do not rise, the importance of the atmosphere becomes apparent because of the following vital activities in it:

(i)   The ozone layer, about 24 km elevation, absorbs almost all electromagnetic radiation in the UV end of the spectrum, i.e. that which is dangerous to Man. This decomposes ozone into ordinary oxygen and atomic oxygen and also ionises high altitude oxygen and forms the ionosphere.

(ii) Condensed water in the atmosphere, clouds, reflect 25% of all outgoing radiation from the Earth.

(iii) Water droplets and dust particles as well as the air itself backscatter one-tenth of the remaining 75% outgoing radiation.

(iv) Water vapour and carbon dioxide are important because they are practically opaque to all but a small part of the infrared region of the spectrum. The narrow wave band in the visible part of the sun's spectrum which strikes the planetary surface as c. 50% of the total incident solar radiation at the top of the atmosphere warms the oceanic surface and the land and they radiate not in the visible part of the spectrum but in the IR part. However, it is solely in the narrow zone lying between the absorption bands of water vapour and carbon dioxide that the IR radiation of the solar heated Earth can escape and this is the 'greenhouse effect', the thermal regulatory mechanism setting the average planetary temperature and keeping it steady.

REFERENCES

1. STARR, V. and PEIXOTO, J. P., 1964. The hemispheric eddy flux of water vapour and its implications for the mechanics of the general circulation. *Arch. Mer. Geophys. Bioklim., Ser. A*, **14**, 111–30.
2. ANON, 1969. Environmental Isotope Data No. 1, World Survey of Isotope Concentration in Precipitation (1953–63). *Tech. Repts Ser. No. 96*, IAEA, Vienna.
3. ANON, 1970. Environmental Isotope Data No. 2, World Survey of Isotope Concentration in Precipitation (1964–5). *Tech. Repts Ser. No. 117*, IAEA, Vienna.
4. ERIKSSON, E., 1968. The source of atmospheric moisture and precipitation. in: *Guidebook on Nuclear Techniques in Hydrology. Tech. Repts Ser. No. 91*, IAEA, Vienna, 21–4.
5. BOYCE, I. S. and CAMERON, J. F., 1962. A low level background liquid scintillation counter for the assay of low specific activity tritiated water. in: *Tritium in the Biological Sciences*, Vol. 1, Symp. 3–10 May 1961, IAEA, Vienna, 231–47.
6. PILGRIM, D. H., 1966. Radioactive tracing of storm runoff on a small catchment. 1. Experimental technique. *J. Hydrol.*, **4**, 289.
7. ERIKSSON, E., 1967. Isotopes in hydrometeorology. in: *Isotopes in Hydrology*, Symp. 14–18 November 1966, IAEA, Vienna, 21–34.
8. LIBBY, W. F., 1963. Moratorium tritium geophysics. *J. Geophys. Res.*, **68**, 4485.
9. DANSGAARD, W. F., 1964. Stable isotopes in precipitation. *Tellus*, **16**, 436.
10. ERIKSSON, E., 1965. Deuterium and oxygen-18 in precipitation and other natural waters. Some theoretical considerations. *Tellus*, **17**, 498.
11. ÖSTLUND, G., 1965. 1965 Hurricane tritium. *Symp. Isotope Techniques in the Hydrologic Cycle*, 10–12 November 1965, Urbana, Illinois, USA.
12. GUIMOND, R. J., ELLETT, W. H., FITZGERALD, J. E., WINDHAM, S. T. and CLUNY, P. A., 1979. *Indoor Radiation Exposure due to Ra-226 on Florida Phosphate Lands*. Criteria and Standards Division, Office of Radiation Programs, US Environmental Protection Agency, Washington, DC 20460.

13. ÅKERBLOM, C. V. and WILSON, CAROLE, 1981. Radon gas—a radiation hazard from radioactive bedrock and building materials. *Bull. Int. Assn Eng. Geologists*, **23**, 51–61.
14. MAGRI, G. and TAZIOLI, G. S., 1970. Radon in groundwaters of dolomitic and calcareous aquifer in Apulia (southern Italy). in: *Isotope Hydrology*, Proc. Symp. 9–13 March 1970, IAEA, Vienna, 835–45.
15. LAL, D., NIJAMPURKAR, V. N. and RAMA, S., 1970. Silicon-32 hydrology. in: *Isotope Hydrology*, Proc. Symp. 9–13 March 1970, IAEA, Vienna, 847–68.
16. WEBSTER, P. J., 1981. Monsoons. *Sci. Amer.*, **245**, 2, 70–81.
17. RODDA, J. C., 1976. The assessment of precipitation. in: *Introduction to Physical Hydrology*, ed. Richard J. Chorley. Methuen and Co. Ltd, London, 77–81.
18. NEFF, EARL L., 1977. How much rain does a rain gage gage? *J. Hydrol.*, **35**, 213–20.
19. BLOEMEN, G. W., 1978. A high accuracy recording pan-evaporimeter and some of its possibilities. *J. Hydrol.*, **38**, 159–73.
20. PENMAN, H. L., 1963. Vegetation and hydrology. *Tech. Communication No. 53*, Commonwealth Bureau of Soils (Farnham Royal), 124pp.
21. OLIVIER, H., 1961. *Irrigation and Climate*. Edward Arnold, London, 250 pp.
22. THORNTHWAITE, C. W., 1948. An approach towards a rational classification of climate. *Geog. Rev.*, **38**, 55–94.
23. FONTES, J. C. and GONFIANTINI, R., 1967. Comportement isotopique au cours de l'evaporation des deux bassins Sahariens. *Earth Plan. Sci. Letters*, **3**, 258.
24. CRAIG, H., GORDON, L. I. and HORIBE, Y., 1963. Isotopic exchange effects in the evaporation of water. 1. Low temperature experimental results. *J. Geophys. Res.*, **68**, 5079.
25. CRAIG, H., 1961. Isotopic variations in meteoric waters. *Science*, **133**, 1702.
26. FRITZ, P., SUZUKI, O., SILVA, C. and SALATI, E., 1981. Isotope hydrology of groundwaters in the Pampa del Tamarugal, Chile. *J. Hydrol.*, **53**, 161–84.
27. ZIMMERMANN, U. and EHHALT, D. H., 1970. Stable isotopes in study of the water balance of Lake Neusiedl, Austria. in: *Isotope Hydrology*, Proc. Symp. 9–13 March 1970, IAEA, Vienna, 129–38.
28. EHHALT, D. H. and KNOTT, K., 1965. Kinetische Isotopentrennung bei der Verdampfung von Wasser. *Tellus*, **17**, 3.
29. CRAIG, H. and GORDON, L. I., 1965. Isotope oceanography: deuterium and oxygen-18 variations in the ocean and the marine atmosphere. Spoleto Meeting on Nuclear Geology, Italy.
30. KOPF, F., 1967. Die Rettung des Neusiedlersees. *Österr. Wasserwirtschaft*, **19**, 7–8.
31. BARRY, P. J. and MERRITT, W. F., 1970. Perch Lake evaporation study. in: *Isotope Hydrology*, Proc. Symp., 9–13 March 1970, IAEA, Vienna, 139–51.
32. GAT, J. R., GONFIANTINI, R. and TONGIORGI, E., 1968. Atmosphere–surface water evaporation from lakes. in: *Guidebook on Nuclear Techniques in Hydrology*, Tech. Repts. Ser. No. 91, IAEA, Vienna, 175–84.
33. GONFIANTINI, R., GRATZIU, S. and TONGIORGI, E., 1965. Oxygen isotopic composition of water in leaves. Isotopes and radiation in soil–plant nutrition studies. *Proc. Symp. Ankara*, IAEA, Vienna, 405.

34. MARTINEC, J. and DANILIN, A. I., 1968. Snow gauging (instrumental). in: *Guidebook on Nuclear Techniques in Hydrology, Tech. Repts Ser. No. 91,* IAEA, Vienna, 25–31.
35. SMITH, L. J. and WILLEN, D. W., 1964. Radio snow gauges: a review of the literature. *Isotopes Radiat. Technol.,* **2,** 41–9.
36. FISCHMEISTER, V., 1956. Die Bestimmung des Wasserwertes einer Schneedecke mit radioaktiven Stoffen. *Osterr. Wasserwirtschaft,* **8,** 86–93.
37. DUNCAN, D. L. and WARNICK, C. C., 1963. Instrumentation for hydrologic measurements at the University of Idaho. *Proc. 31st Western Snow Conf.,* Colorado State University, Fort Collins, 67–73.
38. DANILIN, A. I., 1957. *Priminenije jademych izlucenij v gidrometeorologii.* Gidrometeoizdat, Leningrad.
39. IAEA, 1968. Automatic recording of snow cover thickness by radiography. Contract No. 306, Castagnet A. C., *Tech. Repts Ser. No. 85,* 99.
40. KODAMA, M., NAKAI, K., KAWASAKI, S. and WADA, M., 1979. An application of cosmic ray neutron measurements to the determination of the snow water equivalent. *J. Hydrol.,* **41,** 85–92.
41. WARING, E. A. and JONES, J. A. A., 1980. A snow melt and water equivalent gauge for British conditions. *Hydrol. Sci. Bull.,* **25,** 2, 129–34.
42. ENDRESTØL, G. O., 1980. Principle and method for measurement of snow water equivalent by detection of natural gamma radiation. *Hydrol. Sci. Bull.,* **25,** 177–83.

CHAPTER 3

Rivers

3.1. RATES OF FLOW AND DISCHARGE OF RIVERS

The fresh water cycle may be studied in the river basin and the rate of flow is perhaps the most important parameter which, when assessed, leads to the determination of discharge, the volume of water passing through a given cross-section during a particular time interval. Units of measurement of discharge include cumecs (cubic metres per second) and for small flows litres per second. Earlier measurements may be given in cubic feet per second or cusecs and 1 cusec = 0·028 cumec. On a larger scale, water supply may be measured in million gallons per day (m.g.d.)—1 m.g.d. = 0·053 cumec.

Various methods are available for measuring stream flow rates and conventional instruments for this include current meters. They comprise a propeller attached to a hydrofoil section. Where a stream is sufficiently shallow to permit wading, the current meter is attached to a wading rod having a base plate resting on the stream bed. The metal rod is so calibrated that the current meter can be moved along it to the requisite depth in the stream channel. The number of revolutions of the propeller in a given time is proportional to the stream velocity and this may be counted using a small electric counter. Resultant data are converted to stream velocity measurements. Where large rivers are involved the current meter is lowered from a cable-way to a predetermined depth. A straight, obstruction-free stretch of stream with a well defined channel is selected and its cross-section measured. Then the velocity is determined using the current meter set at the appropriate depth for a number of equally spaced profiles, this number depending upon the nature of the cross-section and the available time. Discharge between any two vertical profiles should not exceed 10% of the total discharge over the entire cross-section. Where current meters are considered to be too expensive, floats may be employed. It has been found that surficial velocity in a given vertical profile exceeds the average velocity for that profile. The usually accepted conversion factor is that the mean velocity in any given vertical profile is 0·85 times the surface velocity. Consequently, if the surface velocity can be measured using a float, the total discharge of the stream can be derived from $Q = VA$ where Q is the river discharge, V is the average velocity of a selected cross-section and A is the area of the cross-section.

Appropriate methods include the following:

(i)   dilution gauging;
(ii) measurement of river velocity and cross-sectional area;
(iii) building artificial stream channels or weirs.

Their applicability may be summarised according to stream size as shown in Table 3.1.

TABLE 3.1.

River type	Dilution gauging	Velocity and cross-sectional area using a current meter or floats	Artificial structures
Small	Useful	Difficult if river is very shallow	V-notch and rectangular weirs
Medium	Feasible using dyes	Cable-way or use of bridge	Feasible using flumes with flows of 100 cumecs
Large	Feasible but undesirable in heavily populated areas	Feasible with use of cable-way	Impracticable because of scale and cost of construction

Measurement of the flow rate of streams may be considered as one of the most fundamental hydrologic problems and it is usually effected at permanent gauging stations. However, as a result of the fact that calibration and recalibration are required, such flow rate measurements are made only a limited number of times annually. Turning now to dilution gauging, the principle involved is that a known quantity of the selected chemical is added to a river and samples of its water collected at various points downstream so as to obtain data indicative of the degree of dilution which has occurred. Non-radioactive and radioactive tracers may be utilised and include dichromates, chlorides, sulphates, nitrites and rhodamine, etc. As noted in Table 3.1, dilution methods are selected when it is impossible to employ a current meter. This may be because of insufficient depth of water, because of turbulence or because the river is transporting materials capable of damaging a current meter. Chemical tracers may be subject to adsorption on the river bed or its contained sediment and in this case radioactive tracers may be substituted. The chemical dichromate, $Cr_2O_7^{2-}$, has chromium with a valency of 6 and is subject to reduction especially in polluted water, the chromium then appearing in cationic form with a valency of 3; the consequence of this is that some of the chromate tracer may be lost due to adsorption.[1]

Another problem is the difficulty of measuring samples by colorimetry. Once more the chromium ought to have a valency of 6 and the re-oxidation of the reduced chromium is a process which cannot be used routinely. NaCl may be utilised and it is measured by conductivity analysis. However, since the background conductivity of some rivers is rather high it is then necessary to employ large quantities of salt so that the background-to-signal ratio may be increased adequately. In fact, it is difficult to measure salt in the field, the more so when suspended sediment occurs. Good isotope tracers are available and these are mostly anionic, not prone to adsorption on river beds, and very practical. Dilution of radioactive tracers has been found to be a very reliable means of measuring flow rates in streams.

There are two basic approaches to the problem and these are outlined below.

3.1.1. Constant Rate Injection Method

In this approach a radioactive tracer in a concentration c_0 is injected at a constant rate into a river with a rate of flow Q. The injection rate may be indicated by q. A certain distance is required in which mixing occurs and subsequently the concentration c across a given section is constant. The tracer balance at any one time may be expressed as follows:

$$c_0 q = \int_s c \, dQ$$

where c is the concentration at a particular point and instant relative to an element $d\sigma$ of the sampling section S in which the rate of flow is dQ. $\int_s$ represents integration over the whole surface of the said sampling section and so may be derived thus

$$Q = \frac{c_0}{c} q$$

from which it is necessary to determine c_0/c. A counter has a linear response as a function either of the concentration or of the total activity of a sample which is labelled assuming that the geometry of detection is not altered in any way. A sample of the river water is compared with a sample of the injected solution and

$$Q = \frac{'N_0}{N} q$$

where N and N_0 represent the counting rates. In order to ensure a linear response in the counter it is necessary to dilute the initial sample aliquot so that

$$Q = \frac{N_d}{N} \lambda q$$

where N_d is the counting rate for the diluted sample and λ is the dilution factor.

3.1.2. Integration Method

D. E. Hull was one of the first to apply this method in 1958.[2] A radioactive tracer which contains activity A_0 is injected into a stream, any technique for this process being suitable so long as the injection is instantaneous and there is minimal dispersion of the radiotracer in the sampling section. The tracer balance may be expressed

$$A_0 = \int_s \int_0^\infty dQ \, c \, dt$$

Subsequent to complete mixing, the expression $c \, dt$ becomes constant in every section of the flow and then

$$A_0 = \int_s dQ \int_0^\infty c \, dt = Q \int_0^\infty c \, dt$$

A sample with a mean concentration c may be obtained by sampling in the appropriate section at a constant rate over a period T which is equal to the passage time of the activity cloud and then

$$\int_0^\infty c\,\mathrm{d}t = \bar{c}T$$

and

$$Q = \frac{A_0}{\bar{c}T} = \frac{A_0}{A}\frac{V}{T}$$

where A represents the activity of the sample having a volume V. Taking an aliquot of the injected solution and thus of the radioactivity

$$Q = \frac{N_{\mathrm{d}}}{N}\lambda\frac{V}{T}$$

There are conditions for employing the radioactive tracer dilution method and these include the following:

(i)   The flow regime must be permanent.

(ii) The radiotracer should be subject to adsorption or sedimentation, i.e. to disappearance from the medium conveying it.

(iii) The mixing ought to be satisfactory and in the constant rate injection method c = a constant, in the integration method $\int_0^\infty c\,\mathrm{d}t$ = a constant.

(iv) As regards timing, sampling should be effected while the concentration in the sampling section is constant and in Fig. 3.1 this is shown as a concentration plateau. The duration of this is equal to $T - \phi$ where T is the continuous injection time and ϕ is the duration of the responding pulse derived from instantaneous injection. As regards spatial considerations the main necessity is to ensure that the sampling section is located downstream from the zone of mixing and far enough from it to ensure that good mixing has occurred.

The problem of selecting the appropriate radioactive tracer may now be considered and perhaps the most widely used one is [82]Br. In 1980 a note regarding its employment in the River Skerne in England appeared from L. Hamill and he stated that it proved to be very reliable with practically insignificant adsorption losses.[3] In his work 40 mCi of [82]Br were injected continuously over 4 h between Ricknall Grange and

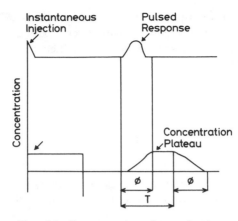

FIG. 3.1. Concentration plateau in time.

Brafferton followed by constant rate injection of 60 mCi of ^{82}Br between Ricknall Grange and Bradbury over a time interval of 6 h.

Other radioactive tracers which have been utilised include ^{131}I, ^{198}Au, ^{24}Na and ^{3}H (T) in the form of tritiated water, this latter for instance by T. Florkowski in the Tana River in Kenya in 1968.[4] Although tritium is environmentally deleterious because of its relatively long half-life of 12·26 years, the radioisotope is almost an ideal tracer because it forms part of the water molecule, is not subject to adsorption except in montmorillonite clays, is not hazardous because of its low level beta energy emission, can be measured in very low concentration by a liquid scintillation spectrometer (down to 10^{-15} mols) and can cope with flow rates up to thousands of cubic metres per second.

As noted in Table 3.2 tritium as HTO is an ideal radiotracer except for

TABLE 3.2
DATA ON APPROPRIATE RADIOACTIVE TRACERS

Radioactive isotope	Half-life $(T_{1/2})$	Maximum permissible concentration $(\mu Ci/m^3)$
^{82}Br	35·9 h	3 000
^{131}I	8·04 days	20
^{198}Au	2·69 days	500
^{3}H (T)	12·26 years	3 000
^{51}Cr	28·0 days	

its long half-life and the fact that it may be retarded or lost by exchange of tritium between the tritiated water and the adsorbed water and interlayer water in clay minerals such as montmorillonite.[5] However, the retardation of tritium is insignificant in soils containing small or negligible quantities of clay and silt. Chloride ion was shown to be an ideal radiotracer also but it is very restricted in practice because of its cost, absence of gamma radiation and very long half-life ($T_{1/2} = 3 \times 10^5$ years).[6] While ^{131}I is in some ways suitable, its very low maximum permissible concentration is a disadvantage. Stable complexes can provide appropriate radiotracers with medium half-lives and such compounds occur among metallic chelates. Such chelates comprise a metal atom closely bound to an organic molecule and may be neutral or charged. A well known chelating agent is ethylene diamine tetra-acetic acid (EDTA) and this may associate as in ^{46}Sc, ^{124}Sb and ^{51}Cr. ^{51}Cr possesses a number of favourable characteristics such as low energy gamma radiation with a concomitantly high permissible concentration level in drinking water. The low level gamma radiation permits excellent localisation of the radiotracer, the only real disadvantage of which is that a mere 8% of the disintegrations produce gamma radiation; also that the cross-section for the formation of ^{51}Cr by irradiation of chromium is relatively small resulting in low specific activity. The stability constant of the ^{51}Cr–EDTA complex is about 10^{24} and the complex itself has a violet colour and is present in acid or neutral solutions as a monovalent ion. ^{51}Cr–EDTA and HTO have been employed together as a double radiotracer in groundwater studies.[5] While tritium activity is detected by liquid scintillation counting, that of ^{51}Cr is detected using a well-type NaI scintillation detector. Since ^{51}Cr causes pulses of similar height to those of tritium (especially owing to the emission of 4·9 keV X-rays) the samples are normally aged before measurement of tritium in order to permit ^{51}Cr to decay to a negligible activity.

As regards the appropriate mixing length this may be defined as the minimum distance at which the mass transfer and the concentration transfer through a small volume at any point of the cross-section are equal. With continuous injection the radiotracer concentration is uniform throughout any cross-section downstream of the mixing length and a rough visual indication of the mixing length may be obtained by introducing a concentrated solution of dye at the injection point and observing its general spread up to the selected point of measurement. Alternatively, a gamma emitting tracer and two radiation monitors located at the centre and close to one bank may be employed. The mixing length is exceeded when the detector readings become equal. In the case of a rapid pulse injection, equal concentration across the river width is never reached because velocities vary across the width and lateral and longitudinal dispersions are not the same. It is possible to calculate the mixing length using G. M. Rimmar's solution in which he assumed that vertical mixing is more rapid than transverse mixing and the problem becomes a two-dimensional eddy diffusion mixing.[7] Then

$$L_{\text{mixing}} = 0\cdot13(B^2/H)(C/g)(0\cdot7C+6)$$

where H is the stream depth(m), B the breadth(m), g (MKS) gravitational acceleration and C the Chezy coefficient. Normally $15 > C > 50$ depending upon the nature of the bed of the river. Assuming that transverse and longitudinal mixing coefficents are equal and that the dispersion is a true Gaussian function the minimum distance for complete mixing is given by

$$L_{\text{mixing}} = 50\, Q^{1/3}$$

where Q is the total mass flow in m^3 per second. Centre point injection is assumed and frictional drag is neglected.

· The actual choice of method in any particular situation depends upon a number of factors. The integration approach is simpler at the injection stage if an aliquot solution has been previously prepared in the laboratory. However, it is more difficult at the stage of sampling because this has to be effected at a constant rate. The constant rate injection method necessitates a larger quantity of the selected radioactive isotope for a given degree of accuracy. The integration approach is usually utilised for measuring higher rates of flow, namely those in excess of 200 m^3 per second.

In order to determine the degree of radioactivity required the sensitivity of the counter has to be taken into account, i.e. the number of counts per μCi m^3, and the statistical accuracy of the measurements must also be determined. Relative standard deviation is obtainable from

$$\frac{\sigma}{N_s} = \frac{1}{N_s}\sqrt{\frac{N_s - N_b}{t_s} - \frac{N_b}{t_b}}$$

where N_s is the counting rate for the sample, N_b is the counting rate for the background, t_s is the counting time for the sample and t_b is the counting time for the background. The radiotracer concentration required in the sampling section may be calculated thereafter. Estimation of the flow rate to be measured must be made and this can be done using a suitable secondary tracer such as Rhodamine B. In fact, chemical tracers of this type are widely utilised in tracer studies in natural water bodies. In the past two decades or more they have, in many situations, come to replace older techniques such as floats and chemical salts and may substitute for radiotracers in locations where the use of these may be hazardous. Actually R. B. Dole employed fluorescein as early as 1906, but Rhodamine B was found to be a much better surface water tracer by D. W. Pritchard and J. H. Carpenter in 1960.[8, 9] As well as these two, hundreds of other commercial dyes are available in a variety of colours. Many are strongly fluorescent but a mere handful show the combination of characteristics required for water tracing (Table 3.3). Actually the four best known are Rhodamine B, Rhodamine WT, Pontacyl Pink and fluorescein itself. They are useful as tracers because

(i)   they are water soluble;
(ii) they are highly detectable, i.e. strongly fluorescent and easily isolated from background;
(iii) they are harmless in low concentrations;
(iv) they are inexpensive;
(v)   they are reasonably stable in a normal stream environment.

The dye recommended by James F. Wilson Jr for discharge measurements or indeed any application necessitating good recovery is Rhodamine WT solution.[10] This, like the other dyes, possesses strong fluorescence and this property may vary with the solvent utilised. However, in hydrologic work the effect is constant because the solvent is always basically water although chemical present in the water may affect fluorescence.

Apart from concentration perhaps the most important factor affecting the fluorescence of dilute solutions is the temperature of the sample. Fluorescence activity increases as the temperature decreases. Temperature correction curves are available. Another significant factor is the pH value of the sample. Fluorescence of the rhodamine dyes is stable in the pH range of 5 to 10, but outside this it decreases. It is interesting to note that the fluorescence of Pontacyl Pink is much less affected by extremes of pH than Rhodamine B. Such a decrease in fluorescence only becomes important in very acid streams where the apparent recovery of the dye could be very much diminished. As regards tracing, fluorescence can be adversely affected by quenching, i.e. by interaction of the dye molecules with other chemicals in the water, because this can result in

TABLE 3.3
RECOMMENDED TRACER DYES[10]

Dye colour, formula, common name	Manufacturer's brand name	Available forms	Specific gravity of solutions	Remarks
Basic violet 10 $C_{28}H_{31}N_2O_3Cl$ Rhodamine B	Rhodamine B extra	Powder		Pro: very high detectability, moderate cost
	Rhodamine B	40% solution by weight	1·12	Contra: fair diffusivity, moderate sorptive tendency combined with moderate photochemical decay rate and high acidity
	Rhodamine BA	40% solution by weight	1·03	
		30% solution by weight	1·03	
	Rhodamine WT	20% solution	1·19	Pro: high detectability, low sorptive tendency, good diffusivity and low acidity
Acid red 52 $C_{27}H_{29}N_2O_4S_2Na$	Pontacyl Brilliant Pink B Sulpho Rhodamine B Fluoro Brilliant Pink	Powder		Pro: fair detectability, low sorptive tendency, good diffusivity, low decay rate, fairly stable at pH extremes
				Contra: much more costly than Rhodamine B
Acid yellow 73 $C_{20}H_{12}O_5$ Fluorescein	Fluorescein	Powder		Pro: cheap, low sorptive tendency and low temperature effect
				Contra: very high photo-chemical decay rates, high potential interference from background

absorption of exciting light of light emitted by the dye as well as degradation of the excited state energy. There is also the possibility that a chemical reaction will alter the chemical nature of the fluorescent compound. A known quenching agent often present in tap water is chlorine and hence chlorinated tap water should not be employed in preparing standard solutions. Photochemical decay can cause a permanent reduction in fluorescence and this is produced by bright sunlight acting on rhodamine dyes. The effect (sometimes termed photodecomposition) increases with time. One of the negative features of rhodamine dyes is the tendency to sorption or adsorption, i.e. adherence to solids—dye molecules physically adhere to surfaces of materials such as river bank and bed sediments, suspended sediments or plant life. Rhodamine B is particularly susceptible to this and significant loss of it may occur in a sample bottle unless this has been prerinsed with the dye solution which it is going to contain.

Fluorimeters are used for detection and there are two fundamental types, namely: (i) fluorescence spectrometers or spectrofluorimeters for spectral analysis; (ii) filter fluorometers.

The filter fluorometer (fluorimeter) is an instrument giving a relative measure of the intensity of light emitted by a sample containing a fluorescent substance. The intensity of fluorescent light is proportional to the quantity of fluorescent substance present. Clearly a fluorometer reading must be compared with that of samples of known concentrations taken on the same instrument under similar environmental conditions. Figure 3.2 shows the basic structure of the majority of filter fluorometers. This comprises six components and of these the filters serve to limit the light intake to that actually fluoresced by the dye. One additional important fact should be noted and that is that ingestion of dyes is dangerous—e.g. Rhodamine B is a forbidden chemical in food because it has carcinogenic properties.

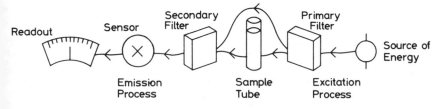

FIG. 3.2. Structure of filter fluorometers.

As regards injection of radioactive tracers, ampoules are usually broken so as to release them directly into rivers and for this purpose a pair of pincers holds the bottle and a crossbow-like device does the actual crushing, aliquot solutions having been previously prepared in the laboratory. An alternative is to use a tank in which the radiotracer is diluted and from this virtually instantaneous injection can be obtained by opening a valve. Continuous injection is effected using a pump connected with a constant level tank. The order of magnitude of tank capacities may be 20 litres for low flow rates (around $200 \, m^3/s$) and 100 litres for higher rates of flow. By reversal of the system it is possible to sample at a constant rate (integration method). Of course great care must be exercised in order to prevent contamination of samples collected at the measuring section by the injected solution—this is especially important because the radiotracer concentrations of such samples are lower, by a factor of 10^6 than concentrations in the injected solution. Subsequent measurement involves counting the sample and the aliquot solution usually with a scintillation counter connected with the sampling tank by a means ensuring reproducible geometry. The appropriate counts include a background count using a sample of river water, a radiotracer sample count and an aliquot solution count (the solution should be prepared using river water).

Experiments in the Tana River, Kenya, were mentioned previously (page 108) and the results are shown in Table 3.4.

Turning now to artificial structures utilised in the determination, these include weirs and flumes and the measurement principle is that a river

TABLE 3.4
FLOW GAUGING IN KENYA[4]

Location	Date	Tritium activity (Ci)	Distance of sampling points from injection points (m)	Surface water velocity (m^3/s)	Flow rate derived from T (m^3/s)	Flow rate from rating curve (m^3/s)
Sagana Kambura	1 November 1967	8·064	1 200–1 800	2·1	104·7	104·8
	8 November 1967	20·16	1 800–2 400	1·9	280	264
	17 November 1967	40·32	1 900–4 000	3·3	569	c. 560

has its flow channelled through a cross-section of known dimensions, the depth of water flowing over the cross-section corresponding to a known discharge. A graph is utilised to convert depth of water (stage) to discharge and this constitutes a stage/discharge rating curve. A flume may be defined as a wooden, sheet metal or reinforced concrete trough or open channel for flushing, sluicing, water conveyance (from a higher to a lower level) or water power and that part of the open channel used for measuring water flow is termed a control flume. Flumes can be used to measure river flows as great as $100 \, m^3/s$ but they can be employed also for much smaller rates of flow. In the case of small streams a thin plate weir may be substituted and this acts as a dam across the stream, the flow passing through a shape of known cross-section. A weir is a concrete, stone or stone mesh overflow wall erected across a stream in order to retard flow and raise the upstream water level to facilitate diversions and measure the rate of flow rather than to store water. Weirs may be constructed in series and possess a notch to permit passage of water. In fact, the optimal weir plate for measuring a small stream discharge is a V-notch weir with the angle of the 'V' being 90°. The head of water flowing over the weir plate corresponds to the stream discharge and the relevant relationship is:

$$Q = 1336 \, H^{2 \cdot 48}$$

where Q is the discharge in litres per second and H is the head of water in metres. Stage/discharge rating curves are available for a great many types of cross-sections for thin plate weirs including rectangular and V-notch kinds.

If regular observations are necessary to monitor the discharge of a river then a rating curve may be constructed so as to give the relationship between the water level (stage) and discharge. Here a stage pole may be installed at the commencement of the period of observation and usually this is marked by metric divisions. Firm installation is essential in order to prevent removal during flooding. This could entail replacing it with another in exactly the same spot which is difficult to determine.

The stage pole is utilised in measuring the actual river level and the discharge is measured on specified occasions and the stage levels noted with a rating curve being built up. Gauging stations used in measurement of river discharge are usually equipped with a continuously recording stage recorder. A sizeable float may be placed in a stilling well so as to reduce the effects of wind ripples and similar surface disturbances. When the movement of the float up and down occurs in response to stage changes it then rotates a drum which is associated with a clock-driven pen recording readings over a week, these being convertible to discharge using the rating curve for the particular site. Recorders also use punch tape recording methods where the tape is supplied directly to a computer which gives a readout of discharge.

There is a detailed network of continuous stage recorders in use in the United Kingdom and other countries. In the UK this is maintained by the Regional Authorities, all records being assembled by the Water Resource Centre at Reading and used in national water planning. If a continuous stage recorder is difficult to construct somewhere then a maximum stage recorder or crest stage gauge may be constructed (Fig. 3.3). This enables the maximum stage attained in any given flood to be recorded and this is important because maximum flows are extremely significant in many hydrologic investigations.

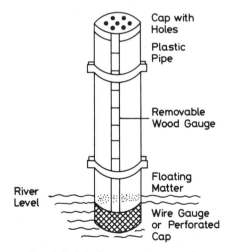

FIG. 3.3. Maximum stage recorder.

One of the most impressive demonstrations of flow measurement by isotope methods in rivers was that effected by T. Cless-Bernert et al. in the Danube in 1970.[11] The exercise was undertaken because it involved large flow rates and the section selected was near Linz in Austria where the river is approximately 200 m wide with a flow rate between 1000 and 7000 m^3/s according to the time of year. The aim was to devise a method based upon radiotracer dilution for measuring the flow rate and also to determine the accuracy of this method. The total count approach was chosen because of the ease of utilising point injections and the fact that measurements can be efficiently effected using dipped probes. The flow rate was calculated using Hull's equation[2]

$$Q = \frac{AR}{N} \, (\text{m}^3/\text{s})$$

where A is the injected activity, N the total count recorded during the passage of the radiotracer and R is a calibration factor, i.e. the relation between the concentration of radioactivity in water and the count rate of the dipped probe (see also page 107). ^{82}Br labelled ammonium bromide was employed as radiotracer and the measuring reach was selected below the town of Aschach. A set of experiments showed that results can be obtained from large rivers using relatively low radioactivity and they were carried out in the summer of 1969. It is believed that, whereas complete vertical mixing was achieved, lateral mixing was attained only in the first experiment. Also non-reproducibility of the results of the two subsequent experiments was attributed to a dependence upon correct selection of injection points in reaches where irregularities on the surface of the river bed exist. Another interesting case of using ^{82}Br was the study of dispersion and other properties in the same river, but this time at Belgrade in Yugoslavia by T. Tasovac and others in 1970.[12] Their work was carried out over several years and both single pulse and continuous injection techniques were used. The experimental zone was 25 km in extent and the properties of the water and suspended material investigated using activation analysis.

Radioactive tracing has been carried out in frozen rivers by J. Balek *et al.* in 1970.[13] Discharge and time of travel were measured in the Moravice and Opava rivers by the dilution method and the radioisotope used was ^{51}Cr diluted in EDTA complex. The detecting equipment was able to measure it at concentrations 100 times lower than the concentration permitted in drinking water in Czechoslovakia.

3.2. THE BASIN HYDROLOGIC CYCLE

River basins are bounded by drainage divides and subject to surficial and sub-surface drainage under gravity to the ocean or interior lakes. Their cycles comprise a series of inputs of precipitation distributed thereafter through transfers into various storages and ultimately output of basin channel runoff, evapotranspiration and deep outflow of groundwater. The appropriate expression is

Precipitation = Basin channel runoff + Evapotranspiration + Changes in storage

Figure 3.4 illustrates the components of the basin hydrologic cycle and their interrelationships. Representative and experimental basins as defined by UNESCO have been used as natural analogues of larger scale systems, but the difficulty is in whether complete accordance can be achieved. One way around this is to construct hardware models either as scale models or analogue models. In the latter there is a radical change in the media representing the basin elements so that, for example, water flow may be represented by electrical flow. Overall synthetic systems may

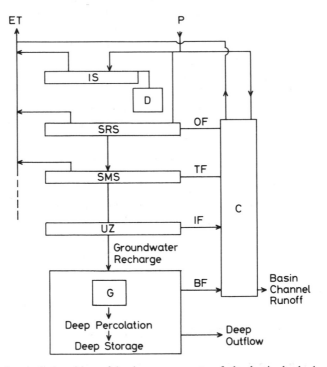

FIG. 3.4. Interrelationships of basic components of the basin hydrologic cycle. Storage: IS, interception; SRS, surface; SMS, soil moisture; UZ, unsaturated zone; C, channel; D, detention. Flow: OF, overland; TF, through; IF, inter; BF, base; P. precipitation; ET, evapotranspiration; G. grandwater.

be employed and analysed by computers but if a lesser level of analysis is required the partial system approach may suffice. This depends upon more restricted assumptions about the basin cycle, for instance that only one parameter may suffice for the precipitation input—the proportion of rainfall infiltrating during any given storm, and one for the output—the proportion of basin discharge contributed by surface runoff as distinct from baseflow. Thus the operation of the partial system is based on the assumption that rainfall excess over infiltration can be equated with the storm runoff component of the hydrograph with infiltration making up the baseflow. Any given storm input is treated in the infiltration sub-system to disentangle the assumed excess of rainfall from the infiltration. The recorded runoff output is treated similarly in the baseflow sub-system in order to separate the assumed surficial runoff from the baseflow. Resultant rainfall excess (calculated) and surface runoff (calculated) are compared and initial assumptions modified until the necessary concordance is attained. Thereafter it is a storm precipitation pattern through time input which can be inserted into the programme so as to provide valuable data relating to possible resultant river runoff—it is hoped.

This last attempt at understanding the basin cycle involves 'black box' techniques in which the basin cycle is regarded as a black box and interest concentrated upon inputs such as rainfall and outputs such as runoff and the establishment of a direct functional link between them. Of course the great complexity encountered in nature and resulting among other things from the chronological variations in components of the basin cycle makes it extremely difficult to find a general mathematical expression relating, say, rainfall and runoff for a stated basin.

The determination of the distribution of travel times of direct runoff in a basin is a fundamental problem in flood hydrology. Ascertaining the mean travel time is important because time of concentration and basin lag are closely related to it. The time of concentration of a basin may be defined as the time required for water to travel to the outlet from the furthest point in it. In unit hydrograph theory the concept of distribution of travel times of direct runoff is elegantly employed. The hydrograph is a graph showing level, velocity or discharge of water in a river channel plotted against time; the term unit hydrograph was introduced in 1932 by Sherman. It is the hydrograph produced by an isolated storm of a given duration and uniform intensity over the entire drainage area which had an equivalent runoff of precisely 1 in. (2·54 cm) of rain. Unit hydrograph (UH) theory is based on the principle that every basin has a characteristic hydrograph, i.e. a characteristic travel time distribution function in response to a uniform rainfall with a unit depth for a specified time interval. A more rigorous concept is that of the instantaneous unit hydrograph (IUH) corresponding to the impulsive response of a network to a unit impulse therein introduced. Both UH and IUH of a basin may be developed utilising records of precipitation and stream flow under high flood conditions. One of the basic assumptions in UH theory is the principle of linearity, but this is valid solely in the case of large scale floods.

Another basin characteristic related to the time of travel is the isochrone curves of surface runoff. It is important to attempt to correlate the distribution function of travel times of a basin with its physical properties such as area, mean channel slope, maximum length of channel etc. so as to develop the synthetic unit hydrograph for use in basins where there is inadequate data on precipitation and stream flow. The synthetic unit hydrograph may be defined as a UH prepared for a drainage basin which is not gauged and it is based solely on the basin's known physical characteristics.

Nuclear techniques may be used to solve the problem of transit time for direct surface runoff and the relevant principle may be outlined. The problem is to describe the travel of water from A to C, two points in a surface drainage network of which C may be the catchment outlet. If instantaneous injection of radiotracer is employed at A then the ordinate of the concentration–time curve of this as measured at C is proportional to the instantaneous unit hydrograph for that elementary area in which the injection is effected. Water at A is labelled and a sample should comprise water travelling during a time dt over a plane perpendicular to the runoff; each flow tube will require an account of radiotracer proportional to the velocity. However, as this cannot be achieved, instantaneous injection is actually carried out. Beyond the mixing distance the following expression may be verified in a section B

$$\int_{0}^{\infty} c(t)\mathrm{d}t = \text{constant}$$

where $c(t)$ represents the instantaneous concentration at any point in the section B. As J. Guizerix and T. Dincer pointed out in regard to the argument, the suitability of the injection point for the radiotracer may be verified if it is established over the whole width of section B that the

curves of impulsive response in the radiotracer $c(t)$ are isochronic and if
it can be estimated that the runoff characteristics are identical in sections
A and B.[14] Radiotracer should not be injected in a zone of weak currents
even if conditions are otherwise favourable. If the curves $c(t)$ are
isochrones then the travel time between the point of injection and the
measurement section is determinable by the time of injection and the
time corresponding to the centre of gravity of curve $c(t)$. If a tributary
exists its distance from the measurement section must be at least the
same as the mixing distance for this part of the runoff. In the case where
the distance between sections A and C is large then the dilution of the
radiotracer at C may be such as to render measurement difficult. Here an
intermediate radiotracer should be injected at a point in a section P. The
principle of the operation may be summarised as follows:

(i)   instantaneous injection of radiotracer at a point A and
      measurement of the $c_1(t)$ curve at P;
(ii) instantaneous injection of radiotracer at a point P and
      measurement of the $c_2(t)$ curve at C;
(iii) calculation of the desired function $c(T)$ for instantaneous injection
      at A by the integral of convolution

$$C(T) = \frac{1}{A} \int_0^T c_1(t) \, c_2(T-t) \, dt$$

The utilisation of the method implies a steady state and linear system
and it is necessary to evaluate the effects of non-steady state on non-
linearity and thus select the time of injection at P. However, the method
described gives the distribution of residence times between sections A
and C and it is independent of whether the system involved is steady
state or non-steady state.[14]

The usual radiotracers (see Table 3.2 above) are available. It is
sometimes desirable to make several experiments simultaneously and
occasionally dyes such as Rhodamine B may be used as well.
Concentrations are measured by means of a suitable probe installed in
the river but not on its bed from which too great a background counting
rate may be derived. Sometimes a boat is used from which the probe is
suspended but movements must not move the probe to a distance greater
than 'infinite radius' from the bed. 'Infinite radius' may be defined for a
probe suspended or placed in water in an infinite homogeneously
radiotracer labelled medium by a hypothetical sphere such that the

radioactivity external to it takes part to the extent of at least 1% in the net signal. Accuracies are difficult to estimate for the method but radiotracers are superior to others in determining the distribution of travel times and with them discharges of approximately $100 \, m^3/s$ can be measured with an accuracy of about 2%.

D. H. Pilgrim has made determinations of the time of travel in a basin as related to the UH and IUH concepts.[15] Storm runoff tracing was effected in a small experimental basin with an area of 96 acres using ^{198}Au and ^{51}Cr–EDTA, both of which proved highly satisfactory. 50 mCi or less activity were injected in liquid form and measurements were carried out using a scintillation counter, a rate meter, a graphic recorder and a scaler. The scintillation counter was mounted in an aluminium waterproof casing attached to a float and then immersed in a stream. Interesting results were obtained. For instance, it was demonstrated that even for a flow hydrograph with no characteristic features to study with routine hydrograph analytical techniques, the hydrograph of the labelled water gave valuable data on the mean time of travel of the water from the injection point to the outlet of the basin. Also the time of travel was found to decrease with the rate of discharge. Especially interesting apropos the UH theory is that the time to peak of labelled water (roughly equal to the mean travel time) asymptotically approaches a constant value when the peak discharge of the stream increases thus showing clearly that the principle of linearity involved in the linear UH theory is only valid for large floods and there is no linear behaviour for relatively small flood flows.[14]

Radioactive tracing of flood flows is very useful indeed and D. H. Pilgrim has given the results of recent studies.[16] These have demonstrated the occurrence of a variety of storm runoff processes including those associated with variable source areas. There is a need for experimental methods in studying the spatial variability of such processes in the field. One is by using radiotracers and here ^{51}Cr–EDTA and ^{82}Br were used.

This was done in a pilot study of sub-surface and surface storm runoff and irregular spatial patterns were observed which proved to be primarily related to the thickness of the surface soil horizon. The experiment demonstrated the value of radiotracers in quantifying horizontal and vertical profiles of flow pathways. Gamma emitters were selected because of ease of measurement in the field and in this case utilised in tandem (5 to 10 mCi for each).

3.3. BASIN MORPHOMETRY

R. E. Horton in 1945 was the first to draw attention to the importance of morphometric analysis which may indeed be termed Horton morphometry.[17] The major practical difficulty is to obtain necessary data and for this to be done it is necessary to define the drainage basin and recognise the drainage pattern in that basin. The basin itself can be delineated from contoured maps by tracing the watersheds enclosing tributaries and slopes and this only leaves the problem of the nature of the drainage pattern. There are two feasible approaches, namely consideration of the active channel network in which water flows or consideration of the valley network which includes not only the presently active channel network but also valleys no longer carrying active flow. Valley networks can be identified from maps, aerial photographs or field observations. For most morphometric studies a 1:25 000 scale is appropriate. The dominant processes within river channels are those of erosion and deposition. The former occurs on the walls or bed of the channel under turbulent flow conditions. The latter takes place when the dimensions of the material to be shifted by the river are too large for movement by any particular set of velocity and flow conditions. Upward eddies under the conditions of turbulent flow tend to remove material and promote erosion whereas downward eddies cause deposition. The power of water to dislodge material on the bed or bank of a stream is a function of the forces generated and their efficiency in overcoming forces resisting movement. The force tending to produce movement is termed shear stress (τ). That which can be generated on a river bed is a function of the specific weight of the fluid, γ, which for water is $1000 \, kg/m^3$, the hydraulic mean radius, R, and the slope, S, of the channel and can be expressed as

$$\tau = \gamma R S$$

τ is sometimes known as the unit tractive force because it is a measure of the shear generated per unit wet area by the flowing water. Minimum bed erosion occurs where the channel slope is low and the wetted perimeter is large as compared with the cross-sectional area of the channel. Turbulence may result from a number of causes such as the roughness of the bed of the river and this latter can be defined in empirical equations using such parameters as Manning's roughness coefficient, n. This appears in the Manning formula which gives mean river velocity, V, by

$$V = \frac{1 \cdot 486}{n} R^{2/3} S^{1/2}$$

V being in feet per second, R in feet and S is the rate of loss of head per foot of channel. As roughness diminishes the flow velocity will increase. Values for n have been assessed under a number of different bed conditions and in fact the US Geological Survey has published relevant data.[18] Approximate representative values may be cited: sand, $n = 0 \cdot 02$; gravel, $n = 0 \cdot 03$; boulders, $n = 0 \cdot 05$. Movement of material along a river bed can be examined through a set of empirical equations dependent upon an assessment of Shield's entrainment function (F_s) and the particle Reynolds number (R_e), the latter indicating the relationship between the forces of inertia and viscosity:

$$F_s = \frac{V^2}{gD(S_s - 1)}$$

where g is the acceleration due to gravity, D is the particle diameter, S_s is the sediment specific gravity and V is the shear velocity. Another expression of F_s is:

$$F_s = \frac{RS}{D(S_s - 1)}$$

and for any one section of a river channel all the right hand side items can be measured and therefore F_s can be calculated.

The particle Reynolds number may be related to measurable properties also:

$$R_e = \frac{(\gamma RS)^{0 \cdot 5} D \rho_f^{0 \cdot 5}}{\mu}$$

where ρ_f is fluid density and μ is the fluid viscosity. When F_s and R_e are plotted against each other on double log axes, it can be seen that the threshold of sediment transport takes place at the minimum values of F_s and when R_e rises above a value of 6. When R_e exceeds 400 and $F_s = 0 \cdot 056$ turbulent flow becomes fully developed and material is removed from the channel bed. The following equation takes into account the fact that full turbulence only exists when R_e is more than 400:

$$(\gamma RS)^{0 \cdot 5} = \frac{400 \mu}{D \rho_f^{0 \cdot 5}}$$

As γ, μ and ρ_f are constants for water at defined temperatures and D and S are known factors for any particular channel, R may be calculated and then related to channel cross-sectional area so as to determine the probable wetted perimeter of the channel when the movement of sediment of a specific size occurs.

As regards channel bank erosion a great deal of the sediment load carried by the river is derived from the walls of the channel. Normally the channel wall material if regolith will remain stable only so long as the angle of slope θ does not exceed the angle of repose of the material ϕ. This latter is related to particle dimensions.

Additionally, on the channel bank of a river there is not only the gravitational force encountered in hill slopes, but also a lateral force generated by flowing water. The gravitational force will be ($W \sin \theta$) and the lateral force is proportional to τ, the shearing force on the stream bed. The resistance to movement results from $W \cos \theta \tan \phi$ and in this case the shearing force is related to the critical shear stress necessary to move a particle, thus

$$\frac{\tau}{\tau_c} = 1 - \frac{\sin^2 \theta}{\sin \phi}$$

where τ_c is the above mentioned critical shear stress and on a side slope

$$\frac{\tau}{\tau_c} = 0 \cdot 75 \gamma \, ds$$

where γ is the specific weight of the fluid, d is the vertical depth of flow and s is the channel slope.

Sediment from the channel banks joins that washed in from valley slopes and eroded from the channel bed to produce the total sediment carried by the river. A lot of sediment may be transported in river systems as a result of the fact that many tributaries may exist. 'Finger tip' tributaries are designated as first order streams and where two coalesce a second order stream results. Third and higher orders result from an extension of the same process. However, if a second order stream is joined by, say, a first order one it remains second order. As regards measurement of suspended load this can be effected by sampling followed by separation and weighing of the solids. Of course this is difficult to do in areas subject to seasonal rainfall and flash flooding. Radioisotope techniques are applicable and offer several advantages:

(i)   water and suspended and bed-transported sediment are undisturbed during measurement which permits greater accuracy than that obtainable using conventional mechanical sampling methods;

(ii)   continuous measurement is feasible.

The appropriate methodology may be summarised. A suspended sediment gauge is utilised which operates on an attenuated transmission principle and relates to the fact that attenuation of a low energy electromagnetic radiation beam from a radioactive isotope source by suspended sediment is dependent upon the sediment concentration in the river water. As early as 1957, a ^{60}Co transmission density gauge for measuring suspended sediment was devised by M. M. Arkhangelski.[19] In 1959 the use of a ^{170}Tm source in transmission geometry for the measurement of high concentrations of up to 50 g/litre and scattering geometry for the measurement of low concentrations up to 6 g/litre was described by V. A. Emelyanov and his associates.[20] In 1965 a ^{109}Cd preferential absorption gauge was developed for the continuous measurement and recording of concentrations exceeding 0·5 g/litre for periods of up to a week.[21] Automatic radioisotope gauges were used to measure suspended sediment transport in natural streams by G. S. Tazioli in 1980 and two were employed, one with a 100 mCi ^{241}Am source and the other with a 150 mCi ^{137}Cs source.[22] They proved to be very practical in torrent regimes and gave a linear response also with high sediment concentrations.

The intensity I of monoenergetic electromagnetic radiation transmitted through x cm of water containing a concentration c (by weight) of sediment relates to the source intensity I_0 in the absence of both water and sediment thus

$$I/I_0 = \exp\left[-\rho_m x(\mu_s c - \mu_w(1 - c))\right]$$

where μ_w and μ_s are the mass attenuation coefficients of water and sediment respectively and ρ_m is the density of the mixture of sediment and water given by

$$\rho_m = \frac{\rho_s \rho_w}{\rho_s - r(\rho_s - \rho_w)}$$

where ρ_s and ρ_w are the densities of the sediment and the water respectively. T. Florkowski has indicated that for practical purposes the intensity I of radiation which is transmitted through a mixture of sediment and water is sometimes related to the intensity I_w transmitted through pure water and since[23]

$$I_w = I_0 \exp(\mu_w \rho_w x)$$

then

$$\frac{I}{I_w} = \exp[\mu_w + (\mu_s - \mu_w)c]\rho_m x - \mu_w \rho_w x$$

Substituting ρ_w from the penultimate equation gives

$$\frac{I}{I_w} = \exp\left[\left(\mu_s - \mu_w \frac{\rho_w}{\rho_s}\right)c\rho_m x\right]$$

The relative sensitivity of measurement S, the ratio of the relative change in radiation intensity to the relative change in sediment concentration is given by

$$S = \left|\frac{\delta I/I}{\delta c/c}\right| = \left(\mu_s - \mu_w \frac{\rho_w}{\rho_s}\right)\frac{\rho_m^2}{\rho_w} cx$$

Sensitivity and precision of the measurements increase with the increasing difference in the mass attenuation coefficients of sediment and water and for this reason low energy electromagnetic radiation is preferable since then μ_s is greater than μ_w and errors due to variations in water density with temperature are relatively small. However, an instrument with lower energy of radiation is more sensitive to variations in the chemical composition of sediments.

A valid correlation between gauge response and suspended sediment concentration can be obtained only when certain requirements are met and these include the following:

(i)   either the dissolved material must make a negligible contribution to the density or its concentration must be determined separately and accounted for;

(ii) variations in the composition of both dissolved and undissolved material must have a negligible effect on the accuracy of the gauge. Minimisation of effects due to variation in the composition of suspended material can be achieved by the appropriate choice of radiation energy. ^{241}Am and ^{109}Cd which have energies of 60 keV and 22 keV respectively are considered as suitable. Laboratory calibration of the gauge is done using materials which simulate sediments such as aluminium or sodium sulphates and must be repeated whenever there is reason to think that a significant change in the chemical composition of the sediment has taken place.

Various types of gauge exist and include the following:

(i) Continuous monitoring comprising two units connected by a flexible cable with a weatherproof shore based control unit and a submersible measuring head. In the shore unit there is a digital printer, counting electronics and relevant power supply. In the measuring head there is the radioactive isotope source, a source switching mechanism and the radiation detector with pre-amplifier. The gauge observes the ratio of X-ray transmission through ambient water containing suspended sediment and a reference liquid which is distilled water. The ratio is a function of the concentration of suspended sediment in the ambient water. The radioactive source in the Parametrics Inc. of Waltham, Mass., USA instrument is ^{109}Cd ($T_{\frac{1}{2}}=470$ days) and an initial radio-activity of approximately 1·3 mCi is designed for a year's operation. The external radiation levels at exterior surfaces of the gauge are lower than 0·1 mR/h so no monitoring is necessary during handling. The concentration range available is from 0·1 to 50 g/litre of sediment of density averaging 2·65 g/cm^3 and accuracy exceeds $\pm 20\%$ in the full measuring range. As regards data retrieval information is recorded permanently at quarter hour or 3 min intervals on tape capable of the continuous reception of it over a period of a week.

(ii) The IAEA portable gauge jointly developed with the USDA Sedimentation Laboratory.[24] This comprises two lightweight portable units which are connected by means of a flexible cable. There is a weatherproof scale and a submersible measuring head. The actual measuring head can either be mounted on a steel rod and operated from the bank of the river or from a boat or bridge or it can be suitably weighted and suspended from a cable. Three minutes is the time required for a single measurement. Prior to a set of measurements being carried out the probe is standardised using a simple device simulating clean water between the radioactive source and the detector. Two types of source have been utilised, namely 1·5 mCi ^{109}Cd and 100 mCi ^{241}Am ($T_{\frac{1}{2}}=458$ years) and the concentration range is from 0·1 to 50 g/litre with an accuracy better than $\pm 20\%$ at the lower end and $\pm 5\%$ at the upper end. The actual measuring system consists of a scaler with count preset and the equipment may be battery operated with approximately eight hours of continuous operation. The gauge is shown in Figure 3.5. It was intended for use in rather shallow streams (up to 10 m deep) and sediment concentrations exceeding 500 ppm.

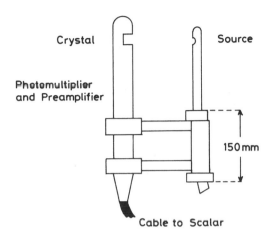

FIG. 3.5. IAEA sediment concentration gauge.

(iii) USDA Sedimentation Laboratory sediment concentration gauge. When the Parametrics gauge was being developed a supplementary lightweight portable gauge was adjudged as necessary and a lower energy gamma emitter than that used in previous determinations of the density of reservoir sediments which was ^{137}Cs was sought. The one selected was ^{109}Cd although ^{241}Am was also tested. The reason why the former was preferred is that its radiations are more strongly attenuated by low concentrations of suspended sediment. The resultant gauge was the MSG–II.

3.4. RIVER LOAD

Material carried by rivers constitutes the load and may be suspended sediment load, bed load or solution or solute load. Generally the faster the velocity of the river the larger the particles it can transport, but this is not the case with particles smaller than 0·5 mm diameter, i.e. medium grade sand. The relation between the velocity needed to move the particle (erosion velocity) and its size is shown in Fig. 3.6. For a particle with a diameter of 1 mm a velocity of approximately 25 cm/sec is required and for one of 10 mm diameter the figure is approximately 100 cm/sec. For those particles which have a grain size smaller than *c*.

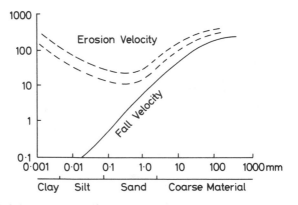

FIG. 3.6. Hjülstrom curve of erosion and deposition for uniform material.

0·5 mm the velocity required for erosion to take place needs to rise as the dimensions decrease. For instance, a particle of silt with a diameter of 0·01 mm needs an erosion velocity of *c*. 70 cm/sec which almost exceeds by a factor of three that for a sand particle with a diameter 100 times larger. Erosion velocity occupies a band because other factors such as the shape of the channel bed influence whether particles are picked up or not. The first description of these results was in the 1930s and the graph is referred to as the Hjulstrom curve after an early worker on sediments. Another feature is shown and this is important for particulate load transport. After attainment of the erosion velocity small particles tend to move as suspended load. Taking a particle with a diameter of 0·1 mm the erosion velocity is *c*. 30 cm/sec and once this is exceeded the particle starts to move as suspended load into water with a lower velocity (less than the erosion velocity curve). Small particles of the type mentioned do not then settle on to the bottom of the stream channel but remain in transport until the lower line of the curve, i.e. the fall velocity, is attained. Of course, for larger particles the difference between the erosion velocity and the fall velocity is quite negligible. It must be borne in mind that the Hjulstrom curve is based on laboratory flume experiments and the situation in the field is more complex, but nevertheless it is an instructive exercise to measure material sizes in a stream channel especially after a flood and also to obtain estimates of the velocities required to move the material using the curve.

As regards bed load this remains in contact with the stream bed and hence moves by a combination of rolling, sliding and slipping. It is the most difficult type of load on which to experiment so as to obtain useful measurements. The main problem is that bed load material usually only moves at high stage times when the velocity at the bottom of the river channel is great—often in times of flood when measuring anything is obviously difficult. Estimates are conventionally obtained using (i) bed load traps, (ii) measuring of materials impounded by artificial structures, (iii) marked pebbles.

Bed load traps can be employed only in small streams and comprise a simple box which is installed in the river channel so that its top is level with the channel floor. After a given time material is collected from the box and measured so as to provide data apropos the size of particles and total weight. Artificial structures parallel dams and in fact dams store reservoir water which often becomes silted, such material constituting a combination of bed load together with a proportion of suspended sediment. A classic case is the High Aswan Dam in Egypt described by Abdel Aziz I. Kashef in 1981.[25] From the time this was planned in 1952 until its completion in 1970 the dam has had sociopolitical and technical problems deleterious to Man and to remedy some of them it is proposed that a channel be constructed from the reservoir downstream to feed, through a branch, the Western Desert areas. The performance of such a channel could be improved by a submerged weir to divert the silts back to Egypt; such action would restore the fertility of the land thus reducing the cost of chemical fertilisers as well as preventing erosion in the Nile and halting the advance of the Mediterranean shoreline.

Radiotracers may be employed in sand movement and bed load studies and in fact are used routinely. They can provide:

(i) quantitative estimates of certain transport parameters such as the ultimate tractive force used in the Meyer–Peter formula;

(ii) checks on bed load transport theories and determinations of the coefficents for the basic hypotheses formulated;

(iii) greater knowledge of the laws of transport and also of the validity of the method used.

The tracing of the movement of sediment requires ascertaining its path from a point of reference during a stated time interval. Data such as the rate of transport, the direction and source must be interrelated with the relevant environmental hydrologic conditions such as the hydraulic characteristics of the channel, the hydraulic gradient and the flow velocity. The principle of radioactive tracing is straightforward and involves, both for suspension and bed load transport, the immersion at a selected point of an activated sediment or a simulator having physical characteristics such as density and shape which closely parallel those of the natural material and subsequent following of its movement using radiation detectors. Many potential radiotracers exist and among the most suitable are the following cited by G. Courtois[26] (Table 3.5).

TABLE 3.5
APPROPRIATE RADIOTRACERS FOR BED LOAD
STUDIES

Radioisotope	Half-life $(T_{\frac{1}{2}})$
^{32}P	14 days
^{46}Sc	84 days
^{51}Cr	28 days
^{95}Zr–Nb	65 days
^{140}La	40 h
^{182}Ta	111 days
^{192}Ir	75 days
^{198}Au	65 h

The chosen radioisotope ought to have a half-life which relates to the duration of the phenomenon being observed and also to the frequency of repeat of experiments. A rule of thumb is:

$T_{\frac{1}{2}}$–length of the phenomenon; 3 $T_{\frac{1}{2}}$–the interval between any two experiments

As the actual duration of experiments is not usually known in advance since it depends upon factors such as dispersion other criteria are applicable and these are:

(i)   examination of suspension transports using half-life less than 8 days such as ^{198}Au;

(ii) examination of bed load transport of sand using a very short half-life for intensive transport and a medium half-life such as ^{51}Cr for normal transport;

(iii) examination of shingle movement using ^{182}Ta or some nuclide with equivalent half-life so as to be able to wait until an appropriate stage increase (flood caused) occurs and is capable of moving the material.

The selected energy ought to be as low as possible so as to minimise health hazards and activities utilised vary from a few millicuries (mCi) to over 100 mCi.

A very interesting approach is the use of radioactive labelling techniques. The irradiation of natural sediments in a nuclear reactor may be undertaken, but much depends on the nature of the sediment. Marking particles in coarse sediments is quite easy and the surficial coating by detectable radioactivity hardly affects the properties. However, this is more difficult where very fine sediments are concerned, i.e. with clay minerals with particle sizes less than 20 microns—this is because surface properties are significant in the suspension of the material. However, it is most important that a satisfactory solution is found because of the fact that sediments of this type are the main cause of siltation in harbours and navigation channels in estuaries as well as along certain muddy coastlines. Activation analysis over such features in populated regions offers a means to obviate large quantity hazards arising from ordinary radioactive isotope applications. It is based upon the possibility of inducing a nuclear reaction in the atoms of the element to be determined as a result of which radioisotopes are formed which can be recognised by their radiation. Additionally, the measured radioactivity of the sample relates directly to the concentration of the element. The optimal nuclear reaction is induced by neutrons from a nuclear reactor (n, γ-reactions) and of course in order to perform the technique rapidly the element must be detectable against the background activity of the natural components of the material which is labelled. Gamma ray spectrometry using a Ge–Li detector or coincidence counting techniques may be applied to the physical determination required. A. J. de Groot et al. used cobalt and tantalum tracers measured by activation analysis in sediment transport studies in 1970.[27] They selected suitable tracers bearing in mind that the choice depended upon the strength of the specific signal from the induced radioisotope and upon the presence of signals in the same region of the gamma spectrum originating from the relevant sample. On that basis an analysis was made of elements which could provide sample sensitivity in the determination of Rhine river sediments. These included Ta, Sb, Co, In, Ir, Tb and Eu and it appeared that Ta, Sb and Co are optimal tracers for Rhine sludge. In work on metal concentrations in sediments transported with river water it is germane to note that these are dependent upon the size distribution of the material and tend to occur most frequently in the finest grain size fractions. Hence linear relationships are found between the contents of the elements and the fraction of particles less than 16 microns in dimension (expressed as a percentage of the $CaCO_3$-free mineral constituents). Such linear relationships facilitate the characterisation of the content of a specific metal in an entire group of cogenetic sediments by a single value and this is thought to represent the content obtained by extrapolation to 100% of the fraction less than 16 microns in dimension. Of course such content values differ widely from one river system to another as may be noted by examining Table 3.6.[27]

TABLE 3.6

CONTENTS OF ELEMENTS IN SEDIMENTS FROM VARIOUS RIVERS EXTRAPOLATED TO 100% OF THE FRACTION LESS THAN 16 MICRONS

Element	River Rhine	River Ems	River Chao–Phrya	River Amazon
Fe × 10^3	54	112	40	44
Mn	2600	3300	1800	1060
Zn	3400	700	30	130
Cr	760	180	100	—
Pb	850	100	30	—
Cu	470	150	50	28
As	310	60	53	—
La	80	80	90	—
Co	24	22	12	13
Sc	12	12	19	—
Sm	7	9	8	—
Ta	1	—	—	—

All contents of elements expressed in ppm.

Experimental work has demonstrated that probably the mobilisation of metals occurs as organometallic complexes and since the degree of this apropos these trace elements mostly varies according to the series of H. Irving and R. Williams it is probable that the stability of such complexes is the dominant factor in the intensity of the process of mobilisation.[28] The formation of the complexes is influenced by the decomposition of organic material in the sediment particles and intensive decomposition in deltas in temperate regions is believed to be responsible for the rapid mobilisation of metals from sediments in rivers like the Rhine and Ems.

However, only a minor decrease in organic matter content was recorded by A. J. de Groot and his coworkers during the transport of sediments to the lower courses of tropical deltas.[27] The geochemical stability of metals depends upon the strength of their bond with suspended matter and suitability of any one for labelling depends upon the natural quantities of it in the relevant water course. Referring to Table 3.6, it may be seen that Fe, Mn, Zn, Cr, Pb, Cu, As and La are all too abundant and Fe, Cr, Zn, Cu, Pb and As very easily mobilise during transport of the sediment. The quantity of Co in sediments in rivers is not high even in polluted rivers like the Rhine and also this metal is not more intensively mobilised before it reaches the marine area along the Wadden coast. Consequently, this metal can be considered as a marker under conditions of not too great dilution of the marked suspension with natural material. Ta seems to be even better and it appears in sediments in truly minute quantities.

As regards the actual marking procedures, these may be considered for the two metals. Fixation of Co to sediment constituents is feasible in a number of ways such as intercalation of Co ions between the layers of clay lattices or as chelated Co fixed to the natural organic matter in the sediments. Another approach is to treat sediments with a pH exceeding 7.7 and containing sufficient $CaCO_3$ with a solution of $Co(NO_3)_2$ under boiling conditions (ratio of solid:solution = 1:10) when $Co(OH)_2$ is actually coagulated on to the particles of sediment. This is transformed into $Co(OH)_3$ by oxidation. This is probably the best method of binding large quantities of Co to the sediment.

Turning to Ta this will adhere to any type of sediment and this may be boiled with a solution of $TaCl_5$ in HF (ratio of solid:solution = 1:10), only a slight increase in pH being necessary in order to hydrolyse the dissolved Ta. The reaction seems to be quite independent of the type of sediment involved, even material completely lacking in $CaCO_3$ having proved to be quite suitable.

The application involves removing a mass, m, selected according to the purpose of the study from the relevant sediment and labelling this with a quantity σm of the tracer, σ being the concentration of the tracer in the sediment. For Co and Ta the maximum permissible concentration is approximately 5% by weight. The marked sediment is then introduced into the system at a specified location so that its behaviour represents that of the natural material. Of course transport follows and the marked material is dispersed over a certain area while becoming mixed with a mass, M, of sediment in that area. This mass is characteristic of the scale of the system and it is proportional to the rate of the dispersion of the sediment and increases with time. The ultimate concentration of the tracer is represented by β and this is in the mass M and of course varies both chronologically and spatially, the average being $\beta = \sigma m/M$. β ought to be higher than the detection limit. Samples are taken from the bottom and also from the suspension in a spatial pattern at fixed times and the dimensions of the pattern ought to increase with time. Generally 100 samples suffice for a spatial picture of the distribution of β. With a set of 10 samplings the total number of samples will rise to about 1000 and this is independent of the size of the cloud. Samples are analysed by irradiation in a nuclear reactor and by subsequent analysis of the activity significant for the element under consideration. The end result is a spatial pattern of β which gradually alters with time and from this the solution to the problem has to be derived. P. Kruger and J. K. Channell have also used activation analysis employing rare earth elements as tracers in estuaries.[29] The characteristics they considered in the evaluation of appropriate tracers included minimal detectable quantity in the estuary, persistence in the water phase being traced and methods together with safety and costs. It was concluded that the most promising elements were in the rare earth group and of course they can be studied together thus facilitating a simpler radiochemical group separation process. The experiments were made in the San Francisco Bay and post-sample treatment of irradiation in a 10 kW nuclear reactor, radiochemical group separation and gamma ray spectroscopy gave detection limits of 1 ng for europium and 20 ng for lanthanum. In the bay the background concentrations of europium and lanthanum are 12 ng/litre and 180 ng/litre respectively. The method is considered suitable for tracing hydraulic flow or for persistence analysis of suspended solids or settleable solid components in the estuary. It was found possible to measure as many as six rare earth elements simultaneously and they may be used together with radioactive rare earth elements so as to extend tracing time or dilution range when the total quantity of radiotracer is limited.

Sometimes glass and exchange resin may be employed as simulants of natural sediments. Glass may be employed by irradiation in a nuclear reactor if crushed to satisfactory particle size containing as impurity an element usually having a high cross-section and which becomes the radioactive tracer. Such glasses are commercially available and may contain tantalum, scandium, lanthanum, iridium, gold and other elements.

As regards exchange resins there are processes which permit the radioisotope to be absorbed in solution on to these. One is IONAC C50

(Green Sand) which is prehardened by heating to between 750°C and 900°C.

Mass labelling can be achieved in this way, i.e. the specific activity remains constant irrespective of the particle sizes involved. Both of the above approaches, glass and exchange resin, entail incorporation of a radioactive isotope into a mass equivalent to the sediment, i.e. mass labelling which must be distinguished from deposition of a radioactive element on to the surface of a natural sediment, i.e. surface labelling. There is a great variety of ways of achieving this, for instance H. Bougault and his associates labelled sands using [198]Au employing a combination of the Petersen method (treatment with tin chloride) and the Campbell method (treatment with silver) after preliminary treatment with nitric acid and soda.[30] In this way it is possible to deposit 125 mg of gold per kg of sediment with an efficiency of 95% (i.e. 10 Ci/kg) using a solution of chlorauric acid. For marking sands with [51]Cr a film of silica gel is deposited initially and radioactive lead chromate is adsorbed on to it; 500 mg of chromium per kg of sand can be fixed with more than 90% efficiency (i.e. 40 Ci/kg). The labelling of silts with [198]Au can be achieved using a neutralised chlorauric acid solution, the gold being reduced on contact with the silt on which it is fixed; 10 Ci/kg of sediment can be fixed with an efficiency of 100%. In marking silts with ^{51}Cr chromium hydroxide is precipitated on contact with the silt and the result is a deposit of 450 mg of chromium per kg of sediment, i.e. 25 Ci/kg of silt with 100% efficiency.

It may be useful to compare mass labelling with surface labelling (Table 3.7)

TABLE 3.7
DISADVANTAGES OF MASS AND SURFACE LABELLING

Mass labelling (glass)	Surface labelling
Difficult to obtain sufficient labelled mass	More difficult to prepare
Incomplete concordance of sediments and glass	Deposited activity is not proportional to the mass of sediment
	Uncontrolled disappearance of surface activity due to wash-off effect of water and interparticulate friction

As regards silt and shingle, silt is very sensitive so that its properties vary according to the nature of the surrounding medium and a variation

in pH, salinity or bound-water content may trigger flocculation
or deflocculation as well as a change in dynamic behaviour. After labelling a silt, efforts must be made to keep the dynamic properties as
constant as possible and this is especially important in estuaries where
salinity and water composition are both extremely susceptible to alteration.

As for shingle, the most suitable labelling method is to place a
radioactive source in a hole drilled in a pebble. This hole is subsequently
sealed up with paraffin or cement, a tiresome procedure as thousands of
pebbles have to be treated. The actual mass of material injected can be as
much as several dozen kilograms and of course there is no actual limit
except that imposed by handling, transport, shielding and funding
considerations. However, if too large a mass is utilised it may deposit as
a hillock and this will interfere with the correct placement of the
material.

The minimal mass of the tracer to be injected is determined by the
statistical fluctuation of the number of particles during detection and in
practice it is considered that the statistical fluctuation of this number on
the edge of the radioactive zone ought to be the same as, or less than, the
statistical fluctuation of the net signal due to the incertitudes of radiation
emission and detection. Taking an NaI(T1) 1 in × 1 in detector moving
at 5 cm from the bottom the following equation can be employed in
dynamic detection by a sled dragged along the bottom:[26]

$$P = 0.37\, d_m^3 (\mu_w I_\gamma + 1.55)\left(1 + 1.05\frac{L_{(h/2)}}{d_m}\right)^2$$

where P is the weight of the sediment to be marked in kg per Ci of
radioisotope, d_m is the mean diameter which would give the same
number of particles per gram as that of the actual distribution

$$\frac{1}{d_m^3} = \int \frac{m(d)}{d^3}\,\sigma(d)$$

$m(d)$ being the proportion of particles with diameter d, I_γ being the dose
factor of the proposed emitter in mR/h Ci at 1 m; μ_w is the mass
adsorption coefficient of the radiation in water per cm and $L_{(h/2)}$ is
the half height width of the differential particle size curve (see Table
3.8).

If core samples are to be taken then the total activity ought to be

TABLE 3.8
NECESSARY MASSES FOR SEDIMENT TRACING[26]

	Detection type				
	Static	Dynamic			
Particle size effect	$1-0.64(L_{(h/2)}/d_m)$	$1-1.05(L_{(h/2)}/d_m)$			
Radioisotope	^{192}Ir	^{192}Ir	^{51}Cr	^{137}Cs[a]	^{182}Ta
Minimal number of particles required per m^2	50	16	17.8	12.2	10.4
P/d_m^3 in kg/Ci m^3	70	22.2	1.24	9.1	16.5

[a] Or emitter of equivalent energy (662 keV).

multiplied by a factor of approximately 10 in order to attain a sufficient strength and the number of particles ought to be multiplied by a factor of 100 to 200 in order to achieve representative numbers in the sample. Sampling is an expensive process in terms of weight and activity of the immersed tracer.

There is a variety of types of radioactive tracer immersion vessels and detection is usually effected using scintillation counters (which have a higher sensitivity than GM counters) incorporated in various kinds of self-contained equipment.

The sled alluded to above is very difficult to design since it must ensure maximal adherence to the river bed regardless of the current velocities encountered there.

The results obtained by the mass and surface labelling techniques may be interpreted qualitatively or quantitatively. In the first case isocounts (isoactivities) curves may indicate the general direction of transport and its distribution over several channels as well as longitudinal and transverse scatter. Variation in such curves between successive detecting operations makes it feasible to relate conclusions derived from these directly to hydrometeorological phenomena such as rain, storm in a catchment area, winds, etc. The same curves may render values for various factors of the observed movement such as transport velocity, velocity of the fastest particles, velocity of the slowest particles, average velocity between two successive detections, width and length of beds affected by transport and the apparent longitudinal and transverse dispersion coefficient. Quantitative information of this type may be amplified by applying the dilution methods used in river discharge measurements to sedimentary transport, i.e. the instantaneous dilution (integration) method and the continuous dilution method. It is difficult to utilise these to solve problems in sediment dynamics because of the difficulties in interpreting the good mixing requirement and length as well as determining concentrations or concentration integrals. Another problem is that the methods are only valid in constant conditions, not in transient circumstances. It is unlikely that transport would remain constant during the passage of a radioactive cloud using the instantaneous dilution method.

The space integration method involves determining separately the mean transport velocity u_m and the transport thickness X and calculating the discharge from

$$Q = I\,u_m\,X$$

where I is the transport width and u_m is determined by the position of the most active particle. X may be determined either by core sampling so as to determine the point of burial of the most active particle or by the limited number of particles method which requires injection of a restricted number of particles, the position and depth of which can afterwards be detected individually (a method very appropriate for shingle).

Another approach to the determination of X is by the overall counting rate method of G. Courtois and G. Sauzay.[31] Here the total number of counts collectable on the radioactive cloud is related to the thickness of transport.

Isocount curves were alluded to above and their preparation is complicated and to some extent subjective. The latter defect may be reduced in impact by using a reference axis, usually the identified direction of transport, and by processing the isocount graph by a digital computer as proposed by P. E. Hartley.[32]

An entirely different approach to the bed load problem involves the environmental isotope approach, i.e. the utilisation of the natural tracers such as:

(i)   natural radioisotopes contained in the sediment;
(ii) radioactive fallout fixed in the sediment;
(iii) nuclear reactor wastes.

Such tracers may be useful for if their movements are followed valuable data can be derived relating to the conjoining of petrographic methods used in sedimentology with hydrological studies.

3.5. RIVER EROSION STUDIES

A great deal of the material transported by rivers is carried in solution and in many streams this amount far exceeds that transported in particulate form. The solution load comprises many different chemical elements and the water can be analysed so as to obtain information on the concentration of each element involved. A useful measure of the total solution load is the parameter termed total dissolved solids which can be obtained by evaporating to dryness a sample of filtered river water and accurately weighing the solid residue. Many rocks comprise a large number of minerals and the chemical composition of the water draining from the area is complex. The principal exception is erosion by solution of limestone; this entails removal of calcium as bicarbonate. Limestone waters can be monitored in order to find out how the calcium content varies with discharge. For streams which flow over limestone before disappearing underground the solute content tends to vary inversely with rainfall and hence with discharge. For springs in limestone regions the calcium content usually remains constant regardless of variations in discharge. To compare the actual rate of erosion in a limestone area with that in another it is normal to express the load in terms of the volumes of limestone removed. The Corbel erosion rate formula may be used and this is

$$X = \frac{ET_{Ca}}{10^d}$$

where E is the effective runoff and is the annual rainfall minus evapotranspiration in litres, T_{Ca} is the calcium content in mg/litre $CaCO_3$, d is the density of the limestone in g/cm^3 and X is the annual quantity of limestone removed in cubic metres per km^2 per year. If density is taken as $2.5 \, g/cm^3$ then the formula becomes

$$X = \frac{4ET_{Ca}}{100}$$

In the case of the Cheddar catchment in the Mendip Hills in England, T_{Ca} is 220 mg/litre, precipitation is 10·3 litres annually and the evapotranspiration is 5·85 litres annually so that X is 39·2 m^3/km^2/year; see Table 3.9 for further data.

In the foregoing discussion it was assumed that limestone consists solely of $CaCO_3$ but many limestones actually contain a proportion of

TABLE 3.9
AMOUNTS OF LIMESTONE SOLUTIONAL EROSION

Location	Mean annual precipitation (mm)	Quantity of limestone removed ($m^3/km^2/year$)
Mendip Hills, UK, temperate	900–1 100	40
Slovenia, Yugoslavia, temperate	1 250–2 000	10–100
Southern Algeria, dry	60	6
Grand Canyon, Colorado, USA, dry	25–40	7
Yucatan, Mexico, wet tropical	1 000–1 500	12–44
Indonesia, wet tropical	200–3 000	83
R. Tanana, Alaska, USA, cold	450	40
Svartisen, Norway, cold	740–4 000	275–5 000

magnesium carbonate also and in this case the Corbel formula is amended to

$$X = \frac{4E(T_{Ca} + T_{Mg})}{100}$$

where T_{Mg} is the concentration of magnesium expressed in mg/litre $MgCO_3$. In the Cheddar catchment case the value of T_{Mg} is 6 mg/litre $MgCO_3$. $T_{Ca} + T_{Mg}$ constitutes total water hardness.

The erosion of soil by water causes loss of agricultural land and siltation and sedimentation problems further downstream and these latter may lead to the infilling of reservoirs and aggradation of the river channels, etc. Soil conservation is a very important activity and in order to determine the best approach to it, it is necessary to relate the rate of erosion to hydrologic and pedological factors. What is required is a quantitative estimate of the rate of erosion and this can be made by collecting products of the process in debris dams and tanks as well as by sediment load measurements. Radioisotopes may be employed by techniques which involve the use of autoradiography by means of which the radioactive patch can be located accurately and every particle revealed. Fast films may be utilised pressed closely against the soil and this technique permits a wide choice of emitters, especially beta emitters. The best tracer is probably ^{32}P where surficial transport is expected.

Scintillation detectors may be used periodically to measure the activity of the injection patch and scanning around this by autoradiography shows up even distant particles if enough activity has been used. The usual labelling processes are carried out and the injection patch is kept rather small (e.g. 5 cm diameter) appropriate activity being of the order of a few millicuries per deposition. S. Kazo and L. Gruber first applied the method in 1962 when they labelled soil particles with ^{32}P in KH_2PO_4 in order to study solifluction on a microscale.[33] This is a soil particle movement caused by rainfall.

3.6. THE FORMS OF CHANNELS

There is great variation in these especially in long profile. This is usually concave from source to mouth but the profile may be interrupted by steps at rejuvenation knickpoints frequently coinciding with the outcrop of rocks which are relatively more resistant. Between such steps channel slope is roughly inversely proportional to the river discharge. The concave profile approaches a graded state at which there occurs a balance between the forces of water and sediment movement within the system and the geometry of the channel. At any given moment there may be a steady state along a part of the river channel when input by water and sediment equals output; such a steady state is independent of time in so far as it may occur at any time. It is clear that in the absence of dramatic changes in climate or geology rivers tend to approach the steady state. The interrelationships between drainage basin morphometry and fluvial processes, as well as between channel form and these processes, are based on the concept that dependent relationships exist between form, process and materials to a degree which permits, under steady state conditions, an empirical predictive relationship to be established. A section of a channel in steady state will lose its input–output balance if any major control parameter alters, e.g. a man-made structure. The relations between sediments and channel characteristics may be expressed by Rubey's equation:[34]

$$SF = \frac{KL^A D^B}{Q^C}$$

where S is the graded slope, F is the optimum form ratio (the depth–width ratio which imparts to a river its maximal capacity for traction), L is the amount of load through any cross-section per unit time, D is the average diameter of the bed load and Q is the discharge through any cross-section per unit time. According to this the general downstream decrease in channel gradient is related not merely to discharge but also to the quantity and the size of the load. J. T. Hack found that channel slope is directly proportional to the 0·6 power of the median size of material for any given drainage area.[35] Thus

$$S = 18 \left(\frac{M}{A} \right)^{0.6}$$

where S is the channel slope in feet per mile, M is the median particle size of bed material in mm and A is the drainage area in square miles.

According to Hack there is a consistent relationship between channel slope and channel length where the latter is taken as the distance in miles from a locality on the river to the drainage divide at the head of the longest stream above it and where S is the channel slope and L its length

$$S = kL^n$$

values of k and n varying according to the lithology of the bedrock. The relationship between lithology and long profile is useful for land analysis, supplying a linkage between form and material as the result of fluvial processes. Channel slope can be related directly to stream flow characteristics in that for many river channels the Manning equation can be simplified as follows

$$V = 50 \, d^{2/3} \, S^{1/2}$$

or

$$S = \frac{V}{50d^{2/3}}$$

As regards the channel patterns of rivers these are, of course, usually meandering and meanders can occur in bedrock or in alluvium. Alluvial meanders are more common and can be classified as tortuous, irregular, transitional or straight. As sinuosity increases so does the width–depth ratio, the percentage of silt and clay in the channel banks and the channel perimeter. As channels straighten the mean annual discharge increases. Sinuosity appears to be determined by the proportions of wash load (suspended sediment) and bed load together with saltation load. Saltation load may be defined as that part of the bed load which is able, in conditions of high energy, to bounce along the channel floor. A wide and shallow channel is associated with the movement of a high proportion of bed material load while a narrow deep channel is associated with the transport of a sediment load primarily maintained in suspension.

Empirical relationships have been proposed between discharge Q and the measurable geometry of alluvial channels, the latter including meander wavelength λ, meander amplitude A_m and channel width w. It has been shown that

$$\lambda = \frac{1890 Q_m^{0 \cdot 34}}{M^{0 \cdot 74}}$$

where λ is the meander wavelength, Q is the mean annual discharge and M is the percentage of silt and clay in channel perimeter (representative of the river load). Clearly it is not possible to consider channel meanders independently of their material properties. In fact S. A. Schumm discovered that channel width may be related not simply to Q_m but rather to the ratio between this factor and M:[35]

$$w = 2 \cdot 3 \frac{Q_m^{0 \cdot 38}}{M^{0 \cdot 39}}$$

and

$$d = 0 \cdot 6 M^{0 \cdot 34} Q_m^{0 \cdot 29}$$

where d is the channel depth.

Turning now to the cross-sectional aspect of channels, the following factors are of importance:

(i)   the velocity of water flow is not constant either across the width or in depth;
(ii) maximal turbulence areas vary with cross-section and thus influence the position of maximum scour;
(iii) the cross-section of a channel can alter very quickly;
(iv) channels differ in cross-section over even very short distances.

Clearly the short-term changes in cross-section observed occur more easily in alluvial channels than in those cut in bedrock. Also the measurement of channel and stream flow characteristics is very much time dependent.

The distinction between alluvial and bedrock controlled channels serves as a convenient classification of them. Bedrock controlled channels are confined between rock outcrops and their morphology is determined by the material forming the bed and the banks. On the other hand alluvial channels obtain their geometries as a response to the hydraulic characteristics of the river.

3.7. FLOOD HAZARDS

Discharge of rivers is usually confined below the banks of channels but when these are unable to contain it water and sediment spill on to, and move across, adjacent surfaces. Next to perennial rivers these surfaces are usually alluvial flood plains created by the fluvial system specifically to accommodate such larger and less frequent flows. In some areas of ephemeral flow floods may spread over the surfaces of alluvial fans. On page 122 flood hydrology in reference to D. H. Pilgrim's work was mentioned.[16] The subject merits further discussion as may be seen from Table 3.10.

TABLE 3.10
ESTIMATES OF AVERAGE ANNUAL LOSS OF LIFE AND PROPERTY IN THE USA FROM FLOODS AND OTHER SELECTED HAZARDS[36]

Hazard	Annual loss (persons)	Annual loss (property) ($m)
Floods	83·4	350–1 000
Hurricanes	84·8	100
Tornadoes	204·3	45
Lightning	600	100

Of course the above estimates are rather crude. For instance, annual flood damage in the USA has been estimated at US$350 million by the US Weather Bureau, over US$900 million by the US Corps of Engineers and at US$1200 million by the US Department of Agriculture. There is no doubt, however, that flooding is a serious environmental problem so that it is not surprising that flood analysis, prediction and control are usually important activities of national, regional river or water administration authorities.

Flood plains result from the storage of sediment within and near the river channel. There are two main processes. Firstly, there is the accumulation of sediment within the shifting river channel. Sediment is frequently deposited on the slip of slopes on the inside of meander bends and produces point-bars. When the river migrates in the direction of the outside of the bend the point-bar will grow and the flood plain deposit become augmented. Much sediment is stored only temporarily in a point-bar and may be moved further downstream occasionally. This kind of within channel accumulation can take place at any point in the valley and is mainly associated with discharges below the banks. Secondly, there is suspended sediment which is carried by discharges over the banks on to the valley floor where it may settle and add to the pre-existing flood plain sediment either over the flooded surface or sometimes locally along the margins of the channel forming levees. Where there is a mixture of fine and coarse material in flood plain sediments most of the coarse part results from deposition by lateral accretion within the channels and some of the fine material may result from overbank accretion. Where the flood plain sediment is mostly made up of fine material it is probable that most of it will be deposited within a channel. The frequency with which bankfull discharge and flooding takes place is rather similar for different rivers even when they are located in different types of environment. The recurrence interval for bankfull flow is in the range 0·5 to 2 years and the similarity of this in contrasted environments plus the fact that channels do not normally deepen as flood plain deposition continues suggest that channels are adjusted to accommodate discharge generated within the watersheds for much of the time, that the flood plain is adjusted to transmit larger flows for the rest of the time and that both features are functionally interrelated.

Flood plains may be defined as areas characterised by distinctive suites of forms and deposits, areas inundated by flood events of particular magnitudes and frequencies. From the hazard point of view floodway and pondage area may be distinguished. The floodway is the area of the flood plain usually marginal to the main channel in which land filling or drainage concentration as the result of constructional activities would significantly increase water levels. The pondage area lies adjacent to the floodway and is the location of storage of water during flooding.

As regards alluvial fans these are rather common landforms in arid and semi-arid areas and normally occur where the ephemeral flows from mountains spread out on to adjacent plains. They vary greatly as regards size but are usually conical in shape (plan view) with apices near the mountain front. Sometimes a set of alluvial fans will coalesce and form composite alluvial slopes. Deposition of material on fans arises from changes in the hydraulic geometry of flows as they quit the major feeder channels from the mountains. Flooding on alluvial fans may occur in two main areas, namely along the margins of the principal supply channels and on the depositional zones beyond the ends of these. There are a number of problems associated with such zones of flooding. One is that because flow on fans is ephemeral so that often there is no flow, the possibility of flooding is frequently minimised. Then flow in alluvial fan systems may vary from 'river' type flows with low sediment concentrations to very viscous debris flows which can move large sized boulders. Also the channels which floods follow can change periodically so that the hazard zones may also change.

Considering the characteristics of flooding and the controlling variables involved in it, the most important physical factors as regards the impact on society are:

(i)   frequency of flooding;
(ii)   the magnitude of flooding;
(iii)   the total flood runoff volume;
(iv)   the increase or decrease in rate of discharge;
(v)   the time lag (time between the centre of mass of a rain storm and that of associated runoff) or flood to peak interval (time between flood elevation at which damage commences and the flood peak);
(vi)   the area inundated;
(vii)   the flow velocity;
(viii) the duration of the inundation;
(ix)   the depth of water;
(x)   the sediment load transported;
(xi)   the season at which the flood occurs.

Figure 3.7 shows a typical flood hydrograph as well as a flood frequency curve. The recurrence interval shown in the latter is that period of time in years in which, on average, a flood is equalled or exceeded and it may be calculated thus:

$$I = \frac{n+1}{m}$$

where I is the recurrence interval, n is the number of years of discharge record and m is the rank number of an individual item in an array. Rank values are flood magnitudes e.g. annual peaks or number of flood peaks above a selected base. It may be correctly inferred that in many parts of the world the historic records are quite inadequate for use in this connection. Recurrence interval, where available, is plotted against an appropriate measure of magnitude on probability graph paper and from

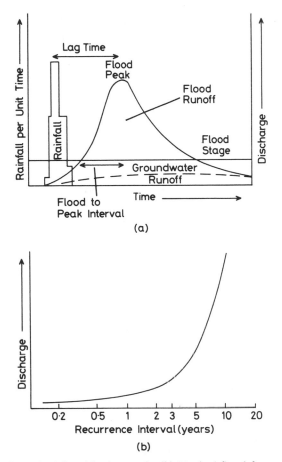

FIG. 3.7. (a) Typical flood hydrograph. (b) Typical flood frequency curve.

such graphs statements may be made relative to the statistical probability of floods. The mean of a series based upon annual peaks, i.e. the mean annual flood, usually has a recurrence interval of 2·33 years and may be written $Q_{2\cdot33}$. It may be inferred that if a flood has, say, a 10 year recurrence interval then there is a 10% chance of it occurring in any particular year. Discharge results from mean depth, width and velocity of flow and its relationship to characteristics such as inundation area and sediment load can be described precisely. Consequently, curves can be drawn relating these variables to the frequency of occurrence. Magnitude–frequency graphs can be constructed and they are useful in hazard forecasting and in deciding what remedial measures need to be undertaken. The flood hydrograph describes the alteration in discharge for any station during a flood and, as may be seen from Fig. 3.7, if the storm rainfall is plotted on it the lag time can be determined.

Among the factors which determine flood characteristics the characteristics of the basin are very important, especially the geometry of the channel. Transient phenomena play a significant role, e.g. release of blockage (due to ice or logs, etc.) may release water suddenly and this can happen also by the collapse of dams. It is feasible to attempt to predict floods and J. C. Rodda has given an important relation:[37]

$$Q_{2\cdot33} = 1{\cdot}08A^{0\cdot77}R_{2\cdot33}^{2\cdot92}D^{0\cdot81}$$

where A is the drainage area in square miles, $R_{2\cdot33}$ is the mean annual daily maximum rainfall in inches and D is the drainage density in miles per square mile. The value of the multiple correlation coefficient was 0·9 and the factorial standard error was 1·58.

A study of 164 drainage basins in New England (USA) by M. A. Benson in 1962 gave the following relationship:[38]

$$Q_{2\cdot33} = 0{\cdot}4 + 1{\cdot}0\log A + 0{\cdot}3\log Sl - 0{\cdot}3\log St + 0{\cdot}4\log F + 0{\cdot}8\log O$$

where $Q_{2\cdot33}$ is the mean annual flood, A is the drainage area in square miles, Sl is the main channel slope in feet per mile, St is the percentage of surface storage area plus 0·5%, F is the average January value of degrees below freezing in °F and O is an orographic factor.

Flood hazards are perceived differently by different human groups and the more complex the technological advancement that exists in the society the more serious they are in their effects. It is important to note that J. Burton and R. W. Kates indicated that the perception of, and adjustment to, flooding are directly related to flood frequency.[36]

Appropriate land practices may be applied to modify floods. Channel change is another approach and here embankments may be employed to confine floods to the floodway. Also, natural channels may be straightened or deepened in order to create diversionary routes for usage in times of flood. Reservoirs may be constructed to store flood waters.

Flooding has been a natural hazard for millenia and indeed constitutes a natural process which is fundamental to the transfer of water and sediment in drainage basins and also is important in modifying valley floors and alluvial fan landforms.

3.8. WATER MOVEMENT THROUGH SOIL

River discharge is affected both by the intensity and distribution of precipitation and these may be affected by interception and evapotranspiration losses and also by storage in the soil before the water reaches a river channel. Of course some of the precipitation falls directly into a river channel, but channels have areas which are only a small proportion of their associated basins and consequently such direct channel precipitation is small although important. Most precipitation falls on surrounding land and therefore has to travel to the stream channel. This travel may take the form of overland flow, but some of it is accomplished by seepage as throughflow or interflow while another part may migrate by very slow seepage through soil and rock strata as baseflow. Water flow arising solely from water contained in permeable bedrock constitutes groundwater flow. Obviously the proportions of each of these components will vary from basin to basin. Observations on daily rainfall and runoff demonstrate that there is a time lag between the actual occurrence of rainfall and the time when that water passes a gauging station. This usually amounts to approximately a day, far too long to be accounted for solely by the mean velocity of the river water itself. The balance is taken up by the downslope movement of water towards the actual stream channel.

It is believed that throughflow (the movement of water downslope through soil layers) is probably the dominant contributor to river discharge. D. Weyman has measured overland flow and throughflow on and in brown soils and peaty podsols overlying impermeable Old Red Sandstone on slopes of about 12° in Somerset, England.[39] These soils can be divided into various horizons and results show that a day elapsed between the peak rainfall and the peak flow from the B-horizon in this soil. Drainage from this horizon went on for no less than 4 or 5 days thereafter and that from the B/C-horizon continued for over 40 days with a peak 5 or 6 days after the actual rainfall. Throughflow drainage did not take place in the uppermost soil horizon and neither did overland flow. The slow flow from the B/C-horizon proved to be sufficient to maintain continuous stream flow throughout the year, i.e. it maintained a 'baseflow' similar to that which would be provided by groundwater from permeable rocks. Relevant data are appended in Table 3.11.[39]

The table illustrates the important contribution of flow through soil horizons to stream discharges, the relative significance of different

TABLE 3.11

THROUGHFLOW RATES ON A 12° SLOPE IN AN UPLAND CATCHMENT IN SOMERSET, UK

	Soil horizon	Bulk density (g/cm^3)	Flows (cm^3/m)	Lag of storm peak	Drainage time
Brown earth soil	A 0–10 cm (organic)				
	B 10–45 cm (sandy loam)	1·6 1·9	0–180	24 h	5 days
	B/C 45–75 cm		1–10	5–6 days	> 40 days
Peaty podsols	A 0–20 cm (peat)			2–3 h via 5 cm pipes at 20 cm depth	
	B 20–60 cm (podsol)				

routes depending upon whether the soil can absorb rainfall as fast as it falls and whether the bedrock can absorb percolating water as fast as it seeps down through the soil horizons. The rates of absorption at these two surfaces act as regulators which control which route is actually selected and followed. The rate at which the ground surface can absorb water is termed the infiltration rate and the capacity of the soil to hold water constitutes its field capacity. Calculation of the probability of surface or overland flow necessitates measurement of rainfall intensity and infiltration capacity of the soil. The former is determined by rain gauges and the latter by appropriate instruments which are extremely simple. For instance, a bottomless container may be sunk into the ground, filled with water to a predetermined level above the ground surface and the time recorded during which the level falls one-third of the way to the ground surface. The experiment is repeated until constant times are recorded and the results are expressed in mm/sec obtained by dividing the difference in levels by the total time taken. After some time the rate of infiltration will decline to a steady level called the saturated infiltration rate.

Information on the movement of water in the unsaturated zone (the zone of aeration) has been obtained using radioactive tracers and the work of K. O. Münnich may be cited.[40] Moisture in a given horizontal plane is tagged with a radioisotope tracer and this is carried along with the infiltrating water. Tritium was employed as HTO and although subject to diffusional spreading nevertheless showed how far the descending water had been displaced. To locate the radiotracer at any given time a soil core was taken using an auger and the tritium concentration of the moisture in the soil core measured and plotted as a function of depth. Standard drying and weighing procedures give the moisture distribution in the core and provided that infiltration is known a water balance can be constructed at any time for any soil. The basic assumption is that water cannot bypass the tagged layer so that this, although in motion, acts as an 'impermeable' layer. A balance can be determined for the moisture above the tagged layer and the moisture flux through any reference plane below the tagged layer is given by the change of total water confined between the tagged layer and this plane. The tagged layer can be regarded as a moving piston. The radiotracer acts like an impermeable sheet moving with the average velocity of the water if lateral exchange between portions of different velocity is sufficiently rapid. This is true of short lateral distances in the range below c. 1 mm for which molecular diffusion provides rapid material exchange between waters moving with different velocities or even between moving and stationary water. Often the soil is sufficiently isotropic and the vertical water movement slow enough for locally different velocities not to show up at all. Then the tagged layer becomes broadened by molecular diffusion in the vertical direction only (longitudinal diffusion).

The application of the tritiated water was carried out with a syringe type injector preferably below the active root zone in the event that groundwater recharge measurement is desired. About 10 to 20 point injections were made along a straight horizontal line at a depth say of 1 m. The amount used for each point was 40 ml at $1.5 \mu Ci/litre \approx 5 \times 10^5 TU$ if the soil moisture is of the order of 30 vol. % or correspondingly less in the case of lower moisture content. Twenty injections were effected in about 2 h and the same time was required to sample five cores. An automatic scintillation spectrometer was used to make analyses. Of course deuterium may also be used as a tracer but it appears to be too expensive. Artificial tritium was used for tracing vertical movements of water in the alluvial plains of northern India in western Uttar Pradesh, Punjab and Haryana by P. S. Goel and his associates in 1978.[41] Extensive data were obtained from sites in the Indo-Gangetic Plains and absolute recharge was calculable at some of these (125 in total). Data on recharge for the past several years prior to 1975 showed a strong correlation of the fractional recharge (recharge over rainfall) with the average clay contents of the soil. There appeared to be a deficiency in the recharge in the areas which are water-logged, i.e. where the water table is very shallow. In Haryana and Punjab the vertical recharge estimated from the tracer displacement is insufficient to replenish the draft. The same technique was applied by P. S. Goel and P. S. Datta with B. S. Tanwar to the measurement of vertical recharge to groundwater in Haryana state using tritiated water.[42] The average recharge for 15 sites during July to November 1973 was equivalent to 9 cm of water (14% of the irrigation plus rainfall). For 18 sites sampled after two monsoons (July 1973 to December 1974) the average recharge was 19 cm and the fractional recharge 0·15. Wide variations in recharge values were noted. P. S. Datta and P. S. Goel in 1977 published data on groundwater recharge in Punjab using tritiated water.[43] Vertical recharge to groundwater due to the 1972 monsoon plus supplemental irrigation has been measured at 21 sites and the average recharge was found to be equivalent to 8·5 cm of water (18% of the average rainfall and 12% of the total watering).

Lysimeters are used also to determine downward movement of soil moisture but they suffer from serious disadvantages. For a start they are expensive and give information only for a single site as well as altering the natural environmental conditions. Many are artificially filled and therefore do not necessarily represent the natural soil. Those containing a funnel to collect water percolating through the horizontal plane in which it is situated are affected notably by the fact that the funnel seriously changes the hydraulic gradient through this reference plane and therefore also alters the moisture flux—especially in those cases where the soil is fine grained. Water which would have percolated through the plane of reference if a soil layer of equal or similar capillary suction were beneath it is retained in the soil filling the lysimeter by capillary forces just as soon as the soil underneath the plane in question is removed and replaced by a funnel. This can be overcome if a special funnel with a porous ceramic plate is placed in contact with the lysimeter soil through which an adjustable water suction can be applied to the lysimeter which to some degree restores the natural conditions at the plane of reference.

Capillary forces tend to bind moisture in soil, the binding energy depending strongly on grain size and the quantity of moisture. The grain size distribution defines the relation between the capillary binding potential and the moisture volume fraction. This potential is a negative hydrostatic pressure and may be represented by the height of a water column measurable by a tensiometer. However, because hydrostatic pressure is usually not important in unsaturated flow the usual situation is

$$H = F + \rho gz$$

where H is the hydraulic potential, F is the capillary binding potential, ρ is the density of the water, g the acceleration due to gravity and z a vertical coordinate normally taken as zero at the water table.

It is important to remember that the relation between potential gradient and rate of flow termed Darcy's Law is more complicated in unsaturated flow than in saturated flow. In the saturated zone the hydraulic conductivity is usually constant with time and relative changes in flow are proportional to corresponding changes in the hydraulic gradient. In the unsaturated zone on the other hand conductivity is a variable dependent upon moisture content and of course the soil may alter its structure where moisture content drops and fissuration occurs. In the unsaturated zone the law may be stated

$$v_f = Kh$$

where v_f is filter velocity and K = Darcy's constant for unsaturated flow dependent upon moisture volume fraction or capillary binding potential.

Another approach to determining soil moisture characteristics is that made by M. de Boodt in 1967.[44] With his associates he effected neutron-logging of moisture and additionally utilised tensiometers to repeatedly measure the hydraulic potential as a function of depth. Sometimes in summer this parameter may have a relative minimum at a certain depth and moisture cannot pass through this level (represented in the above equation by $h = 0$).

REFERENCES

1. GUIZERIX, J., 1968. Surface water: transient measurements of rate of flow. in: *Guidebook on Nuclear Techniques in Hydrology, Tech. Repts Ser. No. 91*, IAEA, Vienna, 32–42.
2. HULL, D. E., 1958. The total count technique: a new principle in flow measurement. *Int. J. App. Isotopes Radiat.*, **4**, 1.
3. HAMILL, L., 1980. A note of the performance of a ^{82}Br radioactive tracer in the River Skerne, England. *J. Hydrol.*, **47**, 307–15.
4. FLORKOWSKI, T., 1968. Use of tritium tracer for river flow measurements. Report to Govt of Kenya, *IAEA Tech. Assistance Rept 358*, Vienna.
5. KNUTSSON, G., LJUNGGREN, K. and FORSBERG, H. G., 1963. Field and laboratory tests of chromium-51–EDTA and tritium water as a double tracer

for groundwater flow. in: *Radioisotopes in Hydrology*, Tokyo Symp., 5–9 March 1963, IAEA, Vienna, 347–63.

6. HALEVY, E., NIR, A., HARPAZ, Y. and MANDEL, S., 1958. Use of radio-isotopes in studies of groundwater flow. 1. Laboratory and field experiments on the suitability of various tracers. *Proc. 2nd UN Int. Conf. PUAE*, **20**, 158.

7. RIMMAR, G. M., 1952. The use of electrical conductivity for measuring discharges by the dilution method. *Trudy G.G.I.*, **36**, 90; Nat. Eng. Lab. Glasgow Translation No. 749 (1960).

8. DOLE, R. B., 1906. Use of fluorescein in the study of underground waters. in: Underground water papers 1906, ed. M. L. Fuller, *US Geol. Surv. Water Supply Paper 160*, 73–83.

9. PRITCHARD, D. W. and CARPENTER, J. H., 1960. Measurement of turbulent diffusion in estuaries and in-shore waters. *Int. Assn Sci. Hydr. Bull.*, **20**, 37–50.

10. WILSON, JAMES F. JR, 1968. Fluorometric procedures for dye tracing. Chapter A12, Book 3 (*Applications of Hydraulics*), Techniques of water resource investigations of the US Geological Survey. US Dept of the Interior, Washington DC, 31 pp.

11. CLESS-BERNERT, T., GEHRINGER, P., RIEDLMAYER, L., and ROTZER, H., 1970. Flow measurements in the Danube. in: *Isotope Hydrology*, Symp. 9–13 March 1970, IAEA, Vienna, 483–96.

12. TASOVAC, T., DRAŠKOVIC, R., RADOSAVLJEVIĆ, R., FILIP, A., VUKMIROVIĆ, V., RADOJČIĆ, M., and VUKOTIĆ, R., 1970. Nuclear techniques in studies of dispersion and some other properties of the Danube. in: *Isotope Hydrology*, Symp. 9–13 March 1970, IAEA, Vienna, 497–507.

13. BALEK, J., RÁLKOVÁ, J. and SOCHOREC, R., 1970. Radioactive tracing in frozen rivers. in: *Isotope Hydrology*, Symp. 9–13 March 1970, IAEA, Vienna, 479–82.

14. GUIZERIX, J. and DINCER, T., 1968. Transit time for direct surface runoff. in: *Guidebook on Nuclear Techniques in Hydrology, Tech. Repts Ser. No. 91*, IAEA, Vienna, 43–50.

15. PILGRIM, D. H., 1966. Radioactivity tracing of storm runoff on a small catchment. I. Experimental technique. *J. Hydrol.*, **4**, 289; II. Discussion of results. *J. Hydrol.*, **4**, 306.

16. PILGRIM, D. H. and HUFF, D. D., 1978. A field evaluation of subsurface and surface runoff. *J. Hydrol.*, **38**, 299–318.

17. HORTON, R. E., 1945. Erosional development of streams and their drainage basins; a hydrophysical approach to quantitative geomorphology. *Bull. Geol. Soc. Am.*, **56**, 275–370.

18. BARNES, H. H., 1967. Roughness characteristics of natural channels. *US Geol. Surv. Water Supply Paper 1849*, 213 pp.

19. ARKHANGELSKI, M. M., 1960. Application of radioactive isotopes for investigating suspended sediments in rivers. *Heat Eng. and Hydrodynamics IV*, AEC-tr-4206, 82–8.

20. EMELYANOV, V. A., NESTEROV, V. E. and SHUMAKOV, B. B., 1959. The problem of measuring water turbidity and the attenuation of a beam of gamma rays. *Sb. trud. Ynzh. NIIGiM*, No. 6.

21. FLORKOWSKI, T. and CAMERON, J. F., 1966. A simple radioisotope X-ray transmission gauge for measuring suspended sediment concentrations in rivers. Proc. Symp. Warsaw 1965, IAEA, Vienna, 395.
22. TAZIOLI, G. S., 1980. The measurement of suspended sediment transport in natural streams using automatic radioisotope gauges. *J. Hydrol.*, **47**, 173–85.
23. FLORKOWSKI, T., 1968. Suspended load. in: *Guidebook on Nuclear Techniques in Hydrology, Tech. Repts Ser. No. 91*, IAEA, Vienna, 51–5.
24. MCHENRY, J. R., COLEMAN, N. L., WILLIS, J. C., MURPHREE, C. E., BOLTON, G. C., SANSOM, O. W. and GILL, A. C., 1967. Performance of nuclear sediment concentration gauges. in: *Isotopes in Hydrology*, Proc. Symp. Vienna 14–18 November 1966, IAEA, Vienna, 207–25.
25. KASHEF, ABDEL AZIZ I., 1981. Technical and ecological impacts of the High Aswan Dam. *J. Hydrol.*, **53**, 73–84.
26. COURTOIS, G., 1968. Sediment movement and transport. in: *Guidebook on Nuclear Techniques in Hydrology, Tech. Repts Ser. No. 91*, IAEA, Vienna. 55–66.
27. GROOT, de A. J., ALLERSMA, E., de BRUIN, M., HOUTMAN, J. P. W., 1970. Cobalt and tantalum tracers measured by activation analysis in sediment transport studies. in: *Isotope Hydrology*, Proc. Symp. 9–13 March 1970, IAEA, Vienna, 885–98.
28. IRVING, H. and WILLIAMS, R., 1962. Order of stability of metal complexes. *Nature*, **162**, 746.
29. KRUGER, P. and CHANNELL, J. K., 1970. Use of rare earth elements as tracers in estuaries. in: *Isotope Hydrology*, Proc. Symp. 9 13 March 1970, IAEA, Vienna, 869–81.
30. BOUGAULT, H., CAILLOT, A., COURTOIS, G. and JEANNEAU, B., 1967. Depots superficiels de radioelements sur les sables et les vases. in: *Isotopes in Hydrology*, Proc. Symp. Vienna, 14–18 November 1966, IAEA, Vienna, 233–62.
31. COURTOIS, G. and SAUZAY, G., 1966. Les méthodes de bilan des taux de comptage de traceurs radioactifs appliquées à la mesure des debits massiques de charriage. *Hoville Blanche 3*.
32. HARTLEY, P. E., 1967. A technique for digital computer processing of data from radioisotope sediment tracing studies. *Int. J. Appl. Isotopes Radiat.*, **18**, 713–20.
33. KAZO, S. and GRÜBER, L., 1962. The investigation of microsolifluction with the aid of tagged isotopes. *Congrès AIHS*, Colloque de Bari, 62–6.
34. RUBEY, W. W., 1952. Geology and mineral resources of the Hardin and Drussels quadrangles in Illinois. *US Geol. Surv. Prof. Paper 218*, 175.
35. SCHUMM, S. A., 1969. River metamorphosis. *J. Hydraulics Div., Proc. Am. Soc. Civ. Eng.*, **95**, 255–73.
36. BURTON, J. and KATES, R. W., 1964. The perception of natural hazards in resource management. *Nat. Res.*, **J3**, 412–41.
37. RODDA, J. C., 1967. The significance of the characteristics of basin rainfall and morphometry in a study of floods in the United Kingdom. *Inst. Assn Sci. Hydr. Leningrad Symp.*, 835–45.
38. BENSON, M. A., 1962. Factors influencing the occurrence of floods in a humid region of diverse terrain. *US Geol. Surv. Water Supply Paper 1580–B*.

39. WEYMAN, D., 1975. *Runoff Processes and Streamflow Modelling.* Oxford University Press.
40. MÜNNICH, K. O., 1968. Moisture movement. in: *Guidebook on Nuclear Techniques in Hydrology, Tech. Repts Ser. No. 91,* IAEA, Vienna, 109–118.
41. GOEL, P. S., DATTA, P. S., RAMA, SANGAL, S. P., KUMAR HANS, BAHADUR, P., SABHERWAL, R. K. and TANWAR, B. S., 1978. Tritium tracer studies on groundwater recharge in the alluvial deposits of Indo-Gangetic plains of western U. P., Punjab and Haryana. in: *Approaches and Methodologies for Development of Groundwater Resources.* Proc. Indo-German Workshop 26–30 May 1975. Nat. Geophys. Res. Inst. Hyderabad, 309–322.
42. GOEL, P. S., DATTA, P. S. and TANWAR, B. S., 1977. Measurement of vertical recharge to groundwater in Haryana state (India) using tritium tracer. *Nordic Hyd.,* **8,** 211–24.
43. DATTA, P. S. and GOEL, P. S., 1977. Groundwater recharge in Panjab state (India) using tritium tracer. *Nordic Hyd.,* **8,** 225–36.
44. de BOODT, M., HARTMANN, R., de MEESTER, P., 1967. Determination of soil moisture characteristics for irrigation by neutron moisture meter and air purged tensiometers. Isotope and radiation techniques in soil physics and irrigation studies, *Proc. Symp. Istanbul,* IAEA, Vienna, 147.

CHAPTER 4

Lakes and Other Surface
Water Manifestations

4.1. GENERAL CHARACTERISTICS OF LAKES

Lakes constitute small to moderately large inland bodies of water, either fresh or saline with surfaces exposed to the atmosphere and without access to the sea or having such access solely by means of rivers. They occupy depressions into the zone of saturation in the environmental soil and rock, derive their water from rain, melted snow, ice, etc. and are small scale agents of erosion in which waves may develop, controlled by the same factors governing them in the oceans. Most lakes have a surface area of less than $250 \, km^2$, although some are much larger than that; the largest fresh water lake in the world (Lake Superior) has an area of almost $80\,000 \, km^2$. Such larger lakes may have tides and develop beaches, bars, spits, wave-cut cliffs and stacks. The origins of lakes are various. They include crustal movement, volcanism, glaciation, river action, wind, the solutional removal of rock and, of course, the activities of Man. Since most lakes are shallow they are usually considered to be evanescent features of the surface of the planet, having a rather short geological life. However, while the average depth is probably not much more than $30 \, m$, some are very deep indeed. For instance, Lake Baikal in the USSR reaches a maximum of $1700 \, m$. Table 4.1 lists pertinent data.

The classification of lakes may be based upon the origin of the depression in which they occur and so they may be divided into tectonic, glacial, volcanic and sink-hole but this does not affect other approaches depending upon factors such as salinity and stratification.

159

TABLE 4.1
CHARACTERISTICS OF SELECTED MAJOR LAKES

Lake	Area (m^2)	Volume (1 000 acre feet)	Shoreline (m)	Dept (ft) Average	Maximum
Caspian Sea	169 300	71 300	3 730	675	3 080
Superior	31 180	9 700	1 860	475	1 000
Victoria	26 200	2 180	2 130		
Aral Sea[a]	26 200	775			
Huron	23 010	3 720	1 680		
Michigan	22 400	4 660			870
Baikal[a]	13 300	18 700		2 300	5 700
Tanganyika	12 700	8 100			4 700
Great Bear[a]	11 490		1 300		
Great Slave[a]	11 170		1 365		
Nyasa	11 000	6 800		900	2 310
Erie	9 940	436			
Winnipeg[a]	9 390		1 180		
Ontario	7 540	1 300			
Ladoga	7 000	745			
Chad[a]	6 500				
Maracaibo[a]	4 000				
Rudolf[a]	3 475				
Athabasca	3 085				
Titicaca[a,b]					

[a] Area fluctuates.
[b] This is the world's highest lake situated in Peru/Bolivia at an elevation of 3 800 m above sea level.

4.1.1 Tectonic Lakes

Tectonic lakes establish themselves in natural catchment basins resulting from differential movements of the planetary crust. Some examples are Lakes Albert, Malawi and Tanganyika in East Africa, together with Lake Baikal in Siberia, USSR. Tectonic lakes usually have an elongated shape, steep sides and great depth since they lie in depressions caused by downward movement of a section of the Earth's crust. The best known examples are probably the Dead Sea and Lake Tiberias in Israel, the former being the lowest lying lake in the world at 396 m below mean sea level. These and the East Africa ones comprise components of a long chain of lakes, location of which is governed by the vast system of fractures extending from Zambia to Lebanon known as the Great Rift Valley.

4.1.2. Glacial Lakes

Glacial lakes are impounded by moraines and in the USSR, Finland and Canada there are a huge number of these accumulations of material which have been transported and deposited by ice and whole networks of winding lakes have been produced. The North American Lakes Superior, Huron, Erie and Ontario all fall into this category and like Lake Onega in Russia are of enormous size. The Great Lakes probably originated in the depositional activity of the glaciers and also in glacial erosion and modification of the pre-existing drainage system of the region by the vast continental ice sheet. Other examples are the Finger Lakes of New York and Jenny Lake at the foot of the Teton Mountains in Wyoming. An interesting minor version of the same lake type is afforded by the innumerable moraine-dammed ponds or tarns of the English Lake District.

When a valley glacier melts in stages several morainic dams may be deposited at successively higher elevations so that not one but a whole series of lakes form. This phenomenon is demonstrated in the glacier valley leading from the Col de la Schucht in the Vosges where three lakes occur at intervals, namely the Gerardmer at 600 m, the Longemer at 660 m and the Retournemer at 700 m.

4.1.3. Volcanic Lakes

Volcanic lakes result when a lava flow dams a valley and impounds water to form a lake having the same shape as the valley itself. Some instances of this include the lakes of Chambon, Aydat and Guery in France, Lake Kivu in East Africa and Lake Chelan in the USA. All resulted from valleys being dammed by Tertiary lavas.

Crater lakes arise similarly and are situated in the craters of extinct volcanoes or in cavities caused by subsidence after subterranean volcanism. Usually they are circular and steep sided, the best known being Crater Lake, Oregon, USA, which fills a crater some 9·5 km wide and 600 m deep. It is surrounded by cliffs ranging from 150 m to 600 m high. Another example is Lake Chala on the southeast slope of Mt. Kilimanjaro in Kenja where tritiated water experiments were carried out in the 1960s. These will be discussed below. The famous 'maare' of the Eifel region of West Germany are crater lakes of recently extinct volcanoes and the largest is the Laacher See. Similar lakes occur in the Black Forest and are also found in the Ruwenzori region of East Africa as well as in several American states and the Chilean Andes.

Many lakes cannot be ascribed to the above categories and some of these may have been formed by simple erosional activity of rivers. If a stream bedded on soft rock runs on to a hard rock outcrop differential erosion will form a basin rapidly and water will accumulate here behind the hard rock bar. Of course such a lake will be shorter lived than the other types because the erosional action will proceed and ultimately wear away the rock bar completely. There are other ways in which rivers may form lakes. For instance, ox-bow lakes develop when a river cuts off its bends or meanders through rejuvenation. Erratic meandering deposits made by the river on its delta frequently create lakes and the Zuider Zee on the Rhine delta was formed in this manner. At the north end of the Gulf of Baja, California, lies the Salton Sea which originated by Colorado River deposition cutting off and separating the terminal portion from the main part of the bay. In limestone areas sink-holes and solution valleys produced by groundwater activity may become blocked by rock debris and then lakes will be impounded. Many of the lakes in Florida and across the Yucatan Peninsula are of this type.

Sand bars may form across bay mouths and estuaries to produce lagoons which are shallow lakes occurring adjacent to the sea. In permafrost areas thaw lakes may appear in the warm season and many can be seen on the coastal plain areas of north Alaska.

Playa lakes are temporary lakes forming after rains in dry regions. They are often saline and sometimes they are termed salinas. In the Black Rock Desert of Nevada a playa lake appears and remains in most winters for at least part of the time and covers an area of $1200\,km^2$ or more. Its depth rarely exceeds a few centimetres however. During storms it turns into mud which later evaporates leaving a mudcrack landscape over a wide area. Meteor craters may contain lakes and one instance of this is Canada's Chubb Lake.

Man creates lakes, for instance Lake Mead in Arizona and Nevada which was produced by damming the Colorado River with the Hoover Dam. Another example is Lake Nasser in Egypt. Both these and others suffer greatly from siltation problems. At Lake Mead the river is building a vast delta at the point of entry into the lake and there is no reason to doubt that eventually this deposit will totally infill the lake. It is estimated that if the present rate of deposition continues this will take about four centuries, but it will happen ultimately.

Very small lakes are called ponds and they form in the same manner as lakes or wherever the ground surface is irregular and the soil impermeable. As a matter of fact, percolating waters may deposit an insoluble iron-pan layer in sandy, permeable soils and above this a pond may form. There are many examples of this in Surrey in England as well as in Sologne, France.

As noted earlier lakes differ widely as regards the salt content of their waters and this may relate to the length of life of the particular lake. Of course most lakes are composed of fresh water, but some are saline and in fact much more saline than the oceans. The latter contain $35\%_{00}$ salts, but, for instance, the Great Salt Lake has a dissolved solids content exceeding this by a factor of four. The Dead Sea is even more saline—it has $246\%_{00}$ salts content. All salt lakes form under desert or semi-arid conditions where the evaporation rate is high enough to prevent an outflow and subsequent discharge of salts to the seas. Some salt lakes are intermittent and exist for only a short period after heavy rains subsequent to which they disappear under intense evaporation.

Lakes with fresh water also differ widely in contents but tend to assume the composite dissolved solids characteristic of the waters of inflowing streams. This is because of the balance between inflow and outflow. If a lake receives an inflow slowed down by marginal vegetation then the waters tend to acquire an organic content. Lakes formed in drainage areas in crystalline rock, volcanic or metamorphic environments tend to have low dissolved solids contents. For instance, Lake Superior has its main drainage from the Laurentian shield and the dissolved solids content is only $c.$ $0.05\%_{00}$. In the Grimsel Lake in the Swiss Alps the dissolved solids contents are even lower at $0.0085\%_{00}$. Of course lakes in a limestone area will have a marked $CaCO_3$ and $MgCO_3$ content. Occasionally gases may occur in lake waters, e.g. in crater lakes in volcanic areas. It is important to mention meromictic lakes. These are lakes in which water is permanently stratified and hence does not circulate at any time during the year. In temperate areas this permanent stratification occurs because of a vertical, chemically produced density gradient. Complete mixing does not take place and there are no overturn periods. This is because seasonal fluctuations in the thermal gradient are over-ridden by the stability of the chemical gradient. The uppermost layer of water is wind-mixed, however, and this is termed the mixolimnion. The denser, bottom layer does not mix with the overlying water layer and is termed the monimolimnion. There is a transitional layer intermediate between these and this constitutes the chemocline. In North America meromictic lakes are restricted to sheltered basins small in area compared with depth, basins in arid regions and isolated basins in fjords. It is interesting that up to 1960 only 11 meromictic lakes had been recorded in North America. In the subsequent decade that number doubled and there are known to be seven such lakes in Washington state, six in Wisconsin, four in New York, three in Alaska, two in Michigan and one each in Florida, Nevada, British Columbia, Labrador and Baffin Island. Unfortunately not many chemical studies have been effected on these lakes but it is known that there is no dissolved oxygen in the monimolimnion and possibly large quantities of hydrogen sulphide and ammonia may be present in anaerobic conditions. In 1968 J. Kjensmo suggested that the accumulation of ferrous bicarbonate in the deepest layers of some lakes might have initiated meromixis under certain conditions.[1] E. S. Deevey and his associates investigated the biological fractionation of sulphur and carbon isotopes in the monimolimnion of Fayetteville Green Lake in New York.[2] They noted that the fractionation factor for sulphur was the highest ever observed.

4.2. DYNAMICS OF LAKES AND RESERVOIRS

Those of interest include the ones relating to water balance and its changes, mixing patterns (especially vertical mixing rates) and stratification. These characteristics can be obtained by mass flow and volume measurements, evaporation estimates based on energy balance or evaporation pans and temperature and salinity surveys of the lake. Environmental isotope tracers such as deuterium, oxygen-18 and tritium can be used for improving water balance estimates and these isotopes plus artificially introduced ones can be used in tracing mixing patterns.

Stratification is permanent in meromictic lakes, but all lakes (except very shallow ones) are stratified for at least part of every year (thermocline) and possibly all saline lakes are permanently stratified. Thus the lake system may periodically, or always, be treated as a two box situation, each a well mixed reservoir. Charles D. Keeling and B. Bolin have discussed the general theory of such reservoir models.[3] On the other hand, a continuous transport model is employed to describe vertical tracer concentration gradients. A steady state profile may be maintained by continuous removal of the tracer by radioactive decay with the boundaries (surface or bottom) acting as source. The diffusion equation

$$v\frac{\mathrm{d}c}{\mathrm{d}z} - D_e\frac{\mathrm{d}^2c}{\mathrm{d}z^2} = -\lambda c$$

at steady state describes the tracer concentration at any depth z where v is the vertical advection rate and D_e a diffusion constant normally exceeding that for molecular diffusion and including turbulent transport by eddies. The vertical diffusion of tritium, $^{14}CO_2$ and ^{222}Rn have been described by similar equations. The vertical mixing rate is characterised by the value of D_e and may be determined from the profile by integrating the equation with the correct boundary conditions. Nevertheless it is very important to ascertain that horizontal displacements at various depths do not occur so that the profile is undistorted. In most cases neither the box model nor the vertical diffusion model is applicable because transport conditions in the lake are usually not ideal enough and so a three-dimensional map of environmental isotopes may be constructed. Injections of radioactive isotope tracers such as ^{82}Br, ^{131}I and $Co(CN)_6^{3-}$ have facilitated determination of spreading and flow patterns of lake water, the dispersion of the tracer cloud usually being followed at once by *in situ* measurement using scintillation counters. These can be carried in boats or permanently mounted on stationary platforms.

4.3. LEAKAGES FROM LAKES AND RESERVOIRS

These can be dangerous where the quantity of available water is reduced to human detriment or where the structural stability of hydraulic works is undermined. It is possible for losses to occur through structures such as earth and rock fill dams and levees and they can take place by seepage or more dramatically by leakage through flowpaths in fractured rocks. If losses are large their magnitude can be determined using mass balance equations for specified time intervals if all other parameters are known (such as evaporation, inflow, etc.). Unfortunately, some of these are very hard to measure—evaporation especially—and quantitative assessment of losses takes second place to the identification of the areas of leakage (so that remedial work such as grouting can be carried out effectively). Nuclear technology is useful in doing this and both environmental and artificially introduced isotope tracers can be employed.

Environmental tracers include deuterium and oxygen-18 and these can be used in determining the sub-surface hydraulic interconnections of lakes, reservoirs and, for that matter, canals carrying water of reservoir origin with groundwater aquifers and springs. Fractionation occurs during evaporation, the evaporating water body becoming progressively enriched in the heavy stable isotopes, as was seen earlier. This enrichment effect is marked in lakes and other surface water bodies where evaporation is high compared with inflow. In lakes and reservoirs with a rapid turnover, the effect is smaller but still significant. Both D and ^{18}O are normally used in studies of this kind. This is better than using one or the other because since the relative enrichment of each isotope is different results so obtained are more conclusive. The accompanying Fig. 4.1 shows the results of a study made in south central Turkey from which it was possible to demonstrate clearly that the hypothesis of interconnection of two large lakes where water is lost through fractured limestone with some large limestone springs is not tenable, as T. Dincer and E. Halevy pointed out.[4] An even more interesting experimental programme involved the crater lake Lake Chala in Kenya, to which allusion has been made earlier; this was described by Bryan R. Payne in 1970.[5] The work commenced as a result of the consideration of the feasibility of using water from this lake for expanding the Taveta irrigation scheme in Kenya and as a part of the investigation isotopes were first used in 1964

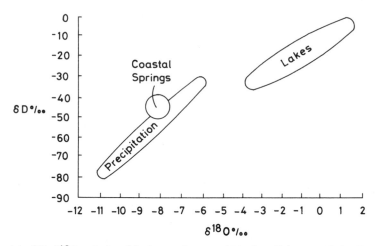

FIG. 4.1. δD–$\delta^{18}O$ relationship in south central Turkey (lakes are Lake Burdur, Lake Beysehir and Lake Egridir).

to examine the relationship of the lake to springs in the area and the turnover time of the water in the lake. Deuterium and oxygen-18 data indicated that there is no major discharge of lake water to the springs.[6] However, the exit point of the lake water had to be determined. Lake Chala has an area of $4\cdot2\,km^2$ with a volume of $3 \times 10^8\,m^3$ and a maximum depth of $100\,m$. It has no surface inflow or outflow hence the assumption that it feeds the springs on the west bank of the Lumi River to the south (this ends in Lake Jipe) is shown to be incorrect. Artificially injected tritium (HTO) was used in estimating the water balance of the lake and over a period of five years mean annual sub-surface inflow and outflow was estimated at $12.5 \times 10^6 \, m^3$ and $8.2 \times 10^6 \, m^3$ respectively. The conclusion was that environmental tritium cannot be used for such a balance estimation. 1900 Ci of tritium were introduced into the lake and the initial tritium concentration was computed as 1600 TU. This is the basis of the determination of the lake volume stated above. Of course some of these estimates depend upon inadequately known parameters such as evaporation and relative humidity. A sensitivity test found, for instance, that a 1% change in this latter could cause a 14% change in the estimate of outflow. Data on the stable isotope composition of the waters in the lake, in Lake Jipe, in the springs and in precipitation are shown on the accompanying δD–$\delta^{18}O$ graph in Fig. 4.2.

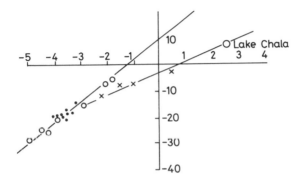

FIG. 4.2. Stable isotope composition of waters in Lake Chala investigation. $\times$, Lake Jipe; ●, springs; ○, precipitation.

This illustrates immediately that the isotopic composition of the springs is completely different from that of Lake Chala and the springs and precipitation values fall along the line of slope 8. By contrast the isotopic compositions of samples from Lake Jipe and Lake Chala lie along a line of slope 4 and this is, of course, characteristic of open water bodies subjected to evaporation. The shift of Lake Chala is thought to indicate that it has a longer residence time and thus is more removed from the precipitation line than Lake Jipe. Continuing the theme of isotopic studies on lakes, the work of J. R. Gat on the environmental isotope balance of Lake Tiberias (the Sea of Galilee or Lake Kinneret) in Israel is very important.[8] The stable isotope composition and tritium content of Lake Tiberias were monitored over a decade and the ^{18}O concentration of the upper water mass was shown to undergo a yearly cycle of average amplitude of $\Delta\delta^{18}O = 0.5‰$. The hypolimnion follows the change at much lower amplitude. Deuterium concentrations change similarly and obey the relationship

$$\Delta\delta D = 5\cdot3 \times \Delta\delta^{18}O$$

The mean annual isotope composition shifts up to $\pm1\cdot5\%$ for ^{18}O as a result of hydrological imbalances between water gain and loss.

The stable isotope inventory of the lake can be expressed as

$$d\delta_L/dt = \frac{1}{V_L}\left[\sum I_i\delta_i - E\delta_E - (O + \frac{dV}{dt})\delta_L\right]$$

where V_L is the lake volume, I_i is the inflow rate of water, E and O are the evaporation and liquid outflow rates respectively and δ_i, δ_E, δ_L are the isotope contents of inflow, evaporative flux and the lake in δ units. This equation applies both to the oxygen-18 and the deuterium balance. Unlike tritium, there is no systematic secular change in the δ values of both the inflow and the lake, but both vary seasonally as well as in response to hydrological imbalances.

As regards the tritium balance, this is given by

$$\frac{d(VT)_L}{dt} = \sum_i I_i T_i - O T_L - \lambda (VT)_L - u(\beta T_L - h T_a)$$

and the hydrological balance of a mixed lake is given by

$$\frac{dV_L}{dt} = \sum_i I_i - (E + O)$$

where V_L is the lake volume, T_L is its tritium content, I_i the inflow rate of water, T_i the respective tritium content, E and O evaporation and liquid outflow rates respectively, β the tritium fractionation factor for the liquid–vapour transition, λ the tritium decay rate, T_a the tritium concentration in atmospheric water vapour, u the exchange rate of surface air with the atmosphere (a function of the wind stress at the surface) and h the atmospheric water vapour content normalised to that of saturated vapour at the temperature of the lake surface (normalised humidity). The last term of the penultimate equation gives the tritium flux into the atmosphere and can be broken up into the flux of tritium carried by evaporation and an exchange flux where $E \neq O$.

A tritium balance equation calculation derived from the above argument was carried out by J. R. Gat for Lake Tiberias which acted as a model for a semi-arid zone lake. In the assumption it is implicit that ideal mixing has occurred in the lake so that no review of the homogeneity of tritium levels in it is required. No areal variations of significance were found except near the mouth of the Jordan River and this conforms with the pattern of salinity. Vertically, the seasonal stratification is reflected by the tritium data and, as expected, the hypolimnion retains the characteristics of the mixed winter lake through the summer, the epilimnion alone responding to changes in the tritium input.

General interrelations are demonstrated in Fig. 4.3. The lake lies about 210 m below mean sea level, is about 170 km² in area and attains a maximum depth of 43 m. It possesses a thermally controlled seasonal stratification which disappears in winter and there are no permanent currents, the Jordan River not actually flowing through the lake. It is interesting that large scale seiches occur.

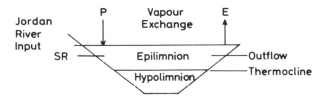

FIG. 4.3. Schema of Lake Tiberias. SR, springs/runoff; E, evaporation; P, precipitation.

Work on Saharan lakes, Lake Neusiedl in Austria and Perch Lake has been discussed earlier (in Chapter 2) because of its relevance to the atmosphere–surface water interrelationship. Environmental isotopes have been used also in establishing the hydraulic connections in a series of lakes and springs near Athens in Greece.[7]

As regards reservoirs, leakage may be a serious problem and the movement of water impounded by an earth dam may be studied by monitoring the behaviour of a radioactive isotope tracer in a piezometer network after an injection is made at an upstream piezometer as E. Gaspar and M. Onescu showed in 1963.[9]

The point dilution method was used in locating a leak at the Rosshaupten Dam which had to be tightened subsequently and at the Krün Dam the adequacy of an injected tightening apparatus was controlled before and after application. J. Mairhofer checked the efficiency of a seal applied to a leaky spot in a reservoir in 1966.[10]

Reservoir waters may be labelled totally in cases where there is no significant enrichment in these with respect to D and ^{18}O and for this purpose an appropriate radioisotope is utilised, for instance ^{131}I. The reappearance of the radiotracer at the suspected outlet(s) provides evidence of the connection between the reservoir with the point of monitoring. The radioisotope alluded to was used by J. Guizerix and his associates in 1966 to label a reservoir of capacity $35 \times 10^6\,\mathrm{m}^3$ with inactive NaI.[11]

An alternative approach is to use the radioactive cloud method which consists of injecting the radiotracer at the bottom of a reservoir where the leakage outlet path is known and then monitoring the evolution of the consequent radioactive cloud with time. Deformations of the cloud may arise as a result of currents, but can be useful indicators of leakiness. At the Kruth Wildenstein earth dam in France, the method was used and the radioisotopes ^{131}I and tritium employed were both injected simultaneously in the reservoir near the dam.[11]

The filter tube method consists of inserting a filter tube for an injection of a tracer in the suspected area of leakage with subsequent monitoring of the acitivity at the suspected exit point. This method uses less radioactive isotope tracer than total labelling or the radioactive cloud method.

Low velocity currents at the bottom of a reservoir may be measured using the deep water isotopic current analyser (DWICA) which comprises a central injection unit and eight peripherally placed detectors. Velocities as low as 1 mm/sec can be assessed, but the disadvantage is that the quantity of seepage which would create such current velocities is rather high.[12]

In 1970 A. Zuber proposed a method for determining leakage velocities through the bottom of reservoirs.[13] This is based upon the flow conservation principle. If a certain area of the bed of the reservoir is covered by a cylinder open at the base and with a pipe inlet at the top, the leakage (filtration) velocity, v_f, can be expressed by

$$v_f = v \frac{s}{S} = \frac{r^2 l}{R^2 t_0}$$

through a covered area S where v is the mean flow velocity in the inlet pipe, s is the cross-sectional area of the inlet pipe, t_0 is the mean transit time of flow along the pipe length l, and r and R are the inner radii of the pipe and cylinder respectively. The instrument is illustrated in Fig. 4.4.

Transit time against filtration velocity measurements show that a reasonably short transit time can be obtained even for a very low

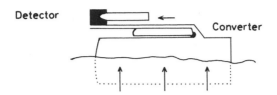

FIG. 4.4. Leakage velocity gauge for inflow.

filtration velocity. Two assumptions are made. One is that the area S is tightly covered so that the flow rate through it is equal to the flow rate through the inlet pipe. The second requires a negligible loss of the potential in the pipe as compared with the loss along the edge of the cylinder which is pressed tightly into the bed material. Thus the presence of the measuring instrument should not disturb natural flow lines and the filtration velocity which is measured may be taken as equal to the natural filtration velocity. Apropos the first assumption this is satisfied by correct design of the instrument. Apropos the second, satisfaction is derived from an electrical analogy. The potential drop in the pipe expressed in cm of water (Δh) for laminar flow is given by

$$\Delta h = \frac{8v\Delta lv}{gr^2}$$

where v is the kinematic viscosity which at $10°C$ is $1\cdot3 \times 10^{-2}$ cm^2/sec, Δl is the pipe length, g the acceleration due to gravity and r the radius of the pipe. As is shown by the Reynolds number calculated for the highest filtration velocity together with the instrument parameters there is laminar flow in the inlet pipe. Two instruments with different cylinder diameters had parameters as follows:
(1) $I = 30$ cm, $R = 19\cdot5$ cm, $r = 0\cdot475$ cm; (2) $I = 30$ cm, $R = 100$ cm, $r = 0\cdot475$ cm and

$$R_e = \frac{2rv}{v} = \frac{2R^2 v_f}{vr} = 69$$

below the critical value. The potential drop in the medium (dh) contained within the cylinder edge is determinable with some simplifying assumptions from Darcy's Law and the equation on page 170.

$$dh = \frac{vr^2 dl}{kR^2}$$

where dl is the thickness of the medium layer within the instrument edge which is roughly equal to the edge length and k is the filtration coefficient in cm/sec. Measurements made on a three-dimensional electrical model gave a function

$$\frac{v_f(\text{measured})}{v_f(\text{true})} = f\left(F, \frac{dl}{R}\right)$$

where

$$F = \frac{\Delta h}{dh} = \frac{8v\Delta l R^2 k}{gr^4 dl}$$

and dl/R is a parameter resulting from the condition of the geometric similitude. Experiments facilitate the determination of the parameter F for an assumed accuracy of v_f and selected dl/R. By the application of the equation on page 170 plus the equation above and with some technical limitations, it is feasible to choose instrument parameters for an arbitrarily accepted maximum value of the filtration coefficient k.

If the influence of the temperature gradient existing in a reservoir is considered then the equation for potential drop in a pipe for laminar flow becomes

$$\Delta h' = \Delta h + \frac{\Delta \rho}{\rho}\delta l$$

where $\Delta \rho$ is the average density difference between the water in the inlet pipe and the surrounding water and δl is the pipe length along which the temperature gradient exists. Further, applying the equation on page 170 and rearranging

$$F = \frac{\Delta h'}{dh} \approx \left(\frac{8v\Delta l R^2}{gr^4 dl} - \frac{\Delta \rho}{\rho v_f}\frac{\delta l}{dl}\right)k$$

From this formula it is clear that the temperature effect is dependent upon the velocity in the pipe or approximately on the true filtration velocity.

The temperature effect is independent of the flow direction but it can hinder measurements of low filtration velocities in very permeable media. If a gradient of 2°C per metre is assumed then if the vertical part of the pipe is 5 cm long the average density difference at 10°C is equal to 5×10^{-6} g/cm^3.

After construction of the instrument the measurements are confined to determination of the mean transit time of a laminar flow in the pipe, bearing in mind that when this is short there is no molecular diffusion. In this case if the injection can be described by the delta function, the first tracer and its maximum concentration appear at a time equal to one-half of the mean flow transit time and a long tail of the breakthrough curve is observed. For long transit times, in the case of small pipe diameter, molecular diffusion becomes dominant and an almost normal distribution of the tracer about the mean flow transit time is observed. Little information is available on interpretation of the mean transit time from breakthrough curves in the intermediate range where such extreme cases may overlap. Attempts to solve this problem were made using experiments effected with a laminar flow in a pipe. Breakthrough curves were calculated for a wide spectrum of velocities and mean transit time calculated from these compared with that known from the flow rate. Counting was effected with a standard 1 inch scintillation detector. It was found that density differences greater than 10^{-4} g/cm^3 can cause serious errors and to avoid density effects a high specific activity radioisotope tracer solution is required. The temperature of the injected solution is the same as that of water in the pipe. In the experiments described, A. Zuber[13] was unable to obtain radioisotopes of high specific activity. The density differences of the active solution actually used were compensated for by adding alcohol and for the highest velocities transit time was of the order of a few seconds. All measurements were interpreted as well using four other methods, namely the mean transit time of the tracer, the transit time of the maximum concentration, the mean harmonic transit time and the transit time of 50% of the tracer. In 1969 measurements were effected in artificial reservoirs on a network of five measuring points and these reservoirs had the dimensions 6 m × 4 m and a depth of approximately 2 m. Results showed good reproducibility and proper response to changes in height of the water table. Particular measurements in the network differed by a factor of 2·5 as a result of differences in permeability of bed material (sands and silty sands). Measurements done after sealing showed a higher scatter of the leakage velocity. Leakage rates obtained from water balance observations (not done simultaneously) were on average 30% lower than those found by the leakage gauge. The reason for this is not known. Of course the method cannot easily be utilised in deep waters nor can it be employed on a rocky bed although modification of the instrument should overcome this latter problem. This might involve using a flange collar which would obviate the necessity for the cylinder edge to be pressed into the bed material.

In this connection the work of A. I. Danilin is relevant.[14] He discussed the results of experiments on moisture conditions in the ground near an irrigation channel and a reservoir and the area of ground affected using neutron moisture gauges and gamma densimeters. Observations of the moisture movement and soil density were made in permanent boreholes up to 16·5 m deep lined with 2 inch steel tubes sealed at the bottom. To measure the moisture use was made of a probe with a high efficiency, low level, slow neutron detector of the LDNM type ($ZnS(Ag)$–B_2O_3) contained therein alongside a $Pu + Be$ neutron source thus facilitating the obtaining of a linear dependence between the thermal neutron count and soil moisture. A portable scaler was used for measurement. In the case of the recording of soil density the LDNM scintillation crystal in the probe was replaced by an NaI(Tl) single crystal and a lengthener with a steel screen with a position on the casing to which it was screwed. The conical end of the lengthener contained a gamma source (^{137}Cs) with an activity given as 2 meq of radium. The length of the probe was 35 cm. These studies enabled determination of the rate at which the soil near the reservoir is moistened and thus established the areas of loessal loams which were moistened by the irrigation channel. The technique is therefore applicable to the problem of measuring the rate of water seepage both from irrigation channels and reservoirs in loessal loams.

4.4 ^{18}O AND D CONCENTRATIONS WITH REFERENCE TO THE WATER BALANCE OF LAKES

Friedman and others studied American lakes in water balance work and compared the deuterium concentration in their inflow with that in the outflow, assuming good mixing.[15] Tritium was used too and its concentrations were measured, subsequent studies being based upon the relation between the inflow capacity ratio of the lakes and the dilution rate of the thermonuclear bomb-produced tritium in their waters. However, molecular exchange between atmospheric water vapour and the lake surface was not taken into account although it is a very important factor needing consideration with regard to evaporating surface water bodies.

The water balance of a lake or reservoir may be expressed as in the equation on page 87 and a variant is as follows:

$$\Delta V = I_s \Delta t + I_g \Delta t + P - R \Delta t - L \Delta t - E \Delta t$$

where ΔV is the volume increment of the water body during a time interval Δt, I_s is the mean rate of surface inflow during the same period, I_g the mean rate of groundwater contribution during the same period, P the quantity of precipitation during the same period, R the mean rate of surface outflow during Δt, L the mean rate of sub-surface outflow during the same period and E the mean rate of evaporation during the same period. Of course, where appreciable seepage losses occur it is difficult to estimate factors such as L and more equations are required to determine the inflow and the losses from it.

Salt or isotope balance equations may be employed to solve the problem and their usage depends upon the feasibility of estimating their concentrations in the terms which are in the mass balance equation. As T. Dincer has indicated in discussing the approach, the use of tracer balance equations is possible only in the case where the tracer concentration in the system's output differs significantly from that in the input as a result of molecular exchange and resulting evaporation in the situation involving the stable isotopes D and ^{18}O as well as tritium or isotopic fractionation or loss of tracer due to radioactive decay or dispersion and mixing processes during storage and transit of water in the system.[16] The isotope tracers of water are actually very advantageous because their concentrations are much less variable spatially and chronologically than are those of non-isotopic tracers. However, their greatest advantage is their resistance to removal by adsorption or other processes owing to the very large relative quantity of water carrier.

An equation valid for any tracer if present in measurable quantities in the lake or reservoir water and not suffering adsorptive or other losses is

$$C\Delta V - V\Delta C = C_i I_i \Delta t - C_g I_g \Delta t - C_p P - C_s R\Delta t - C_L L\Delta t - C_E E\Delta t$$

where C represents mean concentrations connected with volumes and flow and evaporation rates and V is the mean volume of the reservoir during a time interval Δt. If the tracer is radioactive then an additional factor on the right-hand side would be added (λCV, where λ is the fraction of radioactive tracer lost during the time interval Δt). Where precipitation occurs in defined time slots (monsoonal seasons for instance) all terms relating to liquid inflow (including the precipitation) may be lumped together in a simple expression

$$V\Delta C = [I(C_i - C_L) - E(C_E - C_L)]\Delta t$$

and when the mean residence time of the water is long

$$I(C_i - C_L) - E(C_E - C_L) = 0$$

C is the mean isotopic composition of the inflow to the lake including the precipitation over it.

Factors which influence the isotopic composition of lake and reservoir waters include:

(i) Climatic factors, especially the isotopic composition of the atmospheric moisture which has parallel variations to that observed in precipitation. However, the atmospheric moisture does not of necessity have a composition similar to the water vapour which would be in equilibrium with precipitation in the same area.

(ii) Hydrologic factors such as the locations of the inflow and outflow points and the existence of layering (as a result of the latter, isotopically light inflow water can depart from the reservoir through a deep outlet or isotopically heavy water may be discharged through a spillway of a natural river channel). Here the mean isotopic composition of the lake waters will not have significance in relation to the water balance.

The basic equation for evaporation from a water body is as follows:

$$E = k(e_w - e_a)$$

where E is the rate of evaporation, e_w the saturated water vapour pressure at the temperature of the water, e_a the atmospheric water vapour pressure and k a constant under given conditions. Evaporation has been shown to be proportional to the wind velocity and moisture gradients over the evaporating water body and inversely proportional to the atmospheric pressure. In fact, the factor k is primarily a function of the velocity of the wind. An equation taking into account the evaporation of the heavier isotopic species of water (HDO and $H_2{}^{18}O$) is

$$E_i = k_i(e_{wi} - e_{ai})$$

and here the subscript 'i' indicates the relation of the terms to the relevant isotopic species. This is relevant to a pure isotopic species evaporating in an atmosphere in which the partial vapour pressure of the given species is e_{ai}. As a result of the different coefficient of molecular diffusion of the heavier isotopic species in the air the factor k is also different from the factor used in the evaporation of the water containing the lighter molecular species.

In a natural water body with an isotopic concentration of C_w the ratio between the total evaporation and the evaporation of any given isotope species, that is to say the isotopic composition of the net water vapour flux, is given by

$$E_i/E = (k_i/k)\,(e_{wi}C_w - e_{ai})/(e_w - e_a)$$

in the case where C_w is small.

If $e_{ai}/e_a = C_a$ and $k/k_i = K$ and bearing in mind that $e_w/e_{wi} = \alpha$ (the equilibrium fractionation factor) since the vapour pressures are related to saturation it is possible to write

$$C_E = \frac{E_i}{E} = \frac{1}{K}\left[\frac{e_w C_w}{\alpha(e_w - e_a)} - \frac{e_a C_a}{e_w - e_a}\right]$$

Dividing numerators and denominators of the right-hand side of the above equation the result is

$$C_E = [(C_w/\alpha) - hC_a]/K(1-h)$$

where h is (e_a/e_w), the relative humidity normalised to the water surface temperature. In this case C is the isotope ratio in the location where the relative humidity is measured. This last equation can be used to get the isotopic composition of the evaporating water in special conditions. For instance, where $C_E = C_w$, i.e. when an isolated water body reaches constant isotopic content, then the isotope content of the water is obtained thus

$$C_w = \alpha h C_a/[1 - K\alpha(1-h)]$$

This is also the last isotopic content of the evaporating water body when its volume is appreciably reduced by evaporation.

A second case cited by Dincer is obtained by assuming that $C_E = C_a$ and this means that the water has to exchange with the water vapour which originates from itself

$$C_a = C_w/\alpha(K(1-h) + h]$$

K is always greater than unity and so it is apparent that the equilibrium fractionation factor is smaller than the apparent fractionation factor. Cases of this type are observed in very large water bodies such as oceans.

The third case of special relevance to lake studies takes place when part of the water vapour with which the lake water has to exchange is produced by the lake itself with the rest arising elsewhere. Here

$$C_E = \frac{1}{K(1-h)}\left[\frac{C_w}{\alpha} - (mhC_a + nhC_E)\right]$$

Solution of this with respect to C_E gives

$$C_E = \frac{1}{K - Kmh - Knh - nh}\left(\frac{C_w}{\alpha} - mhC_a\right)$$

from which, since $Knh \cong nh$, simplification gives

$$C_E \cong 1/K(1-mh)\,(C_w/\alpha - mhC_a)$$

i.e. a reasonable approximation showing that water vapour produced by the lake has little influence on the isotopic composition of the net water vapour flux from the lake; it is, therefore, enough to know the isotopic composition of the water vapour at the point of measurement of relative humidity irrespective of the relationship of this point to the actual lake area.

Dissolved salts reduce evaporation because they lower the saturated water vapour pressure of the evaporating water which can be estimated using Raoult's Law (valid for dilute solutions) given by

$$X = e_w/e_0 = n_1/(n_1 - n_2)$$

where X is the activity of the water, e_0 is the vapour pressure of the pure solvent at a given temperature, e_w the vapour pressure of the solution at the same temperature, n_1 the number of moles of the solvent and n_2 the number of moles of the solute.

If the fifth equation on page 177 is combined with this and assuming that the presence of salts has the same effect on activities of the various isotopic species the following is obtained

$$C_E = 1/[K(X-h)]\,[(XC_w/\alpha) - hC_a]\,K(X-h)$$

R. Gonfiantini in 1965 showed that the effect of salinity in evaporating water causes a reduced isotopic enrichment of the water.[17] The accompanying Fig. 4.5 illustrates the effect. From it, it may be seen that low values of salinity ought not to affect the isotopic enrichment of evaporating waters. Where $X = 0.97$ (roughly corresponding to the activity of sea water) the effect on salinity is comparable with a 3% variation in relative humidity.[16] The extent of this salinity effect can be checked by comparing points representing fresh lakes with closed lakes in a $\delta D - \delta O^{18}$ graph. If the assumption is made that the inflow waters and atmospheric moisture have the same isotopic composition then a significant departure of a point representing a closed lake from the evaporation line defined by fresh lakes will indicate the existence of an appreciable salinity effect. If

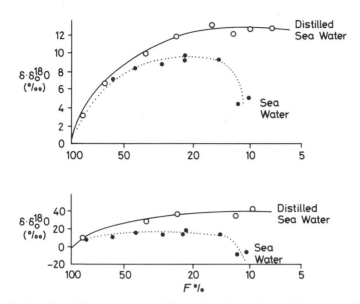

F_IG. 4.5. Gonfiantini's experiments illustrating isotopic enrichment of distilled and sea water during evaporation, F being the volume fraction remaining.[17]

the isotopic composition of the closed lake agrees with the evaporation line this indicates low salinity and the absence of the salinity effect. Taking the case of a deep and closed lake with a constant isotopic composition, C_E may be replaced by C_i in the last equation and to solve for C_a giving

$$C_a = X C'_L / \alpha_{h'} - [K(X - h')/h'] C'_i$$

where the primes indicate that the symbols utilised relate to a closed lake. Assuming—reasonably—that in an area with uniform climatic factors there will be no appreciable variation of isotopic composition of atmospheric water vapour the value of C_a obtained from the equation of the net water vapour flux from a fresh lake may be inserted so as to obtain

$$C_E = \frac{1}{K(1-h)} \left[\frac{C_L}{\alpha} - h \left(\frac{X C'_L}{\alpha h'} - \frac{K(X - h')}{h'} C'_i \right) \right]$$

It is further assumed that the surface temperatures of the lakes are close to the atmospheric temperatures and that the relative humidity does not vary appreciably so that

$$C_E = (C_L - XC_L')/[K\alpha(1-h)] + C_i(X-h)/(1-h)$$

From this it may be seen that no great error can arise in the estimation of C_E in assuming approximate values of K and X. Actually, it is even feasible to assume a value of unity for each.

Referring again to the equation relating to precipitation taking place in well defined periods of the year such as monsoons (second equation on page 175) and inserting the value of C_E from the above equation in that earlier one, the following expression is obtained

$$V\Delta C = I(C_i - C_L)\Delta t - E\left[\frac{C_L - C_L'}{(1-h)} - C_i' - C_L\right]\Delta t$$

This can be utilised to estimate the inflow to a fresh water lake or reservoir using the isotopic composition of a closed lake as a regional index to molecular exchange between the lake waters and the atmospheric moisture. This is providing that an independent estimate of evaporation is made by employing conventional methods, also that reliable estimates of the isotopic concentrations in the lakes and in the inflow waters are available. Dincer suggested that in humid regions where there are no saline lakes, a fresh lake can be used if it has a known water balance (based on a personal communication from J. R. Gat in 1968).[16] In this case the treatment is the same as that described above and an equation similar to the ultimate one above is obtainable. Dincer applied the method in southwestern Turkey where several fresh and salt lakes occur, some being ephemeral. The isotope concentrations in the waters are very well known because the region has been investigated since 1963 and one of the aims of the investigation was to determine possible interconnections between the lakes in the inland region with coastal springs using isotope compositions. The two fresh water lakes of importance are Lake Egridir (elevation 924 m) with a volume of 3.5×10^9 m^3 and a surface area of 470 km^2 and Lake Beysehir (elevation 1125 m) with a volume of 4×10^9 m^3 and a surface area of 700 km^2. Both are utilised as storage for irrigation and hydropower production. There is a long residence time for waters in both and this results in the loss of a great quantity of water by evaporation. Also, there are losses due to sinkholes and fractured limestone terrain. The amounts of these losses are difficult to assess because it is difficult to make such estimates in sinkhole and fractured rock conditions. A water budget has been established for Lake

Beysehir by Dincer and for an average year he gave the following data:[16]

Inflow to the lake	$1100 \times 10^6 \, \text{m}^3$
Precipitation over the lake	$350 \times 10^6 \, \text{m}^3$
Irrigation release	$250 \times 10^6 \, \text{m}^3$
Evaporation	$700 \times 10^6 \, \text{m}^3$
Sinkhole and fractionation losses	$500 \times 10^6 \, \text{m}^3$

In both of these lakes the areas of loss are known, the lake bottoms are flat and they are covered by an impermeable blue clay deposit excluding any possibility of seepage through them. A third lake is Lake Burdur (elevation 1000 m); this has similar temperature and atmospheric moisture conditions to the previous two. It is a saline lake and so the possibility arose of using it as an index for the molecular exchange in the region where all three lakes are situated and to employ the last equation (opposite) to estimate the water balance of the fresh lakes. The total dissolved solids content of Lake Burdur is 23 000 ppm and this is not uninteresting because it means that the salinity effect is not expected to significantly influence the isotopic fractionation in the lake. Areal samplings showed that the lakes can be regarded as fairly homogeneous except for a few pockets near major tributaries and so the isotope values obtained are representative of the mean isotopic composition. No areal survey was made, however, in Lake Burdur.

From the precipitation data here and in Lake Egridir it was possible to state that the mean deuterium and oxygen-18 content for December to April (when most of the precipitation takes place) 1964–65 was $\delta D = -56.5\permille$, $\delta O_{18} = -8.95\permille$. Corresponding values were higher for Konya which lies further inland and is more arid. The above (winter) values are probably on the heavy side because the inflow water to the lakes consists not only of direct precipitation but also of waters originating from the tributary basin which ought to have a lighter isotopic composition owing to the altitude effect.

Groundwater and spring sample values showed the same range of values as winter precipitation and actually carry more weight because they integrate the isotopic composition of several years of recharge.

The intersection of the evaporation and precipitation lines can be used to estimate the isotopic composition of the inflow waters to the lakes (see Fig. 4.1). This point is close to $\delta D = -55\permille$, $\delta O_{18} = -8.75\permille$, which agrees well with the previous estimate of the isotopic composition of the inflow to the lakes. As regards the mean isotopic composition of the lake waters an appropriate time interval must be selected to calculate this and of course variations are significant because they affect the outcome of using the equation for $V\Delta C$ on page 180. The period November 1963 to October 1966 was considered optimal and significant variations are apparent during this time. If the annual evaporation is taken to be constant, then the heavier isotopic composition of lake waters during the water year 1963–64 indicates unusually low inflow to the lakes (especially Lake Beysehir). This was in fact confirmed by the lake level and runoff records which showed that 1963–64 was a very dry year. Evaporation was estimated using Class A pan-evaporation data from the Beysehir meteorological station. α values utilised corresponded to the mean annual atmospheric temperatures in the region of the lakes and for K an approximate value of 1·01 was used. Table 4.2 gives details of estimates of annual inflow (i.e. including precipitation) to Lake Beysehir and Lake Egridir.[16]

TABLE 4.2

$\alpha_D = 1\cdot08$, $\alpha_{18} = 1\cdot009$, $K = 1\cdot01$, INFLOW $\delta_D = -55\%$, $\delta O_{18} = -8\cdot75$, $h = 56\%$ WEIGHTED BY THE SECOND EQUATION, PAGE 180 LAKE BURDUR MEAN ISOTOPIC COMPOSITION $\delta_D = -2\cdot0\%$ $\delta O_{18} = +1\cdot6\%$

Lake	Annual inflow $(10^6 \, \text{m}^3)^a$	Annual losses $(10^6 \, \text{m}^3)$
Beysehir		
$\delta_D = -14\cdot7$	1 157	207
$\delta_D = -17$	1 277	327
$\delta O_{18} = -1\cdot27$	1 265	315
$\delta O_{18} = -0\cdot87$	1 205	255
Egridir		
$\delta_D = -24\cdot4$	1 035	315
$\delta O_{18} = -2\cdot36$	1 033	313

^{a} Includes precipitation over the lake.

This table illustrates the large differences between inflow estimates using D and ^{18}O and these are explicable by a sensitivity test of the equation for $V\Delta C$ on page 180 which demonstrates that the most significant parameter in calculating the inflow is in fact the isotopic composition of the lake waters. An error of only 1% in the estimate of the mean deuterium content, for instance, results in a change of almost 5% in the estimate of the inflow. The answer is to collect a large number of samples for analysis because this facilitates determination of the most accurate value of the mean isotopic composition of the lake waters. An interesting result of the test was that it emphasised the reduced importance of the determination of the fractionation factor, the relative humidity and the factor K used to cover kinetic effects during the process of evaporation, and this arises from the fact that all of these factors are utilised to divide the difference of two isotope ratios or concentrations rather than dividing an actual isotope ratio. Dincer's work is of the greatest importance because it shows that the D and ^{18}O contents of lake waters can be used in determination of the water balance of lakes where some components of this are not well known, a situation common in lakes or reservoirs in fractured rock areas such as karst in which losses difficult to estimate quantitatively will arise. Of course adequate sampling of precipitation, runoff and the lake waters themselves plus other meteorological factors such as atmospheric temperature and humidity is mandatory in the obtaining of conclusive results. The extension of the method to humid regions is feasible.

4.5. THE TOTAL LAKE WATER RESOURCES OF THE EARTH

It has been estimated that the total area of the $c.$ three million lakes on the planet is $2\cdot7 \times 10^6 \, km^2$ and it is not an easy task to evaluate the lake water resources. Some useful information is appended in Table 4.3.

As may be seen the nineteen largest lakes listed in the table account for almost 38% of the total lake area of the planet. G. P. Tamrazyan has indicated that if the six largest lakes in the USSR in the list are excluded then all the remaining lakes in that country (2 814 723 according to him) account for $0\cdot423 \times 10^6 \, km^2$ or a quarter of the area of all the smaller lakes of the planet so that data obtained there and multiplied by a factor of four can be used to characterise the water resources of all the minor planetary lakes.[18] He added that this relation is further substantiated by the fact that 95% of the lakes in the USSR and 85% of their total area are located between the 50th and 75th northern parallels in conditions similar to those of most lakes in other parts of the Earth.

A. P. Domanitskiy and his associates have presented relevant data on the water bodies (lakes and reservoirs) of the USSR which are appended in Table 4.4.[19]

Some interesting relationships are found between the depth of a conventional lake belonging to the category being studied and the total area of all lakes within this category. These are taken from lakes possessing reliable data and are shown in Table 4.5.

TABLE 4.3

THE WORLD'S LARGEST LAKES, I.E. WITH WATER VOLUME ≥ 300 km^3 IN DESCENDING ORDER[18]

Lake	Location	Area $(10^6 \, km^2)$	Water volume $(\times 10^3 \, km^3)$
Caspian Sea	Eurasia	0·424	76·8
Baikal	Asia	0·031	22·8
Tanganyika	Africa	0·034	16·7
Superior	North America	0·082	12·2
Nyasa	Africa	0·031	5·8
Michigan	North America	0·058	5·1
Huron	North America	0·060	4·1
Victoria	Africa	0·068	3·0
Maracaibo	South America	0·013	1·9
Great Slave	North America	0·029	1·8
Issyk-kul'	Asia	0·006	1·7
Ontario	North America	0·020	1·6
Great Bear	North America	0·030	1·3
Aral Sea	Asia	0·066	1·0
Ladoga	Europe	0·018	0·9
Titicaca	South America	0·008	0·7
Kivu	Africa	0·003	0·4
Erie	North America	0·026	0·3
Onega	Europe	0·010	0·3
Total		1·017	158·4
All other lakes together		1·683	7·4
Total		2·710	165·8

TABLE 4.4

WATER BODIES OF THE USSR[19]

Water table area (km^2)	Number of water reservoirs	Total lake area (km^2)
<1	2 814 727	159 532
1–10	36 896	87 075
10–50	2 124	39 974
50–100	234	15 939
100–1 000	159	42 324
>1 000	26	143 596
Total	2 854 166	488 440

TABLE 4.5
AVERAGE DEPTHS OF CONVENTIONAL LAKES AND LAKE CATEGORIES[18]

Category (km^2)	Number of lakes	Total area, $S(km^2)$	Total water volume, $V(km^3)$	$l=V/S$ (m)
50–500	82	11 663	56·3	4·8
500–5 000	17	28 691	260·3	9·1
5 000–50 000	5	117 290	2 381	20·3

$l=V/S$ is the average depth of a conventional lake per 1 km^2 of the total lake area for a certain category of lake.

The factor l in Table 4.5 grows from category to category by a factor of approximately two as the category size gets higher and it is believed that the relation will hold also for lakes with smaller dimensions. On this basis the following average depths for conventional lakes may be anticipated:

2·4 m for the category with an area of $S=5$–$50\,km^2$,
1·2 m for the category with an area of $S=0·5$–$5\,km^2$,
0·6 m for the category with an area of $S=0·05$–$0·5\,km^2$.

The relation between the average area of a lake from each category and the category itself has been examined also and the following data obtained (Table 4.6).[18]

TABLE 4.6
AREA OF AN AVERAGE LAKE IN EACH LAKE CATEGORY

Category (km^2)	Number of lakes	Total area (km^2)	Average area of one lake	Notes
1–10	36 896	87 075	2·4	USSR
10–100	2 360	55 913	23·8	USSR
100–1 000	159	42 324	266·2	USSR
1 000–10 000	120	304 000	2 530	Earth

If the average area of a category is increased tenfold (ascending) then the average area for a lake will be roughly greater by a factor of 10 and will be characterised by the figure series 2·4, 23·8 and 266·2. Designating the average area of a lake as K, then $K=2·4\times10^n$ where n is the category of lake. For category $S=1$–$10\,km^2$, $n=0$; for category $S=10$–$100\,km^2$, $n=1$ and so on. This relation has been employed in order to calculate the total volume of all USSR lake waters, see Table 4.7.[18]

The total quantity of water in lakes where $S<1000\,km^2$ is only 770 km^3 and the proportion of those water bodies of the $S<1\,km^2$

TABLE 4.7
LAKE WATER VOLUMES IN THE USSR

Category (km^2)	Number of lakes	Total area (km^2)	Water volumes $(X\,10^6\,km^3)$	(%)
<1	2 814 727	159 532	0·12	0̄12
1–10	36 896	87 075	0·15	0·14
10–100	2 360	55 913	0·20	0·19
100–1 000	159	42 324	0·30	0·29
1 000–10 000	12	43 830	2·27	2·18
10 000–100 000	4	133 500	24·12	23·21
>100 000	1	424 300	76·80	73·87
Total	2 854 159	946 474	103·96	100·00

category is only 121 km³. In the USSR there are actually 12 natural lakes having $S = 1000$–$10\,000$ with a water volume of $2·27 \times 10^3$ km³, 4 lakes of $S = 10\,000$–$100\,000$ category with a water volume of $24·12 \times 10^3$ km³ (namely Baikal, Ladoga, Aral and Balkhash) and the Caspian Sea with a water volume of about 77×10^3 km³. Tamrazyan stated that the USSR contains 35% of the surfaces of all lakes and over 62% of the lake water volumes of the entire Earth.[18] His data on the total quantity of lake waters on the planet are appended in Table 4.8.

TABLE 4.8
LAKE WATER VOLUMES OF THE EARTH

Category (km^2)	Total lake water volume $(\times 10^3\,km^3)$	(%)	Number of lakes on Earth	Notes
Largest	158·6	95·54	19	Caspian, Baikal, Tanganyika, Superior, Nyasa, Michigan, Huron, Victoria, Maracaibo, Great Slave, Issyk-kul', Ontario, Great Bear, Aral, Ladoga, Titicaca, Kivu, Erie, Onega
Large	2·0	1·20	15	Rudolf, Winnipeg, Van, Nicaragua, Venern, Athabasca, Edward, Dead Sea, Balkhash, Albert, Chad, Tana, Geneva, Sevan, Zaysan

TABLE 4.8 (continued)

Category (km²)	Total lake water volume (× 10³ km³)	(%)	Number of lakes on Earth	Notes
Medium and minor				
1 000–6 000	2·2	1·33	120	
100–1 000	1·2	0·72	600	
10–100	0·8	0·48	10 000	
1–10	0·6	0·37	150 000	
0·1–1	0·4	0·24	1 700 000	
0·1	0·2	0·12	10 000 000	
Total	166	100	11 860 754	

Analysis of the distribution of lake waters with regard to mean sea level showed that most lakes, actually 58%, are located below this datum.

In relation to the oceans, the lakes occupy an area only 0·75% of theirs and lake waters come to a mere 0·012% of the volume of oceanic waters. Nevertheless, lakes are very important for Man because of their fresh water contents and aesthetic characteristics providing scenic beauty and diversity to the continental landscapes.

4.6. SPRINGS

A spring may be defined as a natural outflow of groundwater at the surface and may serve as an important source of fresh water. An exceptional instance quoted by A. Nelson and K. D. Nelson is seven of the Havant and Bedhampton Springs of the Portsmouth Water Company in England which never yield less than 4500 m³ daily, i.e. 1 m.g.d., each.[20] Springs must be distinguished from seepage areas. Seepage is a term describing the movement of water through the ground or any porous medium to the ground surface or to surface water bodies. The movement is slower than is the case with springs. There are many varieties and modes of occurrence of springs and they may be classified according to factors such as cause, rock structure, discharge, temperature and variability. K. Bryan has divided all springs into the following:[21]

   (i)   those which result from non-gravitational forces;
   (ii) those which result from gravitational forces.

In category (i) are volcanic springs and fissure springs which are almost invariably thermal in nature and associated with geothermal resources. Gravity springs result from water flowing under hydrostatic pressure and the following general types may be recognised:

(a) depression springs which are formed where the water table intersects the surface of the ground;
(b) contact springs which arise where a permeable and water-bearing formation overlies a less permeable formation intersecting the ground surface;
(c) artesian springs which are caused by the release of water under pressure from confined aquifers either at an outcrop of the aquifer or through an opening in the confining bed;
(d) impervious rock springs occurring in tubular channels or in fractures of impervious rock;
(e) tubular or fracture springs which issue from rounded channels, e.g. lava tubes or solution channels or fractures in impermeable rock connecting with groundwater.

O. E. Meinzer proposed a classification of springs by discharge which is shown in Fig. 4.6 and Table 4.9. Large magnitude springs are found mainly in volcanic and limestone terrains.

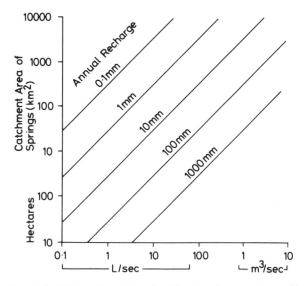

FIG. 4.6. Meinzer's spring classification by magnitude.[22]

TABLE 4.9
THE MEINZER CLASSIFICATION[22]

Spring magnitude	Mean discharge
First	$> 10 \, \text{m}^3/\text{sec}$
Second	$1–10 \, \text{m}^3/\text{sec}$
Third	$0·1–1 \, \text{m}^3/\text{sec}$
Fourth	$10–100$ litres/sec
Fifth	$1–10$ litres/sec
Sixth	$0·1–1$ litre/sec
Seventh	$10–100 \, \text{ml/sec}$
Eighth	$< 10 \, \text{ml/sec}$

The discharge of a spring depends upon the area which contributes recharge to the aquifer and the rate of recharge. Figure 4.6 expresses this relation. There is usually a fluctuation in the rate of discharge in every spring. This may be a response to variations in the rate of recharge and may have periods ranging from minutes to years depending upon the geological and hydrological conditions. There are perennial springs which drain very large aquifers and discharge continuously, but intermittent springs discharge only during those parts of the year when there is sufficient groundwater recharging them to maintain their flow. Regions of volcanoes as well as sandhills are areas containing perennial springs of almost constant discharge. Springs exhibiting regular discharge fluctuations unconnected with rainfall constitute periodic springs and their fluctuations may result from atmospheric pressure changes, from tides affecting confined aquifers or from natural siphons acting in subterranean storage basins.

In coastal areas which have limestone or volcanic rock aquifers, groundwater may be discharged through sub-surface channels, reach openings and enter the sea. Many instances of this may be cited, e.g. from the Mediterranean Sea as well as from Hawaii. If the discharge is large enough it may be feasible to obtain potable water directly from the surface of the sea. Interestingly such a spring was described by the Roman poet Lucretius in the first century B.C. in *De Rerum Natura* as follows 'In the sea at Arados is a fountain of this kind which wells up with fresh water and keeps off the salt waters all around it ... a seasonable help in need to thirsting sailors, vomiting forth fresh waters amid the salt'.

Turning now to springs in relation to geothermal energy, the surface manifestations of this include fumaroles, hot springs, boiling mud pools and geysers, which are hot springs periodically emitting columns of boiling water and steam and resulting from the expansive power of superheated steam which constricts sub-surface channels. Water from the surface and sometimes from shallow aquifers also drains downwards into a deep vertical tube where it is heated to above boiling point. With increasing pressure the steam forces its way upwards and this releases some of the water at the surface thus reducing the hydrostatic pressure and causing the deeper superheated water to accelerate upwards and flash into steam. The geyser then enters the maximum eruption stage for a short time until the pressure is dissipated. After this the filling recommences and the cycle is repeated. Another spring variety called a mudpot may be mentioned; this results when only a limited water supply is available. Water mixes with clay and undissolved particles brought to the surface, forming a muddy suspension by the small quantity of water and steam continuing to bubble to the surface. A fumarole is an opening through which only steam and gases such as CO_2 and H_2S discharge. Such features usually occur on hillsides above the level of flowing thermal springs. Thermal springs are worldwide in their occurrence, but concentrated areas of them are found in the USA (mostly in the western states such as Wyoming, California, Nevada and Oregon), New Zealand (North Island mostly in the Taupo volcanic zone) and the Kamchatka Peninsula of the USSR. Yellowstone National Park in Wyoming actually contains thousands of hydrothermal features constituting the greatest concentration of thermal springs in the world, according to W. R. Keefer.[23] The region represents the site of a tremendous volcanic eruption which took place 600 000 years ago and today temperatures of 240°C are found a mere 300 m below the ground surface.

Hydrogen isotopes in springs in Iceland were studied by B. Arnason and Th. Sigurgeirsson from 1963 to 1967.[24] As early as 1954 water samples from hot and cold springs were analysed for D and ^{18}O contents. In most of the former these isotope concentrations exhibit a linear relationship characteristic of meteoric water derived from the oceans through the processes of evaporation and condensation. This supported the opinion that geothermal water is of meteoric origin but simultaneously demonstrated that some of the hot springs could not have originated from the local groundwater but represented recharge from a rather considerable distance. The results in the later study showed no time variation in D content from samples of cold springs in southwest Iceland whereas samples taken from streams in the same region showed a small variation. Cold springs and rivers have similar D content as the total annual precipitation in their recharge area as judged from monthly samples. Because of the smallness of the time variations, these sources were regarded as useful indicators of the mean deuterium content in the precipitation and its variation with geographic position. Deuterium content varies with distance from the sea and the distribution is modified by the landscape. Samples of steam and liquid water from some boiling boreholes demonstrated that equilibrium is achieved between deuterium concentrations in the vapour and the water phase. This made it feasible to calculate the D content of the recharge water for a hot spring from deuterium measurements of the water phase alone if the base temperature of the recharge water is known. The results gave no reason to believe that the thermal water changes the deuterium content during its subterranean passage. In Iceland the situation is favourable to utilising D analyses in order to trace the recharge area of thermal springs. Often they differ to a marked degree in deuterium content from the precipitation at their locations and the inference drawn from this is that hot water emerging from some of the hot springs and boreholes in southwest Iceland has travelled underground for a distance of 50 km or more.

A very interesting study of seasonal variations in the tritium content of groundwaters of the Vienna Basin in Austria was effected by G. H. Davis et al. in 1965, the results of which were published in 1967.[25] In this work non-thermal and thermal spring waters were analysed. Monthly analyses of this radioisotope from twenty-two groundwater sources in the Vienna Basin were made and the aim of the exercise was to elucidate the complex groundwater–surface water relationship as well as to ascertain the movement of the groundwaters. Four groups of sources were employed, namely:

(i)   non-thermal springs including karst springs of bordering mountains;
(ii) thermal springs ascending along faults bordering the floor of the Vienna Basin;
(iii) wells on the Basin floor;
(iv) large overflows of groundwater on the Basin floor.

The most important findings were that thermal springs believed to be representative of deep circulation showed the effects of mixing with shallow waters recharged from current precipitation (they all contained appreciable tritium contents even at minimal levels). Also the highest tritium contents in well waters were from the upper part of the Basin where water levels are very deep, but streams lose water in crossing alluvium. In addition, well waters in the area of shallow water in the lower Basin were usually lower in this radioisotope than those of the upper Basin but all showed the effect of recharge in the summer of 1965.

R. Margrita and associates have investigated the Fontaine de Vaucluse (spring) using the radioisotopes tritium and carbon-14.[26] Interesting results were obtained and showed that thermonuclear tritium can provide information on the mechanism of functioning of the spring depending upon its hydraulic state. The radiocarbon measurements of the water of the reserve stratum proved that water of greater age is present on the fringes of the rapid feeding and flow circuits.

J. C. Fontes et al. studied oxygen-18 and tritium in the Evian Basin.[27] These isotopic surveys involved precipitation, surface water, test wells and springs and the results made it possible to determine the mean height of the drainage area, also to consider various hypotheses in connection with the hydrodynamics of the water table. Additionally, the exercise made it possible to determine the behaviour of recent meteoric water and its possible contribution to the water table supply. Data derived from conventional hydrologic studies accorded well with the isotopic results and the latter were used also in planning the catchment area equipment and fixing the sites of the test wells. The authors proposed that systematic sampling should be organised on an international scale on the site of the main catchment areas which present serious hydrogeological problems.

4.7. SNOW PACKS AND GLACIERS

The hydrologic pattern in mountainous regions is frequently influenced by glaciers, which underlies the necessity of studying the material balance of these features as well as their response to climatic changes and movements determined by the mechanical properties of their ice. C. Benson has defined characteristic glacier facies, indicating that:[28]

(i) The ablation facies extends from the glacier snout to the firn line, the maximum altitude to which snow recedes in the melting season.

(ii) The soaked facies which is wet during the melting season extends from the firn line to the uppermost limit of total wetting (the saturation line) which in fact is the maximum elevation at which the 0°C isotherm penetrates to the melt surface of the preceding summer.

(iii) The percolation facies is subject to local percolation of melt water from the surface without becoming completely wet. Percolation can take place in snow and firn of sub-freezing temperatures with only the pipe-like percolation channels being at the melting point. A network of ice lenses and layers forms when refreezing takes place. This facies extends from the saturation line to the dry snow line, negligible soaking and percolation occurring above this latter.

(iv) The dry snow facies includes all the glacier lying above the dry snow line and there is negligible melting in it.

Temperature zone glaciers actually only show the two facies below the saturation line whereas one or both facies above the saturation line occur on polar glaciers with ice temperature <0°C. At any given location the net accumulation rate (g/cm^2/year) is the difference between the accumulation (superposition of snow, freezing rain, white frost, refreezing melt water) and the ablation (runoff of melt water and evaporation). The net accumulation rate is negative in the ablation facies, and is positive otherwise as W. Dansgaard has pointed out.[29] The overall budget is the net accumulation rate integrated over the whole area of the glacier. Since the end of the 19th century most glaciers have possessed a negative total budget but since the 1940s there are many which show increasing positive total budgets. Of course the total budgets of the very large ice field regions of Greenland and Antarctica are far from well known. The mechanical characteristics of glacier ice in some ways parallel those of solids at temperatures just below the melting point. Glen's Law expresses the relationship between the shear stress, τ, and the resultant strain rate, ϵ, as

$$\epsilon = k\tau^m$$

k nad m being constant depending upon the temperature and perhaps the pressure as well. It must be borne in mind that this law is the result of laboratory experimentation and it cannot be effected at the extremely low shear stresses found in the central areas of the large ice fields. In the case of valley glaciers, however, it can explain the observed pattern of movement and in fact shows decreasing velocity with increasing depth so that the old ice at the terminus of the glacier and originating from the upper part of the accumulation area is also explained. If the same flow pattern is valid for large ice fields, ice close to bedrock is probably antique and may be as much as 10^5 years old.

Classical methodologies for material balance studies as set out for instance by Østrom in 1966 are widely utilised because they are at once simple and cheap.[30] However, there are difficulties because stake measurements require repeated readings from year to year and in regions of low precipitation the presence of the stake can affect the accumulation around it.[29] Snow density measurements are restricted to uppermost annual layers of the snow cover where the snow is not compressed into solid ice. In recent years environmental isotopes have been used and, as well as deuterium and oxygen-18 plus tritium, lead-210 has been employed.

As regards the use of stable isotopes the principle is as follows. At the middle and in high latitudes the stable isotopic composition of precipitation shows seasonal variation in phase with the condensation temperature. This is of the order of $3‰/°C$ for δD and $0·3‰/°C$ for $\delta^{18}O$. An isotopic stratification of snow results. In the dry snow facies change in this takes place only as a consequence of snow drift and only in regions which have very low accumulation rates (e.g. central Antarctica). In the percolation facies the stratification is still recognisable. In the soaked facies it remains dependent upon the proximity to the firn line. Seeping and refreezing melt water tend to smooth out isotopic gradients. Analysis of a vertical profile of the snow cover facilitates backward counting in time of those δ-minima which correspond to winter snows.

Using this approach permits the measurement of accumulation in individual years of any past time interval represented in the glacier although it does require a great deal of time consuming analytical work. Dansgaard has indicated that to reduce the number of samples which have to be analysed and thus accelerate the obtaining of results, it is advisable to have an approximate idea of the net accumulation rate.[29] Once this is known, even roughly, a core can be taken representing the time interval in question. Half a dozen or so samples may be collected per annual layer and each ought to be about 20 g. The procedure is delicate because of the possibility that evaporation from liquid water may occur which could alter the isotopic composition and this may be obviated by cutting the ice so that it falls directly into plastic bags which are subsequently closed by a knot. These are later placed in warm room and after melting the melt water may be transferred into $20 \, cm^3$ polyethylene bottles (with double stoppers) which have to be filled completely. If storage is necessary for a longer time interval, then the bottles must be maintained at sub-zero temperatures. Mass spectrometric measurements are made and as regards their accuracy this need not exceed $\pm 0.2\permil$ for $\delta^{18}O$ and $\pm 2\%$ for δD. The accuracy of the resultant determination of the mean net accumulation depends upon the number of years and the number of sampling sites considered in the project. As regards ^{210}Pb and naturally produced tritium the accumulation measurements mean dating of old snow layers which implies knowledge of the initial specific activity A_0. There are two extreme cases which are as follows:

(i) A_0 for recent snow is regarded as constant in time and the age t in years of snow with specific activity A is obtained from

$$A = A_0 e^{-\lambda t}$$

where λ is the decay constant in years^{-1}. If x is the depth of the snow layer and a is the net accumulation rate then $t = x/a$ and a may be derived from

$$\ln A = \ln A_0 - \frac{\lambda}{a} x$$

i.e. from the slope of that straight line which is obtained by plotting $\ln A$ against x.

(ii) The total annual fallout $F = A_0 a$ dpm/cm^2/year is constant but A_0 and a vary. Given this assumption a given snow layer cannot be dated explicitly. However, the total activity of a 1 cm^2 column with depth x cm corresponding to t years' accumulation is

$$A_x = F \int_0^t e^{-\lambda t} dt = \frac{F}{\lambda}(1 - e^{-\lambda t})$$

from which t can be found when F and A_x are measured. F may be measured on an entire year's precipitation and on a large ice field F can be found as

$$F = A_\infty \lambda$$

where A_∞ represents the total activity for an infinitely long column (in practice a column representing 100 years—in the case of tritium 100 years back from 1950).

The major difficulty with tritium is that the value of A_0 is not known with certainty because no reliable measurements were made before the injection of artificial pulses of the radioisotope into the atmosphere since 1952. However, there are other difficulties as well and these include the very high possibility of contamination with atmospheric vapour during the collection and preparation of the samples and the problem of excluding the time interval after 1952 (because of the bomb-produced fallout).

The seasonal activity variations in precipitation favour the second procedure outlined above but the determination of F by considering an entire year's precipitation is only applicable if that year is prior to 1952. Consequently, the tritium dating of snow layers on local glaciers requires an excellent knowledge of the stratigraphy which is itself the aim of the investigation.

^{210}Pb has low concentrations and a short half-life ($T_{1/2} = 21$ years) and this, together with the even shorter half-life of tritium ($T_{1/2} = 12.26$ years), imposes an upper limit of a century for ice dating. The procedure outlined under (i) above is applicable to ^{210}Pb and the method can give net accumulation data with an accuracy of $\pm 10\%$. However, the chemistry of this radioisotope is difficult and the preparation and measurement of a sample may occupy several days. In 1967, E. Picciotto and his associates found no systematic change of the ^{210}Pb concentration in a 20 m deep pit in the soaked facies of Kesselwandferner in Austria.[31]

Turning now to artificially produced environmental isotopes, these arose from the atmospheric thermonuclear bomb tests and since that time precipitation has increased its radioactivity. Strata with long lived components of the debris from the tests are relatively undisturbed in the dry snow facies and percolation facies and simple activity measurements gave useful profiles. In the soaked facies of the temperate glacier Kesselwandferner in Austria strata were identified back to 1954 by W. Ambach and H. Eisner in 1965.[32] The total α and β specific activity in the 1954 layer due to the Castle Tests of March 1954 was 100 counts/min/kg.

As regards the movement of glaciers, environmental isotopes have been utilised in determining the mean velocity of glacier ice since it was formed. Radioactive dating of ice in the ablation facies provides the total travel time and its stable isotope composition reflects the actual site of formation in the accumulation zone since the net accumulated material there frequently shows isotope variations relating to the elevation and the inland effects (decreasing values of δ with increasing altitude and distance from the coast). Ice immediately below the firn line can be dated with lead-210 as long as it is not over 100 years old. Older ice can be dated using radiocarbon or ^{32}Si. With ^{14}C the ^{14}C/^{12}C ratio of the CO_2 component in the air bubbles of the old ice provides an adequate basis for the dating. With ^{210}Pb and ^{32}Si the specific activity of the old ice is compared with that of net accumulated material in the accumulation area (in the case of silicon-32 it is necessary to take care that the reference material is not contaminated with thermonuclear bomb-produced ^{32}Si). Quantities required are 20–30 kg for ^{210}Pb dating and 1–5 tons of ice for radiocarbon and silicon-32. 50 mg of carbon are necessary and the ice is usually cut up and later melted *in vacuo* in a stainless steel container, released air being passed through a solution of NaOH for absorption of CO_2. Once the ice has been melted the melt water can be transferred into open containers for the chemical extraction of silicon. A 20 g sample for analysis of the stable isotopes is simply separated from the large quantity of melt water available and the isotopic composition of this is uninfluenced by the seasonal variation at the site of formation of the ice.

Overall accuracy after analysis is given as 30% or so. Use of stable isotopes for determination of the site of formation of the ice is conditional upon the geographic δ-variations in the accumulation facies being much greater than the δ-variations due to possible deviation of the existing climate from that at the time of the formation. If, due to location of, say, local minor glaciers, the condition is unfulfilled then an appropriate correction for climatic change is introduced. A 1°C higher condensation temperature corresponds with approximately 0·7°C higher δ^{18}O.

All the dating methods appear to be applicable both on temperate and polar glaciers. Greenland polar glacier ice was dated by Per Scholander and his associates (including W. Dansgaard) in 1962 using radiocarbon and the results showed unexpectedly young ages of ≤ 3000 years which indicate relatively superficial ice streams in disagreement with Glen's Law.[33] S. Aegeter *et al.* in 1968 found that ages of up to 9000 years exist for ice at the Thule peninsula.[33]

Interesting research was carried out on an Antarctic glacier by Liliane Merlivat and her associates in 1967.[34] Two drillings were made in the ice of Adelie Land near a moraine and two bore samples of ice extracted from 98 m and 105 m. The deuterium contents lay between $\delta D = -370\%$ and $\delta D = -40\%$ and between the surface and $+54$m the value of δD varied around -145% for the two bore samples. This corresponds with coastal precipitation in that part of the continent and from this it is possible to deduce that this ice layer resulted from the transformation of local granular ice. Between $+54$ m and $+34$ m δD dropped rapidly from

$-145\%_0$ to $-350\%_0$ and down to $-9\,\mathrm{m}$ and $+7{\cdot}5\,\mathrm{m}$ $\delta\mathrm{D}$ fluctuated around $-350\%_0$. Basing the interpretation on topographic data for the region and the relationship between $\delta\mathrm{D}$ and the annual mean temperature the origin of this ice on the polar plateau is thought of as being about 900 km from the coast. The ice layer in contact with the sediment has a very high $\delta\mathrm{D}$ value reaching $-40\%_0$ and this is believed to be of marine origin. It was assumed that the deuterium study indicated an ice flow from the polar cap which passed between a layer of local ice and a layer of marine ice.

The exchange of deuterium between ice and water in glaciological studies in Iceland was discussed by B. Arnason in 1970.[35] Iceland is a favourite country for such work because approximately 10% of its area is covered by glaciers and in 1963 a programme of deuterium measurement was inaugurated (see ref. 24 and p. 190). This present work involved collection of ice cores from several boreholes on the glaciers; these ranged in depth up to 100 m. It was found that an extensive homogenisation occurring in the uppermost winter layer during summer thaws is due to an isotope exchange between ice and water and, further, in autumn the deuterium concentrations in ice and water approach isotopic equilibrium (at least up to an elevation of 1300 m). From this was derived a method for estimating the runoff ratio. This plus measurements of the quantity of retained precipitation in previous annual layers give the total annual precipitation in temperate glaciers. Where such estimates were made they accorded well with available and independently obtained data. At an altitude of 2000 m, the deuterium measurements demonstrated that annual precipitation is totally accumulated and therefore at this elevation the deuterium concentration of an ice core collected by drilling through the ice cap may reflect the past climatic change in a similar manner as the $^{18}\mathrm{O}$ does on polar glaciers. Data obtained showed that small variations in the mean annual temperature are reflected in variations of the deuterium concentration of the ice core.

Layers of volcanic ash from recorded eruptions are easily recognised in the ice and so the dating of the ice core is a simple and accurate procedure. No information was available regarding the deepest ice layers but Arnason expected them to be at least several hundred years old.[35] Apropos volcanicity it is known that over the past thousand years many volcanic eruptions have taken place.[36] Several of these and especially the great eruption of the Öraefajökull volcano in 1362 precipitated thick ash layers.

REFERENCES

1. KJENSMO, J., 1968. Iron as the primary factor rendering lakes meromictic and related problems. *Wirt. Int. Ver. Limnol.*, **14**, 83–93.
2. DEEVEY, E. S., NAKAI, N. and STUIVER, M., 1968. Fractionation of sulfur and carbon isotopes in a meromictic lake. *Science*, **139**, 407–8.
3. KEELING, C. D. and BOLIN, B., 1967. General theory of reservoir models. *Tellus*, **19**, 568.
4. DINCER, T. and HALEVY, E., 1968. Leakage from lakes and reservoirs. in: *Guidebook on Nuclear Techniques in Hydrology, Tech. Repts Ser. No. 91*, IAEA, Vienna, 77–83.
5. PAYNE, B. R., 1970. Water balance of Lake Chala and its relation to groundwater from tritium and stable isotope data. *J. Hydrol.*, **11**, 47–58.
6. PECKHAM, A. E. and PAYNE, B. R., 1965. Isotope investigations of the hydrology of Lake Chala and its associated groundwater system. *Proc. 6th Int. Conf. Radiocarbon and Tritium Dating*, CONF-650652, 687.
7. BURDON, D. J., ERIKSSON, E. and PAYNE, B. R., 1963. The use of tritium in tracing karst groundwater in Greece. in: *Radioisotopes in Hydrology*, Proc. Symp. Tokyo, 5–9 March 1963, IAEA, Vienna, 309–20.
8. GAT, J. R., 1970. Environmental isotope balance of Lake Tiberias. in: *Isotope Hydrology*, Proc. Symp. Vienna 9–13 March 1970, IAEA, Vienna, 109–27.
9. GASPAR, E. and ONESCU, M., 1963. Radioactive tracers for the identification of water infiltrations under a dam. *Rev. Phys. Soc.*, **VIII**, 293–307.
10. MAIRHOFER, J., 1966. Strömungsuntersuchungen am Kraftwerk Ybbs-Persenbeug. Report of BVFA to Donau-kraftwerke, Vienna.
11. GUIZERIX, J., MOLINARI, J., GAILLARD, B. and CORDA, R., 1967. Localisation des fuites sur un grand reservoir a l'aide de traceurs radioactifs. in: *Isotopes in Hydrology*, Proc. Symp. Vienna, 14–18 November 1966, IAEA, Vienna, 601–16.
12. ELDER, R. A. and VIGNANDER, S., 1967. Capabilities and potential of USAEC's current meter for ultra-low velocity measurements. in: *Isotopes in Hydrology*, Proc. Symp. Vienna, 14–18 November 1966, IAEA, Vienna, 683–95.
13. ZUBER, A., 1970. Method for determining leakage velocities through the bottoms|of|reservoirs. in: *Isotope Hydrology*, Proc. Symp. Vienna, 9–13 March 1970, IAEA, Vienna, 761–71.
14. DANILIN, A. I., 1970. Neutron investigation of the rate of water seepage from irrigation channels and reservoirs in loessal loams. in: *Isotope Hydrology*, Proc. Symp. Vienna, 9–13 March 1970, IAEA, Vienna, 773–84.
15. FRIEDMAN, I., REDFIELD, A. C., SCHOEN, B. and HARRIS, J., 1964. *Rev. Geophys.*, **2**(1), 177–224.
16. DINCER, T., 1968. The use of oxygen-18 and deuterium concentrations in the water balance of lakes. *Water Resources Research Bull.*, **4**(6), 1289–306.
17. GONFIANTINI, R., 1965. Effetti isotopici nell'evaporazione di acque salate. *Atti. della Soc. Tosc. Sci. Nat.*, A, **LXXII**.
18. TAMRAZYAN, G. P., 1974. Total lake water resources of the planet. *Bull. Geol. Soc. Finland*, **46**, 23–7.

19. DOMANITSKIY, A. P., DUBROVINA, R. G. and ISAYEVA, L. I., 1971. Rivers and lakes of the Soviet Union. *Gidrometeoizdat.*
20. NELSON, A. and NELSON, K. D., 1973. *Dictionary of Water and Water Engineering.* Butterworths, London, 218.
21. BRYAN, K., 1919. Classification of springs. *J. Geol.,* **27**, 522–61.
22. MEINZER, O. E., 1927. Large springs in the United States. *US Geol. Surv. Water Supply Paper 557,* 94 pp.
23. KEEFER, W. R., 1971. The geologic story of Yellowstone National Park. *US Geol. Surv. Bull.,* **1347**, 92 pp.
24. ARNASON, B. and SIGURGEIRSSON, Th., 1967. Hydrogen isotopes in hydrological studies in Iceland. in: *Isotopes in Hydrology,* Proc. Symp. Vienna, 14–18 November 1966, IAEA, Vienna, 35–47.
25. DAVIS, G. H., PAYNE, B. R., DINCER, T., FLORKOWSKI, T. and GATTINGER, T., 1967. Seasonal variations in the tritium content of groundwaters of the Vienna Basin. in: *Isotopes in Hydrology,* Proc. Symp. Vienna, 14–18 November 1966, IAEA, Vienna, 451–73.
26. MARGRITA, R., ERIN, J., FLANDRIN, J. and PALOC, H., 1970. Contribution des mesures isotopiques a l'etude de la fontaine de Vaucluse. in: *Isotope Hydrology,* Proc. Symp. Vienna, 9–13 March 1970, IAEA, Vienna, 333–48.
27. FONTES, J. C., LETOLLE, R., OLIVE, Ph. and BLAVOUX, B., 1967. Oxygène-18 et tritium dans le bassin d'Evian. in: *Isotopes in Hydrology,* Proc. Symp. Vienna, 14–18 November 1966, IAEA, Vienna, 401–15.
28. BENSON, C., 1962. Stratigraphic studies on the snow and firn of the Greenland ice sheet. SIPRE Rept 70, Hanover, NH, USA.
29. DANSGAARD, W., 1968. Snow packs and glaciers. in: *Guidebook on Nuclear Techniques in Hydrology, Tech. Repts Ser. No. 91,* IAEA, Vienna, 83–91.
30. ØSTROM, S., 1966. Glacier mass balance measurements. Dept of Mines and Tech. Surveys, Glaciol. Section, Ottawa, Canada.
31. PICCIOTTO, E., CROZAZ, G., AMBACH, W. and EISNER, H., 1967. Lead-210 and strontium-90 in an Alpine glacier. *Earth Planet. Sci. Letters,* **3**, 237.
32. AMBACH, W. and EISNER, H., 1965. Untersuchung der Radioaktivität der Firnschichten eines Alpengletschers zur Festlegung von Datierungsmarken. *Acta Phys. Austriaca,* **XX**, 58.
33. AEGETER, S., OESCHGER, H., RENAUD, A. and SCHUMACHER, R., 1968. Studies based on the tritium content of E.G.I.G. samples. *Meddr. Grønland,* **177**, 76.
34. MERLIVAT, LILIANE, LORIUS, C., MAJZOUB, M., NIEF, G. and ROTH, E., 1967. Etudes isotopiques en profondeur d'un glacier en Antarctique. in: *Isotopes in Hydrology,* Proc. Symp. Vienna, 14–18 November 1966, IAEA, Vienna, 671–81.
35. ARNASON, B., 1970. Exchange of deuterium between ice and water in glaciological studies in Iceland. in: *Isotope Hydrology,* Proc. Symp. Vienna, 9–13 March 1970, IAEA, Vienna, 59–71.
36. THORARINSSON, S., 1967. The eruption of Hekla in historical times. *Visindafelag Islendinga (Soc. Sci. Islandica),* Reykjavik.

CHAPTER 5

The Oceans

5.1. SEAS AND OCEANS

The Earth is, as far as is known, unique in that its surface is practically covered with liquid water which constitutes 97·2% of the total on Earth (see Chapter 1, Table 1.10). This table also gives the volume of the oceans as $1·37 \times 10^9 \, \text{km}^3$ and since the rate of supply of water by rivers is approximately $36 \times 10^{18} \, \text{g/year}$ (or, as the density of water is about 1, $36 \times 10^{18} \, \text{ml/year}$ or $36 \times 10^3 \, \text{km}^3$ annually) the theoretical time interval required for 'filling' is about 40 000 years. Of course this is really a measure of the mean residence time which as Table 1.10 states is c. 40 000 years, i.e. a measure of the cycling rate—necessarily an average because clearly some of the water molecules will be cycled more frequently or less frequently than others.

The origin of the oceans is not fully understood. It is believed that in the early history of the Earth water vapour, chloride gas, CO_2, CO, CH_4, N_2 or ammonia gas were excluded as gases and only the non-volatile compounds of chlorine, carbon, hydrogen and nitrogen accumulated. Water would have existed in hydrated silicates and other minerals, carbon and nitrogen would be present in low boiling point organic compounds and chlorine as ions substituting for oxygen in silicates or in chlorides. Interestingly, all of these latter have been discovered in that class of meteorites termed carbonaceous chondrites. Incorporation of such material at some phase during planetary growth followed by heating and degassing could have provided the atmosphere. Mantle-derived rocks and lunar and meteoritic data suggest that the terrestrial planets accumulated by a non-homogeneous process, and revolving as a disc around the rotating and condensing sun at a temperature of perhaps 2000 K much material was in a state of vapour at a pressure possibly one thousandth of the current atmosphere. Cooling would have caused high temperature minerals to condense and accrete to form the inner parts of the terrestrial planets while melting and fractionation went on in each primarily through gravitational energy-triggered heating. No volatiles could accumulate up to this point, i.e. the planetary nuclei were, in a sense, dry. The acquisition of carbonaceous chondritic-type material followed and this process could have transported volatiles to the planetary surface. Subsequent melting and recrystallisation ensured their release and, if the dimensions of the planet were sufficient, their retention. While Mercury and the Moon do not appear to have possessed such a volatile-rich coat at any time, Venus and the Earth probably formed with similar quantities of a volatile-rich coat. Mars would have occupied an intermediate position in that its atmosphere indicates probable accumulation of such a coat but its smaller size as compared with the Earth may have led to most of it escaping. The Earth's oldest rocks have been dated at $c.$ 3.7×10^9 years as compared with the planet's age of 4.6×10^9 years and it is clear from these figures that practically the whole of the first aeon of potential rock-recorded history is missing through obliteration so that the above described planetary formation model remains speculative. However, it is thought that the volatile-bearing coat accumulated rather rapidly and therefore it is inferred that a dynamic upper mantle and crust developed soon after this accumulation process due to energy release and heating at the planet's exterior. This is the time interval during which nearly all the volatiles would have been transported to the terrestrial surface and the conclusion is that it is feasible and perhaps also probable that the Earth acquired both an ocean and an atmosphere soon after formation. Both the volume and salinity of the seas would also have been established early even though the atmosphere had a composition certainly quite different from that of today. This latter may have been primarily CO_2, nitrogen and water vapour according to K. K. Turekian.[1] Later ultraviolet light-induced dissociation of water could have created an oxygen reservoir reactive with surficial rocks and the carbon dioxide pressure may have diminished through such reactions. The onset of photosynthesis perhaps in the planet's first aeon caused the rise in oxygen and CO_2 to, and maintenance at, existing levels. This model implies that degassing of the planet was only of minor importance, but other models propose that a continuously degassing Earth existed, e.g. the model alluded to on page 99 in which it is postulated that volcanism played a role. Of course it is known that volcanoes, geysers and fumaroles liberate vast quantities of water vapour and gases into the atmosphere. Much of this material, however, represents recycling of those which derived from sediment alteration and percolation of waters from the planetary surface. Nevertheless evidence exists that there is a continuing, if small, flux of rare gases from the mantle to the surface.

The development of the existing ocean basins will be discussed later, but first it is necessary to examine them in detail.

5.2. STRUCTURE OF OCEANIC BASINS

These have variable topography and structure reflecting internal processes and are of variable duration from which it may be inferred that the oceanic bottom today is dissimilar from that of several hundred million years ago.

Ocean bottom topography may be determined using a remote sensor. In the past this comprised a sounding line for shallow depths, i.e. a hemp line with an attached lead weight, and from the late 19th century until just after the First World War a metal line. Although this is a tedious procedure a great deal of data were accumulated and at that time it was known that the deep ocean bottom is not a plain. After that, echo sounding was developed, a technique which entails reflection of a sound signal transmitted through the water as an echo off the bottom, emission and reception being effected aboard a ship which generates the original signal. The velocity of sound is a function of such factors as temperature, pressure and salinity of the water and so these characteristics must be known in order to convert the transit time of the signal into a depth measurement. The Second World War stimulated improvement and subsequently such soundings have been made using continuous operation precision depth recorders providing bottom profiles. Exact locations of ocean bottom features can also be obtained nowadays because of the improvement in methods of navigation. Although celestial and solar techniques are still utilised, they require accurate assessment of the distance of a heavenly body above the horizon and this is often impeded by cloud. Additionally, currents and wind may adversely affect results. Hence, electronic triangulation (LORAN), an all-weather technique allowing an accuracy of under 1 km, is widely used today as is fixing of location by using artificial satellite signals. The ocean bottom has been found to consist of three large scale topographic features found everywhere and these are as follows:

(i)   The continental margins of which those around the Atlantic
      Ocean comprise shelf, slope and rise proceeding seawards. The
      continental shelf represents the submerged extension of the topog-
      raphy and geology apparent on adjacent land modified by marine
      erosion or the deposition of sediments. Where found, the shelf
      break indicates the maximum extent of the shelf and can be
      anything from 10 to 500 m deep with an average of perhaps 200 m
      (this is roughly the 100 fathom or inner mud line). Relief on the
      shelf is usually below 20 m. The continental slope extends from
      the shelf (above which the gradient is 1:1000) with a gradient of
      1:40 or so and sometimes a series of escarpments down to the
      continental rise with gradients ranging from 1:1000 to 1:700.
      Often this latter is a depositional feature and it may be traversed
      by submarine canyons which channel sediments in a seaward
      direction (e.g. off Trincomalee in Sri Lanka or the Hudson
      submarine canyon off Long Island) and sometimes continue on
      continental slopes and shelves. Deep trenches are found as con-
      tinental margins beyond the shelves in several parts of the world
      and are especially common around the Pacific Ocean basin,
      sometimes exceeding 8 km in depth.

(ii) The ocean basin floor including everything seaward from the
      continental margin except for the third and following topographic
      feature (the major oceanic ridge systems). The floor constitutes
      one-third of the ocean basins of the Atlantic and Indian Oceans
      and as much as three-quarters of the Pacific Ocean basin. Very
      smooth abyssal plains occur adjacent to the continental rises to a
      great degree in the Atlantic and to a lesser degree in the Pacific
      with gradients lying between 1:1000 and 1:10 000 and connected
      by canyons or similar channels to the landward source of sedi-
      ments transported in the form of rather dense slurries and de-
      posited thereon. Some regions such as the Argentine Basin
      possess a rugged topography and the Pacific Ocean floor has a great
      many abyssal hillocks making up a rather hummocky type of
      topography. Such hills may have arisen by the instrusions and
      extrusions of volcanoes. It is relevant to mention seamounts.
      These are sometimes termed guyots and have tops planed flat
      by the action of waves at sea level after which they subsided over
      a long time interval by thousands of feet. Initially these features
      were thought to be as old as the Pre-Cambrian, but the discovery
      of Cretaceous fossils from their summits disproved that hypo-

thesis and, incidentally, showed that the Pacific was not a primordial ocean. The Cretaceous corals alluded to indicate that originally the guyots were in shallow water as compared with their present depths of around 1000 to 1600 m and point to a subsidence history comparable with that of associated atoll groups.[2]

(iii) The major oceanic ridge systems form a series of connected topographically high areas which occur in all oceans and attain widths ranging from 1000 to 4000 km with a relief of 2 to 4 km above the floor of the ocean and occasionally emerging from the surface of the sea as islands. Sometimes this system has been called the mid-oceanic ridge and the best known and most prominent instance is the famous Mid-Atlantic Ridge with topography composed of a mixture of volcanic and rupture features (faults). In its centre lies a discontinuous 'rift valley' which is marked by intense earthquake activity and above average heat flow together with a series of transverse trenches offsetting the axis. Another mid-oceanic ridge system is the East Pacific Rise which has some of these features but not all. Excluding such minor variations, the ridge system seems to extend around the planet except for the offsetting caused by transverse breaks, and B. C. Heezen claimed that it can be traced for 35000 miles.[3] The median valley was first discovered by J. C. Swallow on a cruise of the *Challenger* in 1953 and subsequently it was traced into the western Indian Ocean ridge system by B. C. Heezen and M. Ewing. They postulated on the grounds of similarity of topography and seismicity plus apparent geographic continuity that the axial valley continued into the East African Rift through the Gulf of Aden. Similarly, the East Pacific Rise enters the Gulf of California and was once believed to pass under the high plateau and mountain country of the western USA although now its axis is thought to be linked to the Juan de Fuca ridge southwest of Vancouver Island by the transform fault called the San Andreas.

The above topographic schema of the bottom of the oceans is interesting but takes no account of the relevant sediment and rock structures in order to give an overall picture. These can be examined using appropriate geophysical methods such as seismic refraction and reflection together with gravity measurements.

5.2.1. Seismic Refraction

Seismic refraction results from the energy released during an earthquake (c. 10^{25} ergs). This is transmitted through the planet and the times of arrival of the various kinds of waves at various locations on Earth as determined using seismographs facilitate the determination of the internal structure of the planet. Essentially the same procedure is adopted for ocean bottom analyses except that the waves are produced by man-made explosions detonated from a ship. The sediments and rocks of the ocean basins comprise a layered sequence in which every successively deeper layer has a higher velocity of propagation than the one above with regard to sound waves. The thickness and composition of the layers can be interpreted from such data. Sound can be transmitted in several ways on land, but in the seas because they are liquid it proceeds only by compression and release, i.e. as compressional waves. The different ocean bottom layers have different compressional wave velocities so that any particular sound wave will be refracted at the interface between two layers into the plane of the layer it has entered. In the same way, and as a result of the fact that interfaces between rock strata are good reflectors, a reflection of sound waves may be obtained and this is analogous to echo sounding. Since high frequency sound cannot penetrate deep into the sub-surface, seismic refraction techniques using low sonic frequencies are utilised for crustal examination, preferably in conjunction with gravity determinations. As regards these, the acceleration due to gravity is to a first approximation constant over the planetary surface and hence a pendulum ought to have the same period all over the world since this directly relates to gravity. In fact, the period of a pendulum moved round the Earth is greater at the equator than at higher latitudes indicating that acceleration due to gravity decreases with increasing latitude. The Earth rotates and on such a body the force due to gravitational attraction is partly offset by the consequent centrifugal force. Hence, the equatorial bulge of the planet, which means that the distance from the centre to the surface at the equator is more than at the poles or any point between. The gravitational acceleration is, therefore, diminished at the equator relative to the poles but the effect is responsible for only 35% of the difference in gravitational attraction. The remaining 65% results from the fact that a free body on the Earth's surface is subject to the centrifugal force of the rotating planet and this force is in the opposite direction to the force due to gravity, thus lessening it. As the strength of this counter force is maximal at the equator, the acceleration of a falling body is least at the equator. This information facilitates calculation of the anticipated acceleration due to gravity at any latitude and variations in this parameter can be measured using a gravimeter, if necessary from a ship.

5.2.2. Gravity Measurements

Gravity measurements at sea illustrate differences arising from localised variations in mass distribution resulting from the varying thicknesses of the layers of the oceanic crust and upper mantle. Gravity results may be used with seismic data and with the measured density of the various layers determined by seismic investigation. On the continental margins the location of the famous Mohorovičić discontinuity is not clearly delineated by seismic data although the layer was identified on the basis of seismic refraction studies, but it may be inferred from gravity data bearing in mind the fact that it is a discontinuity between material of different densities, namely the crust and mantle. Crustal structures of the ridge systems can be inferred from both seismic and gravity data. Relevant information is appended in Table 5.1.

TABLE 5.1
OCEAN FLOOR LAYERS

Layer	Thickness (km)	Transmission velocity (km/sec)	Probable composition	Approximate density
Sea layer	4·5	1·5	Sea water	1·0
Layer 1	c.1·0	2·0	Sediments	2·3
Layer 2	c.1·7	5·1	Either consolidated dense sediment or a modified version of layer 3	2·7
Layer 3	4·7	6·7	Gabbro or partly altered basalt	3·0
Mohorovičić Discontinuity				
Mantle		8·1	Ultrabasic peridotite	3·4

Figure 5.1 shows these layers in a section extending across the equatorial Atlantic Ocean from Brazil to Sierra Leone.[4]

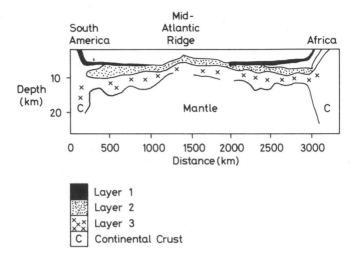

FIG. 5.1. Seismic refraction section across the Atlantic Ocean from Brazil to Sierra Leone. After R. Leyden, R. Sheridan and M. Ewing, 1969, Symp. Cont. Drift, Uruguay 1967.

5.3. OCEANIC CIRCULATION

Oceans comprise a water body which is continuous and heated at the equator by the maximum heat energy flux on Earth arising from the sun. In the polar areas during winter there is almost no direct solar heat flux but heat enters from low latitudes through the movement of oceanic waters and air masses and there is a return movement of cooled water and air. Thus arises a planet-wide circulation powered by solar energy. Ocean water samples are required to elucidate this and tracers must be found in order to determine the actual paths taken by oceanic currents.

Temperature and dissolved salt content must be measured for dynamic studies and may be made *in situ* although this is a complex procedure requiring continuous calibration of instruments as well as diagnostic chemical measurements and total dissolved salt if rates of oceanic circulation are to be determined. Surficial waters may be sampled easily but with deeper waters it is more difficult to accompany sampling with relevant information on depth and temperature and ensure that no mixing occurs during the raising of the sample. However, the sampler bottle devised by, and named after, Fridtjof Nansen in 1940 solved much of the difficulty. Bottles are spaced along a wire as this is let out from a ship using a metered winch so the depth of each one can be roughly determined. A more accurate depth is obtained by measuring the degree of compression of a mercury thermometer in direct contact with the sea water because the increased water pressure at depth gives a different reading from that of a thermometer insulated against the pressure effect. In this way both temperature and depth can be ascertained using two thermometers attached to the Nansen bottle (which can sample 1 to 2 litres of sea water). There are also techniques of sampling utilising remote electronic manipulation and monitoring capacities.

The physicochemical properties of ocean water may be cited. The total quantity of dissolved salts is variable, but the relative proportions of the major elements remain constant. The salinity of the oceans is defined as the number of grams of dissolved inorganic salts in 1000 g sea water and the total range is from 33 to 38‰. Variations in salinity result from causes such as varying evaporative effects, ice floe formation, dilution by fresh water from rivers and dilution through atmospheric precipitation as well as by melting ice (Table 5.2).

TABLE 5.2

CONCENTRATIONS OF MAIN COMPONENTS OF SEA WATER[5]

Component	Concentration (g/kg)
Chloride	19·353
Sodium	10·76
Sulphate	2·712
Magnesium	1·294
Calcium	0·413
Potassium	0·387
Bicarbonate	0·142
Bromide	0·067
Strontium	0·008
Boron	0·004
Fluoride	0·001

These values are for a salinity of 35‰ defined as the mass in grams of the dissolved inorganic material in 1000 g sea water after all bromide and iodide have been replaced with chloride and all bicarbonate and carbonate converted to oxide

In the past salinity was determined by chemically measuring the quantity of chloride but this method necessitated using the conversion

$$salinity = 1·80655 \times chlorinity$$

where chlorinity is the number of grams of chloride equivalent in 1000 g

sea water. This method has been replaced by conductivity measurements often effected using remote probes passing down the wire with a
pressure and temperature sensor. The basis of this is that a salt solution
can conduct an electric current and at any given temperature the higher
the salinity the greater the conductivity measured.

The oceans transfer heat energy from the equator to the poles and this
is done in the surface layers by currents such as the Gulf Stream in a
process paralleling the major transport of heat energy from low to high
latitudes by the atmosphere. The deep oceanic waters are, of course,
much colder than the surficial ones. When water is subjected to pressure
increasing with depth it is both compressed and warmed in an adiabatic
process causing a temperature rise. A temperature probe measures the *in
situ* temperature but knowledge of the equation of state for sea water
enables a correction for pressure to be made and the result is a potential
temperature, an important factor in determining stratification in the
oceans. Temperature profiles of the oceans show that there is a surficial
mixed layer relating to the temperature of the ambient average temperature of the relevant latitude. A bottom deep layer reflects the origin of the
cold waters in high latitudes. Between the two is a thermocline layer
extending from *c*. 100 m to *c*. 1500 m and in which the temperature
generally diminishes from the relatively high surface value to the relatively low deep water value. The thermocline layer is an important
indicator of vertical heat transfer from the surface to deep water and this
occurs by both molecular diffusion and eddy currents, which also mix
salinities.

Sea water increases in density as it cools and this means that as the
surface cools surficial water sinks and displaces deeper water until the
system (if closed) approaches the freezing point. Additional cooling at the
surface produces ice which is isotopically light. The residual sea water
increases in salinity and becomes denser thereafter sinking and displacing
less saline water to the surface to form more ice. Various factors influence
the circulation patterns of the oceans and these include the Coriolis force
discussed earlier as well as vorticity which increases with latitude. At the
surface there is a wind-driven circulation system which involves enormous circular patterns of currents (gyres) moving clockwise in the
northern hemisphere and anti-clockwise in the southern hemisphere, the
most famous being the Gulf Stream. The mechanism of the movement
commences with winds. Heated tropical air is transported polewards in
convection cells and during this process the planetary rotation imposes
itself so as to produce, for instance, the prevailing westerly winds in both

hemispheres. These are balanced by prevailing easterly winds—the trade winds—occurring at about 20° latitude. The winds do not actually push water. The Coriolis force affects the water causing a deflection at an angle to the direction of the applied wind force—to the right in the northern hemisphere so that water in contact with the wind moves to the right of the wind direction, in fact, almost at right angles to it. Representing the surface water column to an observer as comprising horizontal water planes, each one of these in an upper position in motion, will cause the lower placed one to move to the right of its motion, an effect termed the Ekman spiral. On average the water column influenced by wind will move in a path at right angles to the wind direction. The process tends to cause piling up of water at the centres of each hemispheric oceanic basin, but this cannot, in fact, occur for physical reasons. Water 100 to 200 m deep becomes distended in a horizontal direction and this water, which was endowed with the appropriate vorticity of its latitude prior to this, now loses its vorticity because of conservation of angular momentum requirements. Such water moves equatorwards because vorticity there is lower and as it does so it is deflected to the right in the northern hemisphere, i.e. to the west. The southward transport has caused water loss from the gyre system (principally from the 40° to 50° latitude zone) to be lost, hence, a return flow is necessary and this takes place when the water supplied southwards from the centre of the gyre displaces surficial water which flows along the western boundary to replace the missing water. In the Atlantic Ocean this intense warm water flow from the south constitutes the Gulf Stream. On the west coasts of continents surface water is transported by north–south winds as a result of the Ekman spiral. The westward transport of surface waters causes upwelling of deeper waters and these are the repositories of nutrient elements such as nitrogen. Consequently, upwelling areas are also areas of intense biological activity.

Oceanic surface velocities are measurable simply by tracking floating objects and from the results of such observations it is possible to state that at the surface oceans circulate completely in under a decade within each gyre and in a little longer between them in the same ocean. There is interconnection through flow between the Atlantic and Indian Oceans around the Cape of Good Hope and also between the Indian and Pacific Oceans through connections around Indonesia and Australia. However, whether there is surface water transport between the Atlantic and Pacific Oceans is difficult to determine because of the turbulence in the Antarctic Ocean.

There is also the question of deep circulation in the oceans and here the control is density stratification. As noted already water becomes denser with increased salinity and also with decreased temperature, and circulation based on these factors is termed thermohaline. Obviously freezing, evaporation, rain dilution and many other processes can impart distinctive salinity and temperature to a body of ocean water and this will tend to look for its appropriate level in the ocean based upon its consequent density. Continual circulation results from attempts by the oceans to accommodate such water bodies which are constantly being produced. The Atlantic Ocean has been examined in great detail and the following water masses identified therein may be mentioned:

(i) North Atlantic deep water (NADW) forms when warm Gulf Stream water (highly saline because of evaporation in low latitudes) cools by mixing with cold and less saline Arctic water in the neighbourhood of Greenland. The resulting dense water sinks to the bottom of the North Atlantic and then proceeds southwards until it disappears through mixing.

(ii) Antarctic Bottom Water (ABW) forms when water in the Weddell Sea cools in winter so that relatively salt-free sea ice forms and leaves a cold and very saline brine as residue. This then descends to the ocean bottom and on its way down mixes with less saline water, a mixing which decreases its salinity but not its temperature and results in the most dense water in the Atlantic Ocean. It can be traced along the bottom as far as 40°N latitude.

Other water masses form in rather similar ways and occupy levels appropriate to their densities and all of these result from the mixing of various water types. Clearly the further away from the source the greater the degree of mixing with environmental waters and eventually diffusion ought to produce homogenisation at which stage the individual identity of the water mass disappears. The general circulation of the deep oceans is shown in Fig. 5.2. The main sources of deep water are in the North Atlantic south of Greenland and at several locations around the region of Antarctica. As bottom waters flow away from their sources they become intensified at the western boundaries of the ocean basins and as water is supplied through the western boundary currents they spread out eastwards and commence a diffuse flow back to the source areas. During the entire process water also advects upwards towards the oceanic surface. Such deep circulation depends upon the flow of high

FIG. 5.2. Deep water circulation in the oceans. Horizontal shading = major ridge systems; thick lines = major bottom currents; thin lines = return currents. After H. Stommel, 1958, *Deep Sea Res.*, **5**, 80–2.

latitude-formed water and so there is a horizontal advection of water which has a vertical component as mentioned above. As well as advective transport, diffusion occurs. If any changes take place systematically and cannot be attributed to mixing they can be employed to measure the time interval involved during transport. Suitable ones include:

(i) alteration of element concentrations involved in biological pro-
     cesses such as nutrients like phosphorus, nitrogen and carbon;
(ii) radioactive dating isotopes such as radium-226, radiocarbon and
     silicon-32.

The following data are relevant (Table 5.3).

TABLE 5.3
ARTIFICIAL AND NATURALLY OCCURRING RADIOISOTOPES IN THE OCEANS

Radioisotope	Source	Half-life $(T_{1/2})$
^3H	Natural and bomb-produced	$1\cdot26 \times 10^1$ years
^{10}B	Natural	$2\cdot7 \times 10^6$ years
^{14}C	Natural and man-made	$5\cdot73 \times 10^3$ years
^{32}P	Induced	$14\cdot3$ days
^{32}Si	Natural and bomb-produced	$c.\ 6 \times 10^2$ years
^{35}S	Induced	$87\cdot1$ days
^{40}K	Natural	$1\cdot3 \times 10^9$ years
^{51}Cr	Induced	$27\cdot8$ days
^{54}Mn	Induced	300 days

TABLE 5.3 (*continued*)
ARTIFICIAL AND NATURALLY OCCURRING RADIOISOTOPES IN THE OCEANS

Radioisotope	Source	Half-life ($T_{1/2}$)
^{55}Fe	Induced	2·94 years
^{59}Fe	Induced	45·1 days
^{57}Co	Induced	270 days
^{58}Co	Induced	72 days
^{60}Co	Induced	5·27 years
^{65}Zn	Induced	245 days
^{87}Rb	Natural	5×10^{10} years
^{89}Sr	Fission product	50·4 days
^{90}Sr	Fission product	28 years
^{90}Y	Fission product	64·4 h
^{91}Y	Fission product	58 days
^{95}Zr	Fission product	63·3 days
^{95}Nb	Fission product	35 days
^{103}Ru	Fission product	41 days
^{103m}Rh	Fission product	54 mins
^{106}Ru	Fission product	1 year
^{106}Rh	Fission product	30 secs
^{110m}Ag	Induced	249 days
^{113m}Cd	Induced	14 years
^{129m}Te	Fission product	33 days
^{129}Te	Fission product	74 mins
^{137}Cs	Fission product	30 years
^{137m}Ba	Fission product	2·6 mins
^{128}I	Fission product	$1·6 \times 10^{7}$ years
^{141}Ce	Fission product	32·5 days
^{144}Ce	Fission product	290 days
^{144}Pr	Fission product	17·5 mins
^{144}Nd	Fission product	$2·4 \times 10^{15}$ years
^{147}Pm	Fission product	2·5 years
^{147}Sm	Fission product	$1·3 \times 10^{11}$ years
^{131}I	Fission product	8·05 days
^{140}Ba	Fission product	12·8 days
^{185}W	Induced	74 days
^{187}W	Induced	24 h
^{226}Ra	Natural	$1·6 \times 10^{3}$ years
^{228}Th	Natural	1·9 years
^{228}Ra	Natural	6·7 years
^{230}Th	Natural	8×10^{4} years
^{231}Pa	Natural	$3·2 \times 10^{4}$ years
^{232}Th	Natural	$1·4 \times 10^{10}$ years
^{235}U	Natural	$7·1 \times 10^{8}$ years
^{238}U	Natural	$4·5 \times 10^{9}$ years

Fission products arise through nuclear explosions whereas induced radionuclides are produced as a by-product of a generating plant powered by nuclear energy. The above table listing these and natural radioisotopes is adapted from T. R. Rice and D. A. Wolfe, 1971.[6]

Methods utilising many of the radioisotopes have been developed as a means of assessment of the movement rates of water and some results show that water molecules spend from 200 years to 500 years in the deep Atlantic Ocean prior to transfer to another reservoir (here the deep Pacific Ocean through the Antarctic Ocean) and from 1500 years to 2000 years in the deep Pacific Ocean prior to returning to the region of the Antarctic Ocean through southward flows at shallower depths.

More detailed studies in the Mediterranean Sea may be examined since these also relate to flow rate and cover a much smaller area with rather special characteristics. The Mediterranean Sea can be divided into two main basins separated by the Straits of Sicily; the eastern part may be regarded as a 'concentration basin' in which the quantity of water lost by evaporation is greater than the quantity gained by precipitation and the discharge of rivers. Two opposite flows connect this and the western basin through the straits and to compensate for the loss in the water balance more water enters the eastern basin than flows out of it. In order that the quantity of salt remains the same the quantity of salt imported by the entering flow must be equal to that exported by the outflow. Consequently, the upper flow moving eastwards transports more water of Atlantic origin with lower salinity than the deeper westward flow (Levantine Intermediate Water (LIW)) which is characterised by a salinity of $c.$ $38.7\%_{00}$ and a temperature of $c.$ $14°C$. Subsequent to passage by the western sill in the Straits of Sicily the LIW sinks to a level of stability at a depth of approximately $600\,m$ in the Tyrrhenian Sea. Here dense water masses form as a result of enhanced surficial cooling and evaporation during winter and these descend and spread westwards.

Tritium and sulphate ion-^{18}O profiles were made in eight hydrographic stations during 1972 and 1973 by G. Cortecci et al.[7] The stations are located between the Straits of Sicily and $41°$ N latitude in the Tyrrhenian Sea basin. Earlier work showed a deep thermohaline staircase structure in salinity and temperature profiles below the LIW water mass.[8] As regards the technical analytical work, this followed the procedure reported by G. Cortecci and A. Longinelli for measuring the $^{18}O/^{16}O$ ratios in sulphate ions and the graphite-reduction technique also described by these workers and all results were given relative to standard mean ocean water (SMOW).[9,10,11] Isotopic results were obtained together with data on salinity and temperature. Apropos the $\delta^{18}O(SO_4^{2-})$ values, these showed an extremely uniform distribution for both the deep and surface waters and averaged $+9.44\pm0.18\%_{00}$. Unfortunately this made it impossible for $^{18}O/^{16}O$ ratios of sulphate ions dissolved in different water masses to be used as tracers in the circulation and structure studies so far as the low Tyrrhenian Basin is concerned. The tritium values were more interesting and samples for these and the preceding measurements were obtained using Nansen bottles attached above the probe. The surficial and sub-surface tritium concentration values were close to 8 or 9 TU except in that area of the trench where values as high as 12 TU have been recorded at the surface. At about $39°59'$ N and $12°42·5'$ E at a depth of 3500 m in the trench, higher tritium values occurred. The tritium content of LIW decreased northwards and this is ascribed to the β-decay of the radioisotope and also to mixing with deeper water generally considered as poor in this radioisotope. Tritium concentration below LIW in some of the stations was found to decrease monotonically with depth but elsewhere rises were observed and these may have been due to younger advective water layers. Taking into account limitations caused by anticipated experimental error in tritium determinations (usually ± 1 TU) on the basis of the law of radioactive decay, the average flow velocity of the Levantine Intermediate Water was assessed at approximately 110 ± 60 m/day. Further work on the Mediterranean Sea was effected by E. Ozturgut in 1976. He studied the sources and spreading of LIW in the eastern part of that sea.[12]

In 1979 G. Cortecci and his associates described the results of further research on tritium and oxygen profiles in the eastern Mediterranean.[13] This work involved in the hydrographic casts the use of 1·7 litre capacity plastic Niskin bottles for collection of samples for tritium and oxygen analyses. Tritium measurements were made following the method described by J. F. Cameron in 1967, i.e. the water samples were distilled and 250 ml of the distillate electrolytically enriched until 8 or 9 ml remained.[14] The enriched sample was reduced by hot magnesium metal to hydrogen and was subsequently converted with ethylene on a Pd–asbestos catalyst to ethane which was then introduced into a low level proportional counter at a pressure of 1·9 atm. The Winkler method was employed for the dissolved oxygen analyses and the oxygen contents were reported in percent saturation with an accuracy of $\pm 1\%$. Salinity analyses were effected using an Autolab Salinometer. In the various areas selected some interesting results were obtained:

(i)   In the Levantine Basin south of Crete and Rhodes at station 46 the authors found that the upper layer (c. 150 m thick) possessed uniform salinity, temperature, tritium and dissolved oxygen concentrations with values of $39 \cdot 048 \pm 0 \cdot 08\%_{oo}$, $15 \cdot 21 \pm 0 \cdot 06°C$, $10\,TU$ and $96 \pm 0 \cdot 6\%$ saturation respectively and this water was lighter than some noted in the northern part of the basin but denser than the upper layers to the west. Consequently, it may sink and move westwards thus contributing to the LIW flow which appears to be fed mostly by water formed in the northern part of the basin.[12]

At station 30 nearer Crete the more saline layer occurs at 200 m depth and has tritium and oxygen contents of $10 \cdot 9$ TU and $94 \cdot 3\%$ saturation, values close to those measured in the upper layer at station 46 and giving evidence of sinking. Station 77 is located in the middle western part of the basin where there is a cyclonic circulation and here LIW may form but is not yet mixed. From data obtained at this locality a mean tritium content of $c.$ $10 \cdot 5$ TU may be assumed as well as mean oxygen saturation of 95% for the LIW formed in the Levantine Basin. It is a pity that the data are insufficient and that some refer to stations which are less representative than they might be.

(ii) In the Sea of Crete north of that island at station 25 very uniform temperature, salinity, tritium and oxygen values show that water convection reached a depth of about 200 m. The surficial and deeper tritium concentrations are higher than those measured in the Levantine Basin and in the western Mediterranean. A similar result was obtained by H. G. Östlund in 1969 for samples collected in 1965 after the thermonuclear tests of 1961 and 1962 in the central Aegean Basin and in the western Mediterranean where tritium concentrations were 32 ± 5 TU and 18 ± 4 TU respectively down to 100 m depth.[15]

(iii) In the Ionian sea the sub-surface waters above the salinity maximum have higher tritium concentrations moving westwards with 14 TU in the eastern Ionian and 19 TU in the western Ionian. At stations 16 and 20 the authors found that the LIW core layer showed the same tritium and oxygen concentrations and at station 13 the salinity values above $38 \cdot 72\%_{oo}$ gave a profile down to 350 m which is rather flattened as compared with the more eastern one, the maximal salinities being measured at 250 m and 300 m depth. A tritium gradient from $12 \cdot 1$ to $9 \cdot 8$ TU suggests that the LIW flowing through this particular station is formed by upper and lower layers which have undergone mixing with more tritiated overlying and less tritiated underlying waters respectively. They stated that even if it cannot be established with certainty because of lack of knowledge of its flow pattern that this LIW flows through the Straits of Sicily, the same tritium distribution was observed in the LIW at station 8 in the Sicilian channel. Tritium and oxygen concentrations usually decreased with depth but a significant inversion was found at station 20 at 300 m depth (11·9 TU and 90·2% saturation). These higher values are explicable on the basis of an advection of water from the Sea of Crete and at station 25 to the north of this island water with almost the same tritium and oxygen contents (12·5 TU and 90·5% saturation) was measured from 170 to 270 m depth.

(iv) Apropos the Sicilian ridge at station 8 WNW of Malta the water of Atlantic origin with salinity under 37·5‰ in the uppermost 100 m has uniform tritium and oxygen concentrations at 8 TU and 100% saturation respectively, the tritium concentration being close to that measured in surface waters in the south Tyrrhenian Sea.[7] Below the surficial layer there is a transition layer of approximately 150 m thickness where the Atlantic water and the LIW mix. The tritium distribution in this transition layer suggests a tritium concentration of over 12 TU for the upper layer of the Levantine water mass that undergoes mixing, the lower part of the LIW possessing 9·3 TU. Finally, G. Cortecci and his associates referred to the tritium distribution in the LIW core and results here traced to the salinity maximum demonstrated almost the same tritium concentration (c. 10·5 TU ±0·5 TU) from the formation area to the central Ionian (station 16).[13] This uniformity of distribution up to the central Ionian may indicate that the process of lateral mixing as well as vertical mixing with overlying and underlying waters is not important. The LIW core retained its original tritium concentration as the depletion by radioactive decay was negligible because of a relatively high flow rate. An alternative is that it could reflect time variations of the tritium concentrations in freshly formed LIW coupled with the tritium decrease by radioactive decay as the LIW migrates westwards. Cortecci et al. incline to the first hypothesis. This is because the rainwater tritium concentrations measured around the Levantine basin showed rather constant annual average TU values of c. 65 TU ±15 TU from 1968 to 1971 (IAEA Environmental Isotope Data) and through to 1974 (their work) so that the input of tritium in the LIW source areas and its tritium concentrations were probably almost constant from 1968 onwards. Thus the time spent by the LIW to reach the central Ionian is probably under a

year in agreement with the uniform tritium distribution observed
in the LIW core. Apropos oxygen–tritium–salinity correlations, a
general positive result was observed regarding tritium and oxygen
and this proved to be particularly good for waters below 150 m to
200 m depth (except for samples from station 8 in the Straits of
Sicily where the exchange of different waters between the eastern
and western basins rules out such correlation). The same trend
could be distinguished from tritium, oxygen and salinity diagrams. Deviations noted for surficial and sub-surface waters in the
various basins are explicable on the basis of the different meteorological conditions and patterns of circulation which determine particular tritium and oxygen concentrations. G. Cortecci
and his associates explained the tritium–oxygen correlation for
waters below 100–200 m depth by the following proposed sequence of events.[13] When a package of sea water sinks down from
the surface its tritium concentration decreases through mixing
and radioactive decay and its molecular oxygen is consumed
through biological and chemical processes. The greater depletion
of oxygen in the water body probably takes place above 100–
200 m depth just under the thermocline where easily oxidisable
materials are decomposed and respiration processes prevail.
Below this depth oxygen utilisation drops to a very low level and
the   oxygen   concentration   decreases   slowly   with   time.

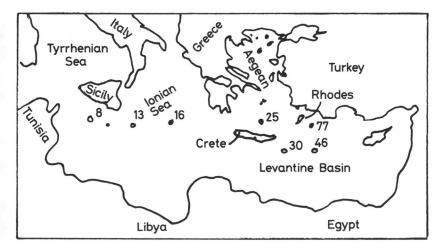

FIG. 5.3. Location of stations where samples were collected in study of tritium
and oxygen profiles in the eastern Mediterranean.[13]

Consequently, deep waters with tritium concentrations around zero show rather uniform and relatively high oxygen contents corresponding to c. 73% saturation. The accompanying Fig. 5.3 shows the station locations to which allusion has been made above.

5.4. OTHER MOTIONS IN THE OCEANS

These include tides, waves, etc. as well as the injection of fresh water into the seas at the mouths of rivers.

5.4.1. Tides

Tides involve periodic rises and falls in sea level, are caused by the Moon and Sun acting on the rotating Earth and vary in amplitude from place to place. In small seas such as the Mediterranean there is practically no tide, but the phenomenon is an impressive twice daily event in countries bordering the great oceans.

The lunar attraction, and to a lesser extent that of the Sun, is responsible for water moving periodically on the terrestrial surface. If the radius of the planet is designated r and the distance between the centres of the Earth and Moon R with the mass of the Moon M, then F, the force due to the joint system on a unit mass of the Earth anywhere along the radius, would be the same if all parts of the planet were rigidly joined to the centre and is given by

$$F = \frac{gM}{R^2}$$

and the force F' on a unit mass on the terrestrial surface not anchored rigidly to the planetary centre (in this case sea water) is given by

$$F' = \frac{gM}{(R-r)^2}$$

so that the difference between the rigid Earth and non-rigid water in terms of force is given by

$$\Delta F = F' - F = gM \frac{R^2 - (R^2 - 2rR - r^2)}{R^2(R-r)^2} = \frac{2r(R-r)}{R^2(R-r)^2} = \frac{2r}{R^2(R-r)^2}$$

and as $R \cong 600\,000$ km and $r \cong 6000$ km, R vastly exceeds r and $(R - r)$ may be replaced by R so that $\Delta F = 2r/R^3$.

Differential force between the rigid Earth and the fluid water of its surface tends to pull the latter moonwards under the sub-lunar point, and on its diametrically opposite side the planet is being differentially pulled away from surface water. The consequence is that water would bulge out at the sub-lunar point as well as on the opposite side were it not for the fact that its chemical bonds are too strong to permit this to happen. In fact, therefore, the tide is not caused by the direct vertical attraction of the satellite on a column of water. There is variation from point to point over the whole water-covered model of the Earth, but only at the sub-lunar point and its diametric opposite is this force vertical in direction. It may be inferred that everywhere else an ever increasing horizontal component will be introduced proceeding away from these two points and it is precisely this differential horizontal force distribution which makes water flow on Earth towards both the sub-lunar point and its opposite. One location on the planetary surface will experience in a day two high tides and two low tides, the semi-diurnal tidal cycle. The solar day is 24 h but 24 h and 50 mins must elapse before the Moon returns once again to the same location on the Earth (because the satellite revolves around the planet) and this means that the commencement of a particular cycle at a point on the Earth is displaced 50 mins every day from the previous day. As regards the solar effect, this is much smaller than the Moon's, amounting in fact to only about 45% of the latter and it is extremely complex because of the difference between the plane of the Moon's orbit round the Earth and the plane of the Earth's orbit round the Sun. It is not surprising therefore that in various parts of the Earth it is possible to find mixtures of semi-diurnal and complete diurnal tidal cycles dependent upon these two effects. When Earth, Moon and Sun are aligned the tidal range for semi-diurnal regions will be maximum because of the combination of influences of both heavenly bodies on the planet and such occasions take place at new and full moons and constitute spring tides. When Sun and Moon are at right angles at quadrature tides have their minimal amplitude and constitute neap tides.

5.4.2. Waves

Waves may be generated by winds which pile up water in their passage over the oceanic surface and the amplitude and periodicity of the ridges so formed depend on the intensity of the winds. However complex the interaction of winds and ocean may appear to be, the pattern so produced may be resolved into a combination of quite regular wave patterns. The depth to which waves influence oceans is a function of their wavelengths and constitutes the wave base. In deep ocean areas this is at a shallow level, i.e. under 50 m, which is a mere 1% or so of the depth of the ocean, but as coasts are approached the wave base will encounter the bottom and this has a great effect on the properties of the waves. In the first case, i.e. in deep water, the velocity of a wave is related solely to wavelength and the expression which can be applied is:

$$v = \sqrt{\frac{gL}{2\pi}}$$

where v is the velocity, g is the acceleration due to gravity (980 cm per second per second) and L is the wavelength. In shoal areas at depths under 25 m the velocity is controlled by depth not wavelength and the relationship is expressed:

$$v = \sqrt{gh}$$

where h is the water depth.

Wave train is the term applied to a pattern of waves and this moves out of the area of generation through wind action which supplies a group velocity although within the wave train the various wavelengths actually move with different velocities according to the relevant equation (that for deep water waves). The longer the wavelength the greater the velocity so that the first waves to arrive from a far-off storm are long ones and they constitute what is termed a swell. The group velocity is approximately half the phase velocity of the longest wavelength in a wave train and the longer waves tend to absorb shorter wavelengths during travel. The consequences are that remote regions receive merely a continuous swell from storm disturbance regions. In shoaling areas wave velocity is a function of water depth only and the modified wave front tends to become a replica of the submerged coastal features. The actual period of a deep water wave is directly proportional to the velocity and thus to the wavelength to which the velocity is related. Long wavelength, high velocity waves are decelerated after they arrive near a coastline. As there cannot be a change in the wave period in shallow waters the wavelength of the incoming wave decreases so that the height of the wave increases and at a water depth of approximately 1·3 times the wave height the wave will break. After this it dissipates on the shore as surf and swash.

5.5. COASTLINES

Solar energy is dissipated along the boundary between land and sea, the Sun driving the wind which makes waves that impinge on the land and also causing evaporation which subsequently condenses and precipitates, often over land, later channelling a return to the seas. Coastal processes are extremely variable and usually proceed with a high level of activity so that the forms and materials of the coastal zones are subject to considerable and often rapid change both spatially and in time. Processes affecting a coast include waves and tides together with winds and these operate so as to influence beach and coast forms in both plan and profile.

Waves can be divided into two categories following the above discussion; these are sea waves (actually being generated in an area) and swell (longer, lower, modified waves which have travelled a long way from the area of generation).

Wave characteristics at a particular location on a coastline are a function of its aspect with respect to generating winds and swell and also of the offshore and coastal plan. Clearly during wave generation energy is transferred from air to water and thus waves increase in size with increasing strength of wind, increasing wind duration and the fetch of open water. This process is incompletely understood, but empirical relationships have been established and curves produced which permit the significant wave height and period to be estimated for any combination of wind variables.[15] The significant height is defined as the mean of the highest one-third of the waves and it tends to mask the variability inherent in practically all wave trains which results from the large number of waves of many different heights and periods which move in a wide range of directions. The three-dimensional wave spectrum can be analysed using Fourier techniques as a result of which the energy assigned to the various actual periods can be obtained, as G. E. R. Deacon has pointed out.[16]

J. L. Davies classified coastlines in terms of wave types into four major groups.[17] These are shown in Fig. 5.4. The storm wave environment is found in high latitudes in areas where strong winds often blow and create steep waves and the relevant coasts frequently possess long stretches of rocky cliffs and wave-cut platforms. They are ecologically important, providing appropriate habitats for seaweeds which are being exploited (for instance off western Scotland) as well as for lobsters, crabs, etc. Lower latitudes are swell-dominated, stormy high latitude-created swells being divisible into west and east coast swells. The west coast swells are

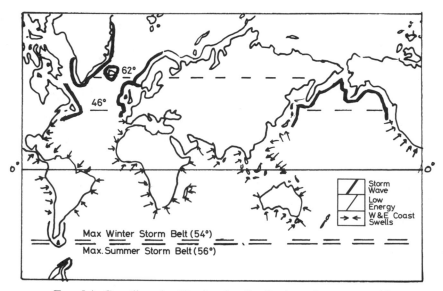

FIG. 5.4. Coastline classification by distribution of wave types.[17]

higher and possess more energy and may have a mean period of 14 secs with a length of over 300 m, hence undergoing a high degree of refraction prior to reaching the coast. The fourth wave type is a low energy one occurring either where the fetch restricts wave growth or where sea ice or some offshore feature prevents effective waves from actually reaching the coast.

In deep water conditions it is feasible to predict wave characteristics from data on winds and waves have a velocity dependent upon their length. Waves cannot influence the bed of the sea at depths exceeding their length. Refraction of long waves is important because it may be a considerable time before they reach the coast. Wave refraction diagrams can be constructed to assess the degree to which energy is converging on or diverging from the pattern of orthogonals (lines at right angles to the wave crests). Relevant expressions are:

$$I_i = K(EC_n)_b \sin a_b \cos a_b$$

$$I_i = K''(EC_n)_b \cos a_b \ (V_t)/U_m$$

where I_i is the immersed load being transported along a coast, K is 0·17, K'' is 0·28 (numerical constants), a_b is the breaker approach angle, C_n is the wave form velocity and V_t is the longshore current velocity, U_m being the maximum horizontal velocity of the water particles in the wave orbit.

These equations fit empirical data derived by measuring material movement using tracers.[18] Short waves approach at a considerable angle to the shore and cause downwave currents which become particularly marked on a gently curving shoreline. These can cause serious erosion where there is inadequate supply of beach material reaching the coast from updrift. An excellent example is Selsey Bill in Sussex, England. Longshore currents determine zones both of accretion and erosion as well as joining with tidal scour in dispersing sewage effluent discharge into the sea. As a result of this beaches downdrift of the sewage discharge points can be polluted.

Radioisotope and other tracers have been used in connection with water pollution studies and the work of J. Guizerix and his associates at Nice and Menton in France is relevant as also is that of G. E. Eden and R. Briggs in 1967.[19] The latter investigated the problem of beach pollution by sewage discharged from submerged outfalls and one of their aims was to find a means of predicting relevant dispersal patterns which could make an important contribution to improving the design of outfall systems. The radiotracer used was ^{82}Br and this was added continuously to the flow of sewage entering the sea through a submerged outfall or alternatively as a single injection to the sea at the site of a hypothetical outfall. Thereafter the dispersal was mapped by scanning the area using γ-scintillation counters which were towed by a catamaran at predetermined depths and were monitored by simple echo sounders. The submersible counters were based upon a scintillation head, AERE type 1653B contained in a waterproof cylinder together with its 1500V EHT supply and an impedance matching amplifier with a gain of 5. The cylinders were fitted into submersible towing vehicles which could be towed at speeds of up to 5 knots. Ultrasonic transducers were mounted on the upper surfaces of the vehicles so that the depth of immersion could be determined from surface echoes which were detected by a commercial battery operated echo sounder. Double tracer techniques were used as well so as to obviate problems which might arise from adsorption. There are a number of classes of radioisotope which were considered by these workers:

(i) radioisotope tracers unlikely to be removed from solution by naturally occurring surfaces, for instance bromide (^{82}Br) and cobalticyanide in which the cobalt is radioactive (^{58}Co or ^{60}Co, see Table 5.3) as well as chloride-^{36}Cl and to a degree tritium in tritiated water in the absence of certain of the clay minerals;

(ii)   species reversibly taken up by natural surfaces with which water comes into contact and including ^{24}Na and the heavier alkali metals;

(iii) species irreversibly taken up by such surfaces including radio-isotopes of polyvalent metals in uncomplexed forms, e.g. zirconium.

Table 5.4 lists relevant details.

TABLE 5.4

THE UPTAKE OF RADIOISOTOPES FROM HERTFORDSHIRE, ENGLAND, RIVER WATERS BY MUD DEPOSITS FROM THE SAME RIVERS.[19] 1 g MUD SHAKEN FOR $\frac{1}{2}$h WITH 10cm^3 WATER CONTAINING THE RADIOISOTOPE

Isotope	Percentage taken up by mud	Concentration factor[a]
^{36}Cl	0	0
^{82}Br	0	0
^{131}I (iodide)	47	48
^{131}I (iodate)	83	263
^{24}Na	8	4
^{86}Rb	43	41
^{137}Cs	97	1 740
^{90}Sr	51	56
^{140}Ba	85	305
^{106}Ru	74	153
^{144}Ce	92	620
Zr/^{95}Nb	97	1 740

[a] Activity per gram of mud solids/activity per gram of total water (assuming 20% dry matter in the mud).

Double labelling techniques involved use of a non-adsorbable tracer such as ^{82}Br for the liquid phase and a highly adsorbed tracer such as ^{198}Au or $^{110/111}$Ag for the solid phase. It is possible to study segregation effects and the technique was employed to demonstrate the short-circuiting of solids in a sludge-digestion system and to compare relative retention periods of dissolved and suspended matter in a percolating filter. By simultaneously adding a non-adsorbed tracer and the radioisotope being investigated it is feasible to detect reversible adsorption on the bed of a river or on the walls of a sewer. Measurement of the ratio of the activities due to the two tracers at a point downstream provides a sensitive means of detecting reversible adsorption.

Waves comprise a constantly varying force which acts on beach material and changes in them result from factors such as wind directional changes. Consequently, beach and waves are rarely, if ever, in a state of equilibrium even though only several hours may be necessary to achieve it (the relaxation time). Variations of this type are of great practical importance. For instance, in storm periods when highly destructive waves attack the shore, the beach is lowered so that the backshore area may be eroded and damage to coastal defences result. The cliff foot support may be removed and this can be followed by slumping or erosion through hydraulic action, the first occurring where unconsolidated materials are involved and the second where hard rocks exist.

From the above it may be seen that beaches, and indeed coastlines, result from the interaction of processes with materials. For instance, storm waves act in different ways according to the nature of the material upon which they operate. Steep storm waves which break on solid rock can sometimes initiate shock pressures that can trigger disintegration and subsequent block formation and attrition, perhaps even comminution. Similar waves breaking on shingle can throw some to the backshore area so forming a storm beach ridge of the type displayed by Chesil Beach in southern England. On sandy beaches storm waves are totally destructive and can create a steep beach scarp at the limit of their influence as well as carrying sand offshore to the break point and there forming a submarine bar.

Coastal features form in response to processes and materials and relate to the total environment which controls the nature of the processes themselves. Studies of the features can provide a great deal of information apropos their originating processes. However, individual material types can be deposited in a number of differing forms of coastal feature, e.g. sand can be found in coastal dunes, berms, bars, barriers, spits, offshore banks and many other places and in fact it is the commonest and most versatile beach material as a result of the fact that its particulate dimensions are optimal for pick-up by moving air or water. Fine sediments on the other hand can be deposited solely in a suitable environment which determines the subsequent morphology. Mud can accumulate only in sheltered areas such as salt marshes, lagoons or the quieter shelf areas and each of these environments differs from the rest. Shingle is less common than sand and creates recognisable beach forms the most important of which are storm shingle ridges conspicuous in the backshore region. This type of ridge can cover very extensive areas of the backshore region and is exemplified by the famous English feature of Dungeness.

Sediments of the type alluded to above may be classified on the basis of their dimensions and the accompanying table gives details (Table 5.5).

TABLE 5.5

SIZES OF COMPONENTS OF SEDIMENTS. THIS IS SOMETIMES TERMED
THE WENTWORTH SCALE

Name	Particle diameter (mm)
Boulders	>256
Cobbles	64–256
Pebbles	4–64
Granules (Gravel)	2–4
Sand	0·062–2
Silt	0·004–0·062
Clay	$<0·004$
cf. the Unified Soil Classification System of A. Casagrande and the US Army Corps of Engineers:	
Gravel (G)	3 in. to No. 4 sieve $(\frac{3}{16}$ in.)
Sand (S)	
coarse	No. 4 sieve to No. 10 sieve
medium	No. 10 sieve to No. 40 sieve
fine	No. 40 sieve to No. 200 sieve
Silt (M) } Clay (C) }	$<$ No. 200 sieve

Clay is defined variously as particles smaller than 5 microns (0·005 mm) or 2 microns (0·002 mm) and silt as fines larger than clay sizes but smaller than No. 200 sieve size.

If.an oceanic floor sediment contains particles which are almost all of one size range then the sediment is well sorted and, similarly, if a sediment is composed of one mineralogical or chemical type it is pure. Of course most sediments are neither well sorted nor pure in nature and it is exactly because of this that so much information can be derived from them regarding their history. Clay-sized material may contain very fine grained calcium carbonate, but mostly it is made up of silicate and oxide minerals of which the most important are the clay minerals. The sand fraction of sediments comprises minerals which are resistant to erosive forces of weathering and of these the most common is quartz. However, in some places denser resistant minerals may become concentrated as sands and even become of economic significance—for instance, cassiterite sands and ruby-bearing sands of southeast Asia and the diamondiferous sands of Namibia.

5.6. THE DEPOSITS OF THE DEEP OCEANS

Particles are transported to the oceans by rivers and less importantly by the atmosphere and glaciers. Air masses moving across the continents acquire as a function of velocity a steady state concentration of suspended matter with various dimensions and once over water these ought to fall out following Stokes' Law. In fact, however, packages of dust-laden air are bounded above and below with air layers having properties sufficiently different to ensure that turbulence maintains the fine particles longer in suspension than would be the case if simple gravity settling alone operated. Particles smaller than 15 microns (0·015 mm) stay up so long that their main removal mechanism is by entrapment in rain and snow. This is, in fact, the reason why radioactive fallout injected into the lower part of the atmosphere (i.e. the troposhere) is removed at any latitude more efficiently in high precipitation areas than over arid regions. As regards glacial transport, continental ice sheets as in Antarctica and Greenland are efficient as agents both of erosion and sediment transport. In the case where glaciers terminate on land their sediments may supply debris to rivers. Where termination is on the margin of the sea or in the sea as in the above two land masses, such debris is contributed directly to the oceanic floor.

\When particles are transported to the oceans they can be distributed by a great variety of forces which may modify the initial pattern of distribution controlled by the supply source on the continent\ One of these forces comprises surficial currents such as the Gulf Stream and in submarine canyons there are turbidity currents, sediment slurries denser than ordinary water which move downslope and are triggered by earthquakes, hurricanes or high sediment discharge in a river system reaching the sea. An instance of earthquake triggering is afforded by the Grand Banks (Newfoundland) earthquake of 1929 which promoted such a large downslope sediment movement that transatlantic cables near this location were ruptured\ In fact it appears that turbidity currents are the primary mechanism of transportation of materials down to the abyssal plains. Another important type of current is the category of bottom currents which are known sometimes to be sufficiently powerful to move sediments. There is much evidence for this assertion. Photographs of the bottom exist which show features which could have been produced only by bottom currents, features such as ripple marks, coarse residues left behind after the removal of fines, etc. Also floats which are able to maintain station at a designated depth in the ocean show strong currents even at very great depths and current meters have been employed in some localities to measure currents occurring at the bottom. On theoretical grounds too, in order to maintain the balance of water moving in the Atlantic Ocean Basin, strong northward-moving bottom currents have to be postulated for the western South Atlantic in order to balance the shallower southward transport. The deep ocean is clearly a sink for materials transported into it by the various mechanisms outlined and a general classification of these is as follows:

(i)   pelagic biogenic deposits, the remains of organisms, calcareous and siliceous tests, organic and phosphatic material;

(ii) non-biogenic deposits, i.e. sedimentary components which did not originate from the processes of life in the oceans and which include (a) pelagic detrital deposits, those components originating near the oceanic surface and thereafter depositing on the sea floor by settlement; (b) bottom-transported detrital deposits, silts and sands and remains of shallow water organisms and materials from the land typically transported by turbidity and bottom currents; (c) indigenous deposits which originate within the ocean basin as a result of several processes such as the submarine reaction of volcanic materials with sea water, the migration and recon-stitution of materials in the sediments and the weathering of volcanic materials exposed above sea level.

Into category (i) falls a very important group of calcareous materials and these include Foraminiferal tests, coccoliths and pteropod tests which usually are under 30 microns in diameter. The first two are calcitic, but the third are molluscs with aragonitic shells. Remains of all of these are preserved in deep sea sediments at water depths usually under 3500 m; the term 'Globigerina ooze' is used for deep sea sediments mainly composed of Foraminiferal tests and coccoliths.

The calcium carbonate concentrations in deep sea sediments reflect the relative rates of accumulation of clay and $CaCO_3$. The regional distri-butions of $CaCO_3$ concentrations in deep sea sediments show some very interesting features which may be listed:

(i)   In the Atlantic Ocean:

(a)   Topographic highs occur with $CaCO_3$-rich sediments.

(b)   In certain but not all areas of biologically very active ocean surface there are high $CaCO_3$ contents in the bottom sediments even at great depths—for instance, along the eastern path of the

Gulf Stream at approximately 40°N latitude and also under the area of oceanic upwell off the coast of Namibia.

(c) There are regions such as the Argentine Basin which, despite the high biological activity in the surface waters, are practically devoid of $CaCO_3$ in the bottom sediments at any depth.

(ii) In the Pacific Ocean:

There is a similar pattern in the East Pacific Ocean where the sediments of the East Pacific Rise are $CaCO_3$-rich as also are sediments underlying the biologically highly productive waters along the East Pacific equatorial current. However, in the North Pacific the same situation occurs as in the Argentine Basin and the $CaCO_3$ contents of the sediments are very low. Generally there is a gradual decrease in calcium carbonate with increasing depth until about 4500 m and at greater depths than this the concentration drops to extremely low average values. The point at which the $CaCO_3$ concentration of deep sea sediments decreases rapidly with depth is usually termed the compensation depth and it constitutes that depth at which the rate of supply of $CaCO_3$ is exactly compensated by an equal rate of solution of the compound. That it should exist at 4500 m is surprising because laboratory experiments show that the level at which supersaturation relative to calcium carbonate changes to undersaturation for the compound ought to be 500 m. Consequently, a kinetic model for the explanation of the dissolution of the compound at depth is left and evidence was obtained from a Pacific experiment in which accurately weighed and polished spheres of calcite were precisely located along a wire suspended in the ocean.[20] After subjection to the dissolving action of sea water and subsequent removal, it was found that spheres below 3800 m showed greater dissolution than those from shallower levels. The rates of solution must be related to the changing properties of the appropriate water column even below the supersaturation level of 500 m and upwards, i.e. even in the undersaturated level. Repetition with Foraminiferal tests took place and the same effect was noted. The Foraminiferal tests in deep sea deposits show a distribution helpful in interpretation of the behaviour of $CaCO_3$ in ocean water profiles and two main types can be distinguished on the basis of the shell structure, namely fragile spinose tests and dense, rather flattened and non-spinose tests. Above a particular depth (about 3800 m in the central Pacific Ocean) both types are found in the sediments in large quantities, but below that depth practically all of the fragile tests are dissolved and leave a residue only of the more robust ones. This boundary is termed the lysocline and it represents a change in efficiency of dissolution with depth in the oceans. It has been shown in the laboratory that the lysocline can be explained by a sharp alteration in the degree of undersaturation in the ocean. Above the lysocline the deposition rate of calcium carbonate exceeds the solution rate determined by the properties of the water column involved. Once $CaCO_3$ commences to accumulate, the local pore waters and that microboundary layer which exists at the interface between sediment and water become saturated with respect to calcium carbonate. This effectively halts the dissolution of falling tests as they reach the bottom. At the lysocline the solution rate is near the deposition rate and the accumulation of calcium carbonate is diminished. If the solution rate equals the rate of deposition then the compensation depth and the lysocline are identical. In areas where there is very high surface water organic productivity it is possible for the deposition rate to exceed the solution rate at all depths sampled below the lysocline and under such conditions the establishment of a saturated pore water and microboundary layer at the sediment–water interface will act to preserve the calcareous tests as they fall out on to the ocean floor. The compensation depth will be deeper.

As well as calcareous materials, siliceous ones contribute to category (a) above because there are several groups of organisms which occur in deep sea sediments—these are diatoms, radiolarians, sponges and silicoflagellates. Diatoms constitute the majority in terms of quantity and like the coccolithophorids they are photosynthetic organisms whereas radiolarians, like Foraminifera, are particle-eaters. Silica in the form deposited by such organisms is very soluble in sea water so that the accumulation of tests on the floor of the ocean depends upon the facility with which a particular test is dissolved while descending through ocean waters. There is no equivalent to the lysocline, the rate of solution being a function of the size of the test, the concentration of silica in the relevant water column and the protective chemical bondings with organic compounds or elements such as magnesium on the test surface. Siliceous sediments occur mostly at high latitudes, in the equatorial Pacific Ocean and in regions were upwelling of waters takes place.

Turning to non-biogenic deposits these fall into three major groups, namely sands, silts and clays, volcanic products and metalliferous materials.

Clays and associated minerals are distributed according to a number of factors and may be pelagic, bottom-transported or indigenous. Clay sedimentation in the Atlantic appears to be mainly influenced by continental sources and evidence for this is provided by, for instance, the distribution of gibbsite (hydrated aluminium oxide), the common end-product of intense tropical weathering and a principal component of bauxite (the most important aluminium ore). It occurs where continent-derived materials are dominant. Reinforcement is provided by the variation in the kaolinite/chlorite ratio in the Atlantic, a ratio especially useful as it represents the maximum effect of climatic zones on weathering products. Kaolinite is again a product of weathering in tropical climates and in such circumstances chlorite is rather easily destroyed. On the other hand, weathering in temperate and arctic conditions results in either the formation or the preservation of chlorite. Consequently, there is a sharp decrease in the kaolinite/chlorite ratio with increase in latitude as has been recorded from the Atlantic Ocean.

As regards the Pacific Ocean, this is bordered peripherally by deep trenches which trap bottom-transported material deriving from the continents. It is believed, however, that in the past continuous canyons and other transportation channels down the continental rise must have existed in the northeast Pacific Basin to result in the large abyssal plains found there. Apropos sands and silts, these are transported to the oceanic floor by a number of mechanisms and constitute an important part of the abyssal plain deposits. Often brought down from the continental margin by turbidity currents is a silt component which is transported by western boundary currents from the glacial debris from high latitudes. Minerals resulting from comminution and crushing of continental rocks by glaciers include quartz, amphibole, etc., and detrital silt-sized material is also contributed by aeolian transport from arid terrains. A high level of quartz has been detected in the eastern Atlantic Ocean deriving westward from the Sahara and wind-blown quartz has been identified in the Hawaiian soils. This latter probably originates in the Gobi Desert because there is practically no quartz in the volcanic mineral assemblage of that basaltic island group.

There are three types of volcanic product on the bottom of the oceans, namely rock fragments, volcanic glass and minerals such as montmorillonite produced by the interaction of hot water and volcanic material. Volcanic islands are mainly basaltic in composition so that it may be expected that basaltic rock fragments are very common on the sea floor around them. Ocean ridges and sea mounts have provided samples of basalt and volcanic glass in deep sea deposits is also mainly basalt although occasionally pumice is found. Pumice is a more acidic glass originating in continental volcanism. Basaltic glass can also occur and may be either relatively unhydrated hyaloclastite or hydrated palagonite. The former is stable but the latter devitrifies in sea water and forms the zeolite phillipsite and montmorillonite. Zeolite minerals in deep sea sediments may derive indigenously and they comprise lattice-type silicates many of which have strong ion-exchange and ad-sorption capacity. Usually they occur in volcanic regions as late phase products of hot water activity. Phillipsite is the commonest in Pacific Ocean sediments, is rich in potassium and may comprise over 50% of the sediments in areas with a low rate of clay accumulation and a high rate of volcanic activity.

Metalliferous deposits include the ferromanganese nodules found throughout the oceans. Ferromanganese or manganese nodules, i.e. nodules of hydrous manganese and iron oxides, are common on the deep sea floor and these compounds may occur also as coats on minerals and as concretions. Consequently, there is a great variation in size from under 30 microns to 850 kg mass. The average composition is given in Table 5.6.

TABLE 5.6

AVERAGE COMPOSITION OF MANGANESE NODULES. AFTER J. MERO.[21]

Element	Weight percentages (dry weight basis)		Element	Weight percentages (dry weight basis)	
	Pacific Ocean	Atlantic Ocean		Pacific Ocean	Atlantic Ocean
B	0·029	0·03	Fe	14	17·5
Na	2·6	2·3	Co	0·35	0·31
Mg	1·7	1·7	Ni	0·99	0·42
Al	2·9	3·1	Cu	0·53	0·2
Si	9·4	11·0	Sr	0·081	0·09
K	0·8	0·7	Y	0·016	0·018
Ca	1·9	2·7	Zr	0·063	0·054
Sc	0·001	0·002	Mo	0·052	0·035
Ti	0·67	0·8	Ba	0·18	0·17
V	0·054	0·07	Yb	0·0031	0·004
Cr	0·001	0·002	Pb	0·09	0·1
Mn	24·2	16·3			

Manganese nodules have been located by dredging and underwater photography. They have proved to be most common in regions with low accumulation rates for clay and $CaCO_3$, specifically areas scoured by bottom currents, e.g. the Drake Passage between Antarctica and South America, and areas of slow pelagic clay deposition, e.g. the central Pacific Ocean. The sources of the component elements in the nodules are probably detrital oxides of manganese and iron from continents together with manganese and iron derived from the reaction of submarine volcanic products with sea water. Nodules and concretions grow at various rates which, according to radioactive dating measurements on ferromanganese deposits both on the continental margin and along the Mid-Atlantic Ridge, may sometimes be very rapid. However, deep sea nodules from the ocean bottoms show evidence that their growth rates may be as low as $5 \, mm/10^6$ years (again as determined by radioactive dating). Although some nodules may be sediment-covered, many lie at the interface between water and sediment. Some recoveries suggest that the former may be blanketed under as much as a metre of sediment.

As regards the origin of the nodules, there is probably not just one but several. However, a certain number of common conditions are necessitated and it appears that all Mn and Fe in them has undergone a solution phase. Under the oxidising conditions of most of the sea floor at depth the solubility of these elements is extremely low. They can be supplied in solution either by the flushing of hot sea water through a newly emplaced and cooling basalt deposit on the sea floor or by diffusion from pore waters of buried sediments which have become reduced at depth resulting in an increase of dissolved Fe^{++} and Mn^{++} (the reduced ionic species of iron and manganese). It has been observed that in nearshore deposits bacterial reduction of sulphate in anoxic sediments causes the migration of iron and manganese; this is a mechanism of transport of these elements from deep sediments to the oxygenated sediment–water interface where they will undergo oxidation and precipitation of the oxides. Unfortunately, this does not explain the high metal contents of the nodules because under the conditions indicated other metals than iron and manganese will be immobilised. A probable practical source for much of the iron and manganese found is fine-grained particulate transportation through pelagic sedimentation, particles rich in these metals slowly reaching the ocean floor after which remobilisation and reprecipitation take place as a result of the intervention of specific bacteria. Other metals may arrive in association with the very adsorbent ferromanganese particles and subsequently attain inclusion in the growing nodules.

The major oceanic ridge systems are characterised by concentrations of metals which are higher than those in adjacent areas and this probably results from the different environmental conditions favouring such concentrations such as submarine volcanism, increased elevation over the oceanic floor preventing the receipt of large quantities of bottom-transported detritus, etc. The Red Sea is a particularly interesting and unusual environment which in some ways resembles an oceanic ridge except in that it is a narrow sea bounded by continental rocks. Deep hot brines exist in some basins within it and underlying them are metal-rich deposits containing manganese, lead, copper and zinc. Hot saline waters flow through these deposits and enter the deep basins simultaneously transporting the metals and depositing them within the basins. This sea has been discussed in detail by the author and H. A. Gunatilaka in their book *Copper: Its Geology and Economics* published by Applied Science Publishers in 1977.[22] The region appears to be a locus for the generation of new oceanic crust.[23] Data from it and from the Salton Sea in California confirm that their metal-rich hydrothermal emanations are chloride-rich and sulphide-poor brines which are denser than sea water and form brine pools. On discharge on the sea floor the metal-rich brine contacts a large reservoir of oxidised sulphur formed either by sulphate-reducing bacteria or (perhaps and) by other reactions involving organic matter. The penetration of metal-rich fluid through the H_2S-charged interstitial sediment causes a massive sulphide deposition. In the Red Sea, two hot brine pools have a copper content of 0·014 to 0·8 ppm compared with the normal content of sea water which is 0·003 ppm and one dredged sample contained 0·5% Cu, 2·6% Zn and 0·15% Pb, perhaps the first known syngenetic concentration of base metals actively formed in a marine setting. It has been estimated that the metal content in the sediments is equivalent to about US$6 billion at mid-70s prices.[24] Cooling is probably going on. The importance of the Red Sea and similar regions is that they demonstrate the role of saline brines as metal carriers and perhaps identify new ore areas.

The sulphate reduction alluded to above may occur in sediments and anoxic waters and is a function of the availability of organic matter, as E. T. Degens pointed out in 1965.[25] Reduction rates for the Black Sea have been given as 0·5 to 42 g S/m^2/year for surficial silts and below 5 m depth the rates of H_2S production dropped by 50% to 90%. However, the presence of readily utilisable organic matter increased the rate of H_2S

production in surface sediments by a factor of up to 100. Some measured rates of sulphur and organic matter production in some representative modern environments are shown in Table 5.7.

TABLE 5.7
RATES OF H$_2$S GENERATION AND SULPHUR PRODUCTION IN MODERN ENVIRONMENTS

Locality	SO_4^{2-} content (mg/litre)	Rate (mg H$_2$S/litre/day)	Rate (g S/m^2/year)
Barents Sea littoral	up to 2 700	9·09–24·26	181–445
Black Sea	up to 2 200	0·027–2·31	0·49–42
Krasnovodsk Bay	up to 2 200	3·87–8·41	7·1–153

RATES OF PRIMARY ORGANIC MATTER PRODUCTION

Locality	Gross organic production (g/cm^2/year)	S equivalent based on 10% utilisation of organic matter (g S/m^2/year)
Black Sea	100	4·5
Long Island Sound	770	34
Continental Shelf	270	12
Sargasso Sea	320	14

All data from P. A. Trudinger et al., 1972[26]

Oceanic sediments accumulate under gravity and form deposits in which, where no disturbance occurs, a backwards and continuous sequence through time is given by passing downwards through them. This may be effected by coring which provides a stratigraphic record, parts of which may be dated using radioactive methods, a tool providing valuable information apropos the rate of sediment accumulation. Coring can be carried out with a gravity corer which is a tube with a weight attached and which is dropped into the sediment. This cannot penetrate far, however, so that a piston corer may be substituted if depths greater than about a metre are desired. This can reach depths up to 20 m. Both implements create uncertainty regarding the recovery of the topmost sediments near to the water–sediment interface due to the fact that they normally have rather small diameters. A third type, the box corer, can obviate the problem and provide a practically undisturbed record of the sediment but only down to a metre or so. In recent years the same power techniques applied to oil well drilling on land have been extended to the sea. Ships equipped for research such as the *Glomar Challenger* can use them and indeed have done so in programmes such as the Deep Sea Drilling Programme of the National Science Foundation. The management of this particular enterprise was the Scripps Institution of Oceanography. Coring can be effected in waters of great depth such as 5000 m and penetrations in excess of 400 m have been made successfully. Three types of radioactivity have been used in geochronometry, the dating of core sediments, namely:

(i)   Primary involving nuclides which have a half-life of adequate length to ensure that even five aeons after solar system formation they still exist in measurable quantities. Among these are potassium-40, rubidium-87, thorium-232, uranium-235 and uranium-238.

(ii) Secondary involving nuclides associated with the uranium decay series and having half-lives of the order of 100 000 years, e.g. thorium-230, actinium-231 and uranium-234.

(iii) Cosmic ray-induced nuclides which are continuously being created at present mainly through cosmic rays impinging upon the upper atmosphere. The best known examples are tritium, radiocarbon, silicon-32, beryllium-7 and beryllium-10, all relatively short-lived and sustained in the atmosphere and in the oceans at roughly constant levels when naturally formed (i.e. artificially introduced pulses being excluded), their continuous production making up for the radioactive decay losses.

Conditions which have to be fulfilled before any of the above can be used in the measurement of geologic time include the following:

(i)   The radioactive species acting as a clock must be isolated from its daughter at the time of deposition if the growth of the daughter is to be measured or, in the case of a decay series, from its radioactive parent if the decay of the species is to be measured.

(ii) The system must be closed, i.e. there must be no input or output of the radioactive species selected as the clock (this applies to the daughter if growth is being used).

(iii) The half-life of the radionuclide must be appropriate to the particular time interval being investigated and hence cannot be either too long or too short for the application.

Some of the above-mentioned radioisotope clocks have been discussed earlier and it has been seen that tritium and radiocarbon are optimal for transit time measurements for water in aquifers from measurements made in them, some of which have been alluded to by the author in his book *Ground Water*.[27] As regards radiocarbon, the quantity of this produced in the upper atmosphere annually has been determined to be approximately 9800 g for the Earth and bearing in mind the half-life ($T_{1/2} = 5730$ years) it is possible to calculate that about $8 \cdot 1 \times 10^7$ g of carbon-14 are maintained on the planetary surface, i.e. *c.* $8 \cdot 29$ g/cm². The general distribution is summarised in Table 5.8.[28]

TABLE 5.8
CARBON-14 DISTRIBUTION

Reservoir	$g\,^{14}C/cm^2$
Atmosphere (mostly CO^2)	0·12
Biosphere (organic)	0·33
Mostly dissolved organic carbon compounds in oceans	0·59
Oceans (H_2CO_3, HCO_3^-, CO_3^{--})	7·25
Total	8·29

Clearly the main reservoir is the ocean and $CaCO_3$ tests and organic compounds in deep sea sediments can be dated using radiocarbon. In fact, samples as old as 40 000 years can be dated and such work on deep sea cores has indicated measurement of the length and end of the last major glacial period. It has been shown that this terminated effectively some 11 000 years ago and on the continents this was marked by the retreat of glaciers which originally covered large tracts of Europe and North America, the oceans concurrently expanding in volume with both depth and sea level changes also occurring. Foraminiferal evidence supports this interpretation of the recent history of the planet.

As well as radiocarbon (and tritium), silicon-32 has been employed in attempting to date deep sea sediments and so has beryllium-10. This latter has a half-life of $2 \cdot 5 \times 10^6$ years and assuming a constant rate of deposition in a particular locality the decay of this radioisotope can be followed through a core of sediment.

Turning now to the uranium decay series, this has important applications. Some of these relate to the use of the series in dating the deeper parts of cores, i.e. those parts which extend back several hundred thousand years. The decay schemes involved are as follows:

$$^{238}U \xrightarrow{4\cdot49 \times 10^9 \text{ years}} {}^{234}Th \xrightarrow{24\cdot1 \text{ days}} {}^{234}Pa \xrightarrow{1\cdot18 \text{ min}}$$

$$^{234}U \xrightarrow{2\cdot48 \times 10^5 \text{ years}} {}^{230}Th \xrightarrow{7\cdot5 \times 10^4 \text{ years}}$$

$$^{226}Ra \xrightarrow{1622 \text{ years}} {}^{222}Rn \xrightarrow{3825 \text{ days}} \text{ and stepwise down to stable}$$

$$^{206}Pb, \quad {}^{235}U \xrightarrow{7\cdot13 \times 10^8 \text{ years}} {}^{231}Th \xrightarrow{25\cdot6 \text{ h}} {}^{231}Pa \xrightarrow{3\cdot43 \times 10^4 \text{ years}}$$

stepwise down to stable ^{207}Pb

In the dating of deep sea sediments probably the most important radionuclides are ^{230}Th and ^{231}Pa which have rather similar chemical properties differing markedly from those of uranium. In rocks the ratio of ^{232}Th to ^{238}U is approximately 4:1 but in sea water this is very different at 0·0005. The reason for this lies in the differences in chemical properties alluded to above. The oceans are slightly basic and contain dissolved carbonate and bicarbonate ions actually constituting a solution in which thorium cannot dissolve. On the other hand, uranium can dissolve by forming strong bonds with carbonate ions. It is not surprising therefore that the concentration of uranium in sea water is 3×10^{-6} g/litre whereas that of thorium is a mere $0·0015 \times 10^{-6}$ g/litre. ^{230}Th and ^{231}Pa are produced in sea water as a result of the radioactive decay of uranium. They are rapidly removed as insoluble phases and are, in fact deposited on the floor of the oceans. An interesting consequence is that they are found to occur in deep oceanic sediments in excess quantities greater than would be expected for them in equilibrium with uranium in detritus originating on land. In the oceans there will be no excess of uranium because of its high solubility (i.e. formation of soluble complexes with carbonate).

As regards potassium–argon dating, only one isotope of potassium is radioactive, i.e. ^{40}K, and this has a half-life of $1·24 \times 10^9$ years. Of its decay products, 88% comprise ^{40}Ca, the common calcium isotope, and 12% are ^{40}Ar, a rare gas. The latter if trapped in appropriate rocks and minerals will accumulate if the temperature stays below 300°C. This is a useful dating tool and as such it has a very wide range in time, from about 100 000 years back almost to the age of the planet. As a result of the presence of relict argon originating from the weathering of continental materials in clay minerals in deep sea sediments, it is difficult to date such non-biogenic layers although they are rich in potassium. $^{40}K/^{40}Ar$ dates can be obtained from associated volcanic layers, however, because during their molten phase all included argon was lost so that all argon now measured has to be a result of the decay of potassium-40.

Magnetic reversal dating is another interesting technique; it is based on the fact that the polarity of the planet is known to periodically undergo reversals and evidence for this has been obtained partly in connection with the development of ideas apropos plate tectonics. Magnetic field measurements were made at sea using magnetometers with gyrostabilised platforms which were towed behind ships or aircraft. Nearly all the magnetism assessed comes from magnetite-bearing basalts of the oceanic floors. Such data constitute a record of magnetic anomalies recorded graphically on continuous traces and they represent minute departures (in milligauss) from the mean value of total magnetic intensity measured in the direction of the geomagnetic field of the Earth. In the late 1950s a persistent north–south alignment of such anomalies was discovered in the eastern Pacific Ocean and on east–west traverses these demonstrated a very characteristic and oscillatory pattern of positive and negative values about the mean. They were thought to delineate elongated bodies of magnetite-bearing rock (inferred to be basalt) aligned north–south, having magnetisation patterns sharply contrasting with those of their east and west neighbours. Similar phenomena were also found in the Atlantic Ocean. F. J. Vine and D. H. Matthews in 1963 in a classic paper analysed the problem and suggested a solution which marks a giant step forward for geology.[29] Earlier information strongly implied that geomagnetic field reversals occurred during the past few million years. Now computed magnetic profiles assuming normal magnetisation of the ocean floor did not resemble the observed profiles so the approach became to use an alternative model with 50% of the crust reversely magnetised in alternating bands. The reasoning is that if such magnetic reversals actually occur and if the sea floor spreads (as H. H. Hess proposed[2]) then basaltic magma ought to well up at the axis of the oceanic ridge, becoming magnetised in the direction of the prevailing geomagnetic field as it cooled below the Curie temperature, thereafter forming a massive dyke subsequently spreading laterally away from the said axis. Repetition of the process with the dyke being split axially would cause the creation of a series of blocks with alternately

242   SURFACE WATER

normal and reversed magnetisation and becoming progressively older
with increasing distance away from the axis.

Using this model a good agreement with the observations was obtained and so the Vine–Matthews hypothesis came to be accepted
generally. It is a potential magnetic recorder for determination of the
velocity of the oceanic conveyer belt involved in spreading of the sea
floor and provides an accurate time scale for reversals.[30] Existing
polarity is believed to have commenced about 700 000 years ago and
prior to that the geomagnetic field was reversed (except for brief episodes
of present polarity) for approximately 2×10^6 years. Two significant
advances assisted in this interpretation. One was undoubtedly the improvement in potassium–argon dating technology for lavas and the other
was the demonstration that the anomaly patterns are parallel with the
mid-oceanic ridges and symmetrical so that the two sets of anomalies on
each side of the ridge mirror each other. The accompanying Fig. 5.5
correlates magnetic epochs based upon the polarity time scale and is
derived from A. Cox *et al.*[31]

Further examination of the sea floor spreading concept was made
during the JOIDES (Joint Oceanographic Institutes Deep Earth
Sampling) project which was financed by the US National Science

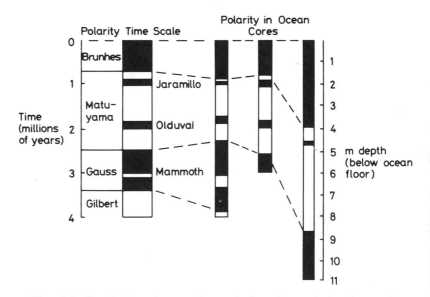

FIG. 5.5. Correlation of magnetic epochs based on polarity time scale.

Foundation, particularly during the third leg of the series of cruises across the South Atlantic at about 30°S. Drillings reached the Upper Cretaceous as well as basaltic basement and the age of the sediment directly overlying the latter as determined from micropalaeontological evidence was found to increase systematically away from the axis of the mid-Atlantic Ridge and implied a spreading rate of 2 cm per year. JOIDES data suggest that the rate of spreading is more constant than had at first been thought and M. Ewing among others believed that it was greater during the past ten million years than it had been previously.

Deep sea cores afford a great deal of information apropos past climates. For instance it has been possible to detect past glacial episodes causing a lowering of sea level by approximately 100 m at maximum about 18 000 years ago. The abundances of certain microorganisms in cores are useful indicators also. For instance the Foraminifer *Globorotalia menardii* is a temperature index and the higher the percentage of the species in fossil assemblages, the warmer the temperature of the surface palaeoocean must have been. One of the best tools for palaeoclimate determination is the oxygen isotopic composition of Belemnoidea, Foraminifera, etc. In the case of calcium carbonate deposition from sea water an isotope exchange reaction can be written for the two common oxygen isotopes oxygen-16 (99%) and oxygen-18 (1%) thus:

$$\tfrac{1}{3}CaCO_3{}^{16} + H_2{}^{18}O = \tfrac{1}{3}CaCO_3{}^{18} + H_2{}^{16}O$$

and for this reaction the equilibrium constant K is given by

$$K = \frac{(\text{Number of molecules } CaCO_3{}^{18})^{\frac{1}{3}} \times (\text{Number of molecules } H_2{}^{16}O)}{(\text{Number of molecules } CaCO_3{}^{16})^{\frac{1}{3}} \times (\text{Number of molecules } H_2{}^{18}O)}$$

At equilibrium calcium carbonate has a different ratio of isotopes from water because the chemical bonds differ for the two molecules. Although removal of the compound from solution as a precipitate alters the isotopic composition of the water, this has no effect with regard to ocean water which constitutes an almost infinite sink. Thus the ratio $H_2{}^{16}O/H_2{}^{18}O$ can be taken as constant. However, at different temperatures, different quantities of the heavier oxygen isotope will occur in the $CaCO_3$ relative to sea water (K is temperature-dependent) and in 1948 the Nobel Prize winning chemist Harold C. Urey calculated the expected temperature controlled variation in the process, see Table 5.9.

TABLE 5.9
OXYGEN ISOTOPE FRACTIONATION AS A FUNCTION OF TEMPERATURE
BETWEEN WATER AND CALCIUM CARBONATE

Temperature (°C)	$^{18}O/^{16}O$ water	$^{18}O/^{16}O$ crystal
0	$\dfrac{1}{500}$	$\dfrac{1\cdot026}{500}$
20	$\dfrac{1}{500}$	$\dfrac{1\cdot022}{500}$

In Table 5.9 it is assumed that the isotopic composition of sea water is constant so that the colder the water in which the calcium carbonate forms, the more enriched in oxygen-18 (i.e. the heavier) it is. Assuming isotopic constancy of sea water, a measure of the oxygen isotope composition of a calcium carbonate shell or test deposited from it will be a measure of its temperature. Of course the isotopic composition of sea water has varied greatly throughout Earth history, but as a first approxi-

TABLE 5.10
DATING TECHNIQUES FOR THE DEEP OCEANS

Method	Dating range (years)	Datable materials
^{14}C	0–45 000	Carbon-containing materials
^{32}Si	0–2 500	Diatoms and radiolarian-rich deposits
^{231}Pa	0–120 000	Deep sea sediments, manganese nodules, corals
^{230}Th	0–40 000	Deep sea sediments, manganese nodules, corals
$^{40}K/^{40}Ar$ fission tracks	60 000–several hundred thousand	Volcanic materials
^{10}Be	Up to 10×10^6 years	Manganese nodules
Magnetic stratigraphy: (i) based upon K–Ar	0–4·5 million	Deep sea sediments
(ii) based upon extended chronology	4·5–150 million	Deep sea sediments

mation the method has provided interesting results and in fact appropriate corrections have been devised for the glacial phases of the ice age, for instance by Cesare Emiliani. These take into account the preferential storage of the lighter isotope ^{16}O in snow and ice accumulating on continents. This increases the $^{18}O/^{16}O$ ratio in the oceans concomitantly with increase in salinity and the result is that any calcareous tests precipitating in the oceans during glacial episodes will have a higher $^{18}O/^{16}O$ ratio even if the sea water temperature was the same as it is at present. The palaeotemperature tool has been discussed by the author in detail in his book *Paleotemperature Analysis* (Number 2 in the series *Methods in Geochemistry and Geophysics*).[32]

A tabular summary of dating techniques is appended (Table 5.10).

5.7. THE HISTORY OF THE DEEP OCEANS

Planetary crustal movements appear to be largely concentrated in three types of structural feature characterised by earthquakes and volcanicity, i.e. mountain ranges (including island arcs), mid-oceanic ridges and major faults with large horizontal displacement. In 1965, J. Tuzo Wilson suggested that such mobile belts form a continuous network dividing the surface of the Earth into a number of large and rigid plates.[33] Any feature at its apparent termination could be transformed into either of the other two and such a junction was termed a transform. Associated faults constitute transform faults. As noted earlier, mid-oceanic ridges expand and produce new crust according to the sea floor spreading hypothesis and as this happens residual and inactive traces of the former positions of the faults remain behind in their topography. On the other hand as the ocean crust moves down beneath the convex side of island arcs the distance between two such island arcs linked by a transform fault and convex with respect to each other will ultimately diminish as crust is consumed. These ideas underwent complete theoretical formulation and development and the transform fault concept was extended to a spherical surface. The Earth's surface was divided into 20 blocks of various sizes and divided by boundaries of three types:

(i) Oceanic rises in which new crust is created.
(ii) Oceanic trenches in which crust is destroyed.
(iii) Transform faults where crust is neither created nor destroyed.

Tectonic activity in the lithosphere had long been known to be mainly confined to a series of narrow zones marked by earthquakes and volcanicity, the best known being the Girdle of Fire around the periphery of the Pacific Ocean. These zones are now referred to as the boundaries of six major and perhaps twice as many minor plates according to the theory of plate tectonics which has been called a revolution in the earth sciences,[34] a revolution leading from continental drift to a new global tectonics, in fact. As a result the above categories in modified form appear as:

(i)   Constructive plate margins at which new crust is created by upwelling of material from the mantle and marked by the mid-oceanic ridges.

(ii) Destructive plate margins at which crust is destroyed by being pushed downwards beneath island arc–oceanic trench systems or mountain belts with cold lithosphere descending into the asthenosphere as far as 700 km, such commonly curvilinear features being termed subduction or Benioff zones.

(iii) Conservative plate margins at which crust is neither created nor destroyed, the plates sliding laterally past each other and characterised by transform faults which frequently offset the ocean ridge axis. Since the transform faults may have inactive extensions beyond the offset ridge axis these may define circles of rotation for the previous motions and therefore provide a possible key to the direction, if not the rate, of the past plate movements.

The place of meeting of two plate boundaries or three plates is termed a triple junction, the sole manner in which the boundary between two rigid plates can end. As seen earlier magnetic anomalies can provide much useful information including the amount of spreading away from the ridge axis.

Plate tectonics have been applied to the problem of the break-up of the original super-land mass of Pangaea; the first disruption appears to have taken place in the southern part of the North Atlantic, northwestern Africa moving apart from North America during the early Jurassic. The spreading zone subsequently moved progressively north and south so that Africa and South America began separating in the Middle Cretaceous and Europe and North America started to move apart at roughly the same time. There is a great deal of palaeomagnetic evidence for this hypothesis, incidentally. The Indian Ocean seems not to have existed earlier than the Cretaceous, but by the end of this period India is thought to have been moving northward across the Tethys towards Asia with Australia–Antarctica parted from Africa. It was believed that tensional subsidence and marine transgression marked tension between the components in the Cretaceous with sea floor spreading commencing in the early Tertiary.[34] B. D. Johnson *et al.* in 1980, however, presented a revised model of sea floor spreading between India and Australia from the inception of the phenomenon 125 million years ago to the change to a new system 90 million years ago stemming from the wide recognition of the M-series of magnetic anomalies off the southwest margin of Australia from a revised pole of opening between Australia and Antarctica and by the extension in the central Wharton Basin of the late Cretaceous set of magnetic anomalies.[35] The phase of spreading which is represented by the later anomalies has been extended back to 90 million years so as to give a resolved pole that describes the rotation of India from Australia consistent with the M-series anomalies, DSDP (deep sea drilling programme) site ages and fracture zone trends. An abandoned spreading ridge in the Cuvier abyssal plain is believed to indicate a ridge jump (within the first ten million years of spreading). Elsewhere two types of ridge jump (one to the continental margin of Australia or India and the other by propagation of the spreading ridge into adjacent compartments thereby causing them to fuse) are postulated to account for other observations. I. O. Norton and J. G. Sclater in 1979 also gave a model for the evolution of the Indian Ocean and the breaking up of the southern super-remnant continent originating from the splitting of Pangaea and termed Gondwanaland and they used magnetic anomaly and fracture zone data to present a self-consistent tectonic history both of the Indian and South Atlantic Oceans.[36] Clearly both the Atlantic and Indian Oceans are rather young in terms of Earth history but curiously the Caribbean appears to be older. K. Burke and coworkers believed that ocean floor in this region was formed mainly during the Jurassic and Cretaceous.[37] Subduction of the young Caribbean ocean floor started by late Jurassic times according to them and persisted until the Eocene on its northern and southern borders. By the late Eocene the Caribbean area was occupied by what they termed a buoyant mass of abnormally thick and shallow oceanic crust modified from more normal crust by the intrusion of great thicknesses of late Cretaceous sills. At the beginning of the Oligocene a cordon of extinct arcs surrounded the buoyant ocean area and transform motion replaced subduction along the northern and southern edges. Subduction was restricted to boundaries with the American and Cocos plates that were being consumed on the east and the west respectively. Convergence at the rate of about 1 cm per year between the North and South American plates since 38 million years ago appears to have been accommodated largely by internal deformation of the Caribbean plate producing a pattern of faults with an intriguing resemblance to the slip lines in a modified Prandtl cell (the authors do not explain this). Studies on the region in question have also been carried out by a number of other workers, e.g. G. L. Freeland and R. S. Dietz in 1971.[38]

The evolution of a young ocean basin has been studied by J. R. Cochran in the area of the Gulf of Aden in 1981.[39] In this case new marine geophysical data are used to describe the structure and history of this gulf. Magnetic anomaly data show sea floor spreading magnetic anomalies on Sheba ridge from the axial anomaly to anomaly 5 (10 million years before the present), between the Owen fracture zone and 45°E and to anomaly 2' (3 million years before the present) or anomaly 3 (4 million years before the present) west of 45°E. The data actually do not support the two episodes of sea floor spreading recently proposed. Landwards of the sea floor spreading anomalies is a magnetic quiet zone of uncorrelatable anomalies. This has a boundary which is also a structural one marking the edge of Sheba ridge with deeper basement lacking a significant topographic gradient found on the landward side. A magnetic quiet zone occurs not only where Sheba ridge splits continental lithosphere but also on east Sheba ridge where the ridge splits the old oceanic lithosphere of the Owen and Somali Basins. There the position occupied by the continental margin within the gulf is marked by non-magnetic ridge complexes that stretch from the continents to the Owen fracture zone. The magnetic quiet zone boundary is not an isochrone in either the Gulf of Aden or the Red Sea suggesting that significant horizontal motions can occur prior to the initiation of sea floor spreading. The offset on the Dead Sea rift is used to estimate that from 80 to 160 km of opening (amounting to between 65% and 200% extension of the initial rift valley) occurred in the Gulf of Aden and Red Sea prior to establishment of a mid-oceanic ridge. It is suggested that the development of a new ocean basin occurs in two stages, namely:

(i) a first stage involving extension over an area perhaps 100 km wide in a rift valley environment without an organised spreading centre;

(ii)   a second stage involving concentration of the extension at a single axis and the inception of true sea floor spreading.

The Galapagos spreading centre at 86°W has been extensively studied and a detailed geothermal field investigation was carried out recently by K. E. Green and his associates and entailed 443 heat flow measurements in an area of 570 km^2, revealing the general planform of the geothermal flux.[40] They also permitted the first true areal estimate of the near axis conductive heat flux to be made. The instrusion process and associated hydrothermal circulation dominate the surficial heat flow pattern with circulation apparently continuing beyond the limits of the survey. The actual average of the conductive heat flux is 7·1 ± 0·8 HFU (295 ± 33 mW/m^2), about one-third of the heat flux predicted by plate models. The remaining heat is apparently removed by venting of hydrothermal waters at the spreading axis and through basalt outcrops and hydrothermal mounds off axis. The pattern of surficial heat flux is lineated parallel to the axis of the strongly lineated topography. Sharp lateral gradients in the heat flow greater than 10 HFU/km near escarpments (commonly expressed as high heat flow at the tops of the scarps and lower heat flow in the valleys) may indicate a local concentration of the circulation by surface fault systems and/or variable sediment thickness. Other important papers on the Galapagos rift at 86°W include the following:

(i)   A regional morphological and structural analysis by R. W. Allmendinger and F. Riis who presented analysis of a detailed topographic survey with a multi-beam bathymetric survey system of the crest and upper flank of the Galapagos rift between 85°20′ and 86°17′ W.[41] The morphology of the area is lineated because of elongated ridges and troughs parallel to the ridge axis. The magma source appears to be shallow and so magma is available everywhere along the axis.

(ii)   A study of the volcanism, structure and evolution of the rift valley was carried out by T. H. van Andel and R. D. Ballard using an Angus towed camera system.[42] Unlike the terraced rift valley of the mid-Atlantic ridge, the Galapagos rift valley comprises a single trough a few hundred metres deep between faulted walls leading to low crestal ranges.

(iii) R. D. Ballard examined sheet flows, collapse pits and lava lakes of the rift valley and noted that the sheet lava flows had various surface forms such as smooth, rippled or jumbled.[43] Collapse pits usually have numerous lava pillars around them. It is suggested that the sheet flows may be submarine equivalents of surface flow pahoehoe (this last word refers to a type of lava having a festooned and ropey type of surface structure).

The accompanying Fig. 5.6 shows part of the Galapagos rift where active hydrothermal fields are known to occur. The structure and morphology of these hydrothermal fields and their relationship to the volcanic and tectonic processes of the rift valley have been examined by Kathleen Crane and R. D. Ballard in a paper which appeared in 1980 and from which the above mentioned figure has been taken.[44] In that work the Angus camera system was also used. The Angus camera system comprises a survey camera with lighting system mounted in a heavy duty steel frame capable of being towed within a few feet of the ocean floor on a conventional trawl wire. It has a 16 mm wide angle lens and takes 3000 photographs (35 mm) per lowering.

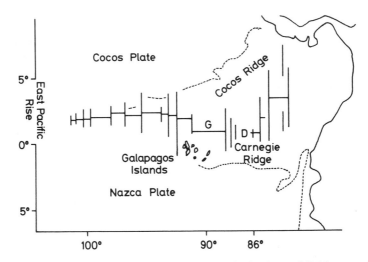

FIG. 5.6. Part of Galapagos rift where active hydrothermal fields occur.[44]

Some important evidence on the history of the oceans derives from investigations into the origin of mountain belts since a significant feature of most of these comprises ophiolite complexes, masses of basic or even ultrabasic igneous rocks such as basalt, gabbro and peridotite occurring as enormous thrust slices and especially characteristic of melange terrains. The composition as well as the structure of these strongly suggest oceanic crust or uppermost mantle which has been sheared from descending plates and forced upwards under compression into the overlying rock. Ophiolites commonly have associated with them radiolarian chert, a siliceous sedimentary rock thought to derive from a deep sea deposit. Ophiolites give significant clues to the presence of former subduction zones now enclosed by continents, i.e. they mark the line of joining of continents which have collided due to sea floor spreading. Hence the ophiolite belt showing thrusting of late Cretaceous age and running from Oman through the Zagros mountains in Iran and the Taurus mountains in Turkey appears to mark either closure of the African–Arabian continent on Eurasia or possibly a subduction zone in the Tethys between Africa and Eurasia (Tethys is the name given to a Mesozoic geosyncline which developed between Gondwanaland and Laurasia, the southern and northern pieces which split off from the original super-land mass Pangaea, and covered southern Europe, the Mediterranean and the Himalayan region perhaps extending even into Burma and SE Asia).

Two types of mountain building resulting from plate movements are known and are:

(i)   island arc-Cordilleran type which develops on leading plate edges above subduction zones and is marked by metamorphic belts and divergent thrusting;

(ii) collision type forming after the impact of continent upon continent or continent upon island arc and showing dominant metamorphism of blue schist type, thrusting being dominantly towards and on to the consumed plate.

Orogenic (mountain building) belts provide important clues to the creation and disappearance of oceans throughout long time intervals, but it must be stressed that much remains to be learned about them. For instance, some geologists think that Pre-Cambrian orogenic belts may be fundamentally different from younger ones arising in the last few hundred million years and there may be something in this idea if, for instance, the planetary crust was thinner in the early Pre-Cambrian era. One major problem has arisen in the case of the late Palaeozoic era Hercynian orogeny in western Europe. This attained its maximum perhaps 250 or 260 million years ago and does not demonstrate extensive ophiolitic complexes. It extends its folding and thrusting phenomena over a wide area which cannot by any stretch of the imagination be construed as a narrow belt.

Taking all difficulties into account, however, there can be no doubt that plate tectonics have been very successful in explaining lateral movements of the crust. A simple model of plate dynamics and mantle convection has been proposed very recently by B. H. Hager and R. J. O'Connell in an attempt to quantitively relate plate tectonic motions with thermal convection in the mantle which is deemed to drive them.[45] They suggest that cooling and thickening of lithospheric plates with age and subduction cause large scale horizontal density contrasts tending to drive both plate motions and mantle flow. They quantified these driving forces associated with the density contrasts to determine if they can drive the observed plate motions. First two-dimensional models were computed to evaluate the effects of assumed rheologies and boundary conditions. They were unable to obtain plate-like behaviour in viscous models with traction-free boundary conditions. However, the piecewise uniform velocities distinctive of plate motion can be imposed as boundary conditions and the dynamic consistency of the models evaluated by determining whether the net force on each vanishes. If the lithosphere has a Newtonian viscous rheology, the net force on any plate is a strong function of the effective grid spacing used, leading to ambiguities in the interpretation. Incorporating a rigid–plastic lithosphere which fails at a critical yield stress into the otherwise viscous model removes these ambiguities. The model is extended to the actual three-dimensional (spherical) plate geometry. The observed velocities of rigid–plastic plates are matched to the solution of the viscous Stokes' equation at the lithosphere–asthenosphere boundary. Body forces from the seismically observed slabs, from the thickening of the lithosphere obtained from the actual lithospheric ages and from the differences in structure between continents and oceans are included. Interior density contrasts such as those resulting from upwellings from a hot bottom boundary layer are assumed to occur on a small scale compared to plate dimensions and are not included. The driving forces from the density contrasts within the plates are calculated and compared to resisting forces resulting from viscous drag computed from the three-dimensional global return flow and resistance to deformation at converging boundaries; the r.m.s. residual torque is $\sim 30\%$ of the driving torque. The density contrasts within the plates themselves can reasonably account for the plate motions. Body forces from convection in the interior may provide only a small net force on the plates. At converging boundaries the lithosphere has a yield stress of ~ 100 bars; drag at the base of the plates is ~ 5 bars and resists plate motion. The net driving forces from subducting slabs and collisional resistance are localised and approximately balance. Driving forces from lithospheric thickening are distributed over the area of the plates as is viscous drag. The approximate balance of these two forces predicts plate velocities uncorrelated with plate area as observed. The model represents a specific case of boundary layer convection; the dynamical results are stated as consistent with either upper mantle or mantle-wide convection.

East–west aligned features are characteristic of some ocean basins, e.g. in the eastern Pacific there are a number including the Mendocino Escarpment off California which suggested faulting. There are also a number in the Atlantic. Once the concept of triple junctions was introduced, very interesting developments occurred and their geometry as related to the famous San Andreas transform was studied by W. R. Dickinson and W. S. Snyder in 1979.[46] They believe that understanding the evolution of the feature is a key both to broad aspects of regional geology and to the development of specific structural provinces. Though stable in the regional sense, the paired triple junctions at the ends of the transform have had transient unstable configurations wherever the trends of the prior trench of the newly developing transform were locally not collinear. The resulting instabilities were mainly of kinds inferred to induce extensional tectonics within a nearby region. Passage of the Mendocino fault–fault–trench triple junction northwards along the central Californian coast coincided well with pulses of initial subsidence in Neogene sedimentary basins near the continental margin and with eruptions at local volcanic centres in the coast ranges. Passage of the Rivera ridge–trench–fault triple junction southwards was associated with the rifting events which formed the Californian continental borderland and the Gulf of California.

Seismic images of the deep structure of the San Andreas fault system have been examined in 1981 by G. Zandt.[47] He stated that three-dimensional inversion of teleseismic P-wave travel time residuals recorded at the US Geological Survey central California array has resolved small scale ($\sim$ tens of km) crustal and upper mantle heterogeneity down to depths of 90 km beneath the Californian coast ranges. Upper crustal velocity variations of $\pm 8\%$ correlate closely with surface geology. Lower than average velocities are associated with thick Tertiary sedimentary fill and higher than average velocities with basement exposures. Lower crustal velocity heterogeneity of $\pm 4\%$ appears to reflect variations in crustal thickness. A thinner crust is indicated southwest of the San Andreas fault and northwest of San Pablo

Bay. A linear zone of low velocities (0 to -4%) sub-parallel to the San Andreas fault was resolved in the upper mantle. The preferred interpretation is that the low velocities indicate a narrow upwarp of asthenosphere to unusually shallow depths (~ 45 km) beneath the coast ranges. Such an unusual upper mantle structure may have been produced by the northwest migration along the Californian coast of a transiently unstable Mendocino triple junction (see ref. 46). The inversion results also indicate the possibility of partial decoupling of the crust from the upper mantle.

Research into passive margins has proceeded apace in recent years and X. Le Pichon and J. C. Sibuet in 1981 discussed the stretching model of D. McKenzie,[48] applying it to passive continental margin formation assuming local isostatic equilibrium.[49] The quantitative implications and the fit to the IPOD (international phase of deep drilling) data from DSDP (deep sea drilling programme) investigations on the Armorican and Galicia continental margins of the northeast Atlantic Ocean are also discussed. The amount of brittle stretching observed in the upper 8 km of the prestretched continental crust attains a maximum value of c. 3. This large degree of thinning is comparable to the thinning of the whole continental crust observed by seismic refraction measurements and required by the model for the entire lithosphere. The authors suggest that the agreement amounts to establishing the simple stretching model as a good first approximation to the actual physical process of formation of the margin. They add that it is thus possible to compute simply the thermal evolution of the margin and to discuss its petrological consequences. It is also possible to obtain a quantitative reconstruction of the edge of the continent prior to break-up. Finally, the large slope of the base of the lithosphere during the formation of the margin results in a force similar but opposite to the 'ridge-push' force acting on accreting plate boundaries.

5.8. THE CHEMISTRY AND BIOLOGY OF THE SEAS

Clearly the oceans represent the fount of the existing biological world since, as is believed, life originated in them. Original unicellular organisms ultimately produced the complex life forms existing today, many in the multitudinous environments of the oceanic system.

The chemistry of water involves three main processes, namely:

(i)   concentration and speciation of ions;
(ii) acidity;
(iii) oxidation–reduction potential.

The accompanying table (Table 5.11) records the most insoluble trace element compounds in sea water with the maximum concentrations compatible with the major anionic composition of sea water.

TABLE 5.11
SOLUBILITY CONTROLS ON CONCENTRATION OF TRACE ELEMENTS IN SEA WATER[20]

Element	Insoluble salt in normal sea water	Expected concentration (log moles/litre)	Upper limit of observed concentration (log moles/litre)	Expected concentration in sulphide-rich sea water (log moles/litre)
Lanthanum	$LaPO_4$	−11·1	−10·7	—
Thorium	$Th_3(PO_4)_4$	−11·8	−12·7	—
Cobalt	$CoCO_3$	−6·5	−8·2	−12·1
Nickel	$Ni(OH)_2$	−3·2	−6·9	−10·7
Copper	$Cu(OH)_2$	−5·8	−7·3	−26·0
Silver	$AgCl$	−4·2	−8·5	−19·8
Zinc	$ZnCO_3$	−3·7	−6·8	−14·1
Cadmium	$CdCO_3$	−5·0	−9·0	−16·2
Mercury	$Hg(OH)_2$	+1·9	−9·1	−43·7
Lead	$PbCO_3$	−5·6	−9·8	−16·6

The expected concentrations at 25°C are calculated on the basis of the following thermodynamic concentrations, a (activities) of the anions: $\log a_{PO_4^{--}} = -9\cdot3$; $\log a_{CO_3} = -5\cdot3$; $\log a_{OH^-} = -6\cdot0$; $\log a_S = -9\cdot0$ and Ag, Hg and Pb form strong chloride complexes.

Clearly the oceans are undersaturated with respect to the trace elements and, for that matter, the major elements except possibly for lanthanum and other rare earth metals.

As regards acidity, this depends upon the concentration of hydrogen ions; these can be produced during the dissociation of water thus:

$$H_2O = H^+ + OH^-$$

and the equilibrium product constant for the reaction may be expressed

$$K_{dissociation} = [H^+][OH^-]$$

The value of this at normal pressure and 25°C is $K_{dissociation} = 10^{-14}$ so that the hydrogen ion concentration of pure water is 10^{-7}. On the (logarithmic) pH scale, the equivalent pH value is 7. However, the oceans are not composed of pure water so that variations occur and the chemical compounds involved in regulating the changes are CO_2 (as carbonic acid) and calcium carbonate. It is possible to relate the pressure of carbon dioxide in the atmosphere to the acidity of sea water on the basis of equilibrium with calcium carbonate so that

$$P_{CO_2} = (K_p K_1)^{-1} \left(\frac{2K_{SP}}{K_2}\right)^{\frac{1}{2}} \left[H^+\right]^{\frac{3}{2}}$$

where

$K_p\ \ = 10^{-1\cdot47}$ CO_2 (gas)$+H_2O$ (liquid)$=H_2CO_3$ (aqueous)
$K_1\ \ = 10^{-6\cdot4}$ H_2CO_3 (aqueous)$=H^+$ (aqueous)$+HCO_3^-$ (aqueous)
$K_2\ \ = 10^{-10\cdot3}$ HCO_3^- (aqueous)$=H^+$ (aqueous) $+CO_3^{--}$ (aqueous)
$K_{SP} = 10^{-8\cdot3}$ $CaCO_3$ (solid)$-H_2O$ (liquid)$=Ca^{++}$ (aqueous)$+CO_3^{--}$ (aqueous)

and

K_W will be 10^{-14} H_2O (liquid)$=H^+$ (aqueous)$+OH^-$ (aqueous)

Carbon dioxide, the respiratory waste of animals and the beginning of photosynthesis in plants, dissolves to form carbonic acid with water and this reacts with calcium carbonate increasing the pH thus:

$$H_2CO_3 + CaCO_3 = Ca^{++} + 2HCO_3^-$$

Hydrogen ions from the dissociation of carbonic acid are partly utilised to form bicarbonate ions from carbonate ions derived from dissociation of $CaCO_3$. The appropriate chemical reactions have been expressed above together with K, their associated equilibrium constants (including dissociation constants and solubility product constants) at 25°C.

Turning to oxidation–reduction in the oceans, the half reaction in normal sea water which determines the oxidation–reduction potential (Eh) is:

$$2H_2O = 4e^- + O_2 + 4H^+$$

Oceanic water is a highly oxidising solution. However, in near-shore areas and restricted basins the effect of organisms in depleting the dissolved oxygen content is to lower Eh causing more reduced states in some of the elements.

Nutrient elements occur in the oceans and include carbon, oxygen, nitrogen and phosphorus as amino acids (the constituents of proteins), fats, sugars, etc. which are important plant and animal compounds, and as dissolved bicarbonate, nitrate and phosphate). Carbon is fixed by photosynthesis and nitrogen and phosphorus are also extracted from solution in the uppermost few hundred metres of the seas where light penetrates (the photic zone). Some organic particles settle through the water, others are removed by organisms. In the deeper layers bacterial action destroys much of this and returns the nutrient elements to ionic form. The overall consequence is enrichment of the deeper layers and depletion of the surface layers in the nutrient elements and steady state concentration gradients arise. In some areas aeration is too slow compared with the rate at which biologically usable organic material is supplied. Here the result is stagnation at depths in which organic compounds are employed by anaerobic bacteria deriving oxygen by reduction of sulphate to sulphide. Some instances are the Black Sea and the Cariaco trench in the Caribbean as well as some fjords.

Other nutrient elements occur and a number of their distributions have been studied. For instance Cd, Zn, Ni and Cu distributions in the North Pacific Ocean were described by K. W. Bruland in 1980.[50] Cadmium concentrations were found to average 1·4 pmol/kg in the surface waters of the central North Pacific and appear to show a strong correlation with the labile nutrients such as phosphate and nitrate increasing to values of 1·1 nmol/kg at depths corresponding to the phosphate maximum. Zinc is depleted in surficial waters of the central gyre to an average value of 0·07 nmol/kg and increases to a deep maximum of 9 nmol/kg in correlation with the nutrient silicate. Nickel averages 2·1 nmol/kg in surface central gyre waters, increasing to a deep maximum of 11 nmol/kg correlatable to phosphate and silicate. Copper averages less than 0·5 nmol/kg in the central North Pacific surface waters, increasing to 5 nmol/kg in bottom waters, profiles showing evidence of intermediate and deep water scavenging.

As regards particle settlement in the oceans, S. Krishnamurti and his associates in 1981 described their chemical and radiochemical investigations of surface and deep particles of the Indian Ocean.[51] The mean settling velocities were investigated and calculated from particulate ^{230}Th data using a one-dimensional settling model and came out at c. 2×10^{-3} cm/sec. This is incompatible with the particulate ^{210}Pb depth profiles probably because these two isotopes are scavenged by different size populations of particles. ^{230}Th and ^{210}Pb concentration profiles were found to increase monotonously with depth probably due to *in situ* scavenging of the isotopes from the water column by settling particles. Comparing the Indian Ocean with the Pacific and Atlantic Oceans it appears from the composition and settling velocities of particles and their geographical distribution that they are controlled by similar processes throughout the marine hydrosphere.

Many elements enter into the biological composition of plankton. For instance Co is a requisite for the structure of vitamin B_{12} and Cu is necessary for haemocyanin in the blood of Crustacea while many shell-forming elements exist such as calcium, silicon, strontium, magnesium, barium and even radium. Metals may be accumulated through bonds in polysaccharides which constitute components of chitinous and mucous tissue. The accompanying table is relevant (Table 5.12).

TABLE 5.12

PLANKTON: CHEMICAL COMPOSITION (IN UNITS OF MICROGRAMS OF ELEMENT PER GRAM OF DRY WEIGHT PLANKTON)

Element	Phytoplankton (microscopic photosynthesising organisms such as diatoms and Coccolithophoridae)	Zooplankton (primarily Crustacea, Foraminifera, Radiolaria and larvae)
Si	58 000	—
Na	110 000	68 000
K	12 000	11 000
Mg	14 000	8 500
Ca	6 100	15 000
Sr	320	440
Ba	110	25
Al	200	23
Fe	650	96
Mn	9	4
Ti	≤ 30	—
Cr	≤ 4	—
Cu	8·5	14
Ni	4	6
Zn	54	120
Ag	0·4	0·1
Cd	2	2
Pb	8	2
Hg	0·2	0·1

A number of metals become concentrated in plankton in comparison with sea water and this parallels the situation with nitrogen and phosphorus. It may be stated that, to a first approximation, trace elements are concentrated with the same degree of efficiency as the nutrient elements.

Since it is known that nitrogen and phosphorus are regenerated as dissolved species within the uppermost 500 m of the seas and very little actually reaches the ocean floor, it would be interesting to ascertain the fate of the trace metals as plankton is processed in the food chain. Probably most are returned to the sea water at a rate similar to the return rate for nitrogen and phosphorus. However, some element-transporting debris does reach the ocean floor (deep sea oozes, for instance) and this biogenic material provides reactive surfaces on which further reactions can take place during their descent through the water column. That this happens is verified using ^{210}Pb produced from dissolved radium-226 in the ocean. As this isotope of lead has a half-life of 22 years and the deep ocean water is two orders of magnitude older, ^{210}Pb ought to be in equilibrium abundance with radium-226 and any departure from the equilibrium ratio would indicate that lead-210 is being removed by adsorption scavenging by particles falling through the water and the same argument applies to thorium-230. As noted earlier, this does occur and indeed the higher the biological productivity in the overlying water, the greater the scavenging of these isotopes from the deep water column.[51]

Where rivers meet oceans they sometimes produce estuaries and the circulation in them is driven by the supply of fresh water. Local modification of the composition of the ocean may occur. Biological productivity is high in estuaries and depth is relatively shallow so that a large organic flux reaches the bottom and there joins the load flux ultimately derived from storm transport and erosion. Such organic-rich deposits are an excellent food source for benthos and organisms such as Crustacea, and Mollusca can metabolise it with oxygenated water from above through mechanisms such as bioturbation. At greater depths and in anaerobic environments the sediment contains anoxic interstitial sea water and here, as noted earlier, sulphate-reducing bacteria can convert the dissolved sulphate to H_2S and metabolise the organic material thus:

$$2CH_2O + SO_4^{--} = 2HCO_3^- + H_2S$$
(organic
matter)

Hydrogen sulphide has a great effect on the solubility of metals (see Table 5.11). Most metals are immobilised in anoxic sediments, but reduction of iron from Fe^{3+} to Fe^{2+} and manganese from Mn^{4+} to

Mn^{2+} will greatly increase their solubilities. Consequently, bioturbating organisms release a flux of such reduced metal ions to overlying water and on encountering oxygenated water these are reoxidised and may precipitate as oxides. Later transportation to the deep sea in particulate form may influence the composition of deep sea sediments.

In Long Island Sound which is adjacent to heavily urbanised areas, sediments accumulate at a rate of 0·45 cm/year according to J. Thomson and his associates.[52] As a first approximation, it is suggested that this rate can be assumed for most of the East Coast of the USA estuarine areas. If these have an average depth of 40 m then all should be filled with sediment in under 10 000 years and a reshaping of the coast may be anticipated within the next 10 000 years. The more recent sediments are found to be richer in metals than the older ones and this applies both to coastal and lake sediments. It is believed that this may be ascribed to the industrialisation of the region, some of the metals arriving as a result of atmospheric processes and some being transported through the activity of rivers, outfalls from sewers and dumping barges.

A material balance may be constructed for many of the major dissolved species which are transported to the seas by river systems and the total quantity of such material is thought to be approximately 36×10^{14} g/year, the supply of detritus exceeding this by perhaps a factor of five. Obviously because of climatic and rock variability there will be a great variation in the composition of streams in different parts of the Earth, but the average is suggested in Table 5.13.[20]

TABLE 5.13
AVERAGE STREAM COMPOSITION

Component	Measured concentration		Amount due to marine aerosols	Derived by weathering	
	mg/litre	mM/litre	mM/litre	mM/litre	mg/litre
HCO_3^-	58·4	0·957	—	0·957	58·4
SO_4^{--}	11·2	0·116	0·011	0·105	10·1
Cl^-	7·8	0·219	0·219	0	0
NO_3^-	1	0·016	—	0·016	1
Ca^{++}	15	0·375	0·004	0·371	14·8
Mg^{++}	4·1	0·171	0·022	0·149	3·6
Na^+	6·3	0·274	0·188	0·086	2
K^+	2·3	0·059	0·004	0·055	2·1
SiO_2	13·1	0·211	—	0·211	13·1

Calcium and magnesium derive mainly from weathering of limestones and dolomite, the primary agent being carbonic acid. Sulphate is formed by the oxidation of sulphide minerals.

The marine budgets of Ca, Si, Na, K, Mg and S may be considered. The first, calcium, is removed from sea water mainly by deposition as shell material by certain groups of organisms. The oceanic balance is thought to be as shown in Table 5.14.

TABLE 5.14
$CaCO_3$ BALANCE IN THE OCEANS

	Average percentage of $CaCO_3$ in deep sea sediments	Average clay accumulation rate $(g/cm^2/1000\ years)$	Total $CaCO_3$ accumulation rate $(10^{16}g$ $CaCO_3/1000\ years)$
Atlantic	43·7	1·2	77
Pacific	37·8	0·3?	30
India and all others	—	—	30
Total			137
Rates of Atlantic Ocean and all other oceans equal			154
Rate of all other oceans equal to half the Atlantic Ocean rate			115
Stream supply			122

The average clay accumulation rate in Table 5.14 is required because many cores are unusually rich in $CaCO_3$ and hence give a biased sampling as regards this compound unless this correction is made. The table demonstrates that far more calcium carbonate is being deposited in the Atlantic Ocean than elsewhere and, since this ocean is not bounded by subduction zones, it will be retained in deep sea sediments until such time as new spreading patterns arise to destroy the existing floor.

There are two methods of removal of silicon from sea water, namely:

(i)   through inorganic reaction with clay minerals;
(ii) through organic removal by diatoms, radiolaria, etc.

Deposition of this element occurs in some places, notably the Gulf of California where the total rate of deposition is a hundred times greater than the supply from local streams. Actually the major dissolved fluxes both of silicon and calcium are in the Atlantic Ocean north of 20°S latitude where almost two-thirds of the stream water of the Earth enters the sea. Most of the calcium is deposited as carbonate in the Atlantic as stated above but because of the long residence time of this element in the oceans there is no direct relationship between supply area and area of deposition. The mean residence time of silicon is much shorter, $c.$ 10^4 years as compared with 10^6 years for calcium, and oceanic circulation is rapid enough to separate supply points from points of deposition. Table 5.15 shows relevant information.[20]

TABLE 5.15

SILICON BALANCE IN THE OCEANS

Supply	10^{14} g SiO_2/year
Stream supply rate	4·3
Submarine alteration of basalts	0·003
Solution of glacial debris	?
Total	4·303

Removal in oceans	10^{14} g SiO_2/year
Antarctic	0·11–0·38
Pacific sub-arctic	0·2
Equatorial Pacific	0·005
Berin Sea	0·1
Okhotsk Sea	0·15
Gulf of California	0·15
Total	0·99
Silica removed, e.g. in upwelling areas mostly in the Pacific	3·34

Sodium, potassium and magnesium are not biogenically deposited to any sizeable degree and although magnesium can substitute for calcium in carbonates no dominant pelagic calcium carbonate has been found to contain more than $c.$ 0.05% magnesium. Hence the Mg/Ca ratio deposited biogenically may be given as $c.$ 0.001. Streams supply these elements in the ratio 0.2 and about 5% goes to pelagic $CaCO_3$ with 95% being accounted for in other repositories. Even stricter constraints act on sodium and potassium because even less of these find a repository in $CaCO_3$ than is the case for magnesium. All three of these elements may be trapped as part of the pore waters in marine sediments.

The marine budget of sulphur may be examined. The element is brought to the seas as sulphate ion which is reduced by anaerobic bacteria in anoxic muds in shallow continental shelf areas with high organic contents. H_2S produced does not usually reach the overlying oceanic water in large quantities because it reacts with iron oxide in sediments to produce iron sulphide. Sulphate may also be removed from sea water by precipitation as calcium sulphate in regions of high evaporation such as the Persian Gulf or the Mexican salinas. Gypsum deposits are formed at low temperatures in such environments and evaporite formations preserved.

Some recent research of great interest in deep sea isotopic investigations should be mentioned. A high resolution global deep sea chronology for the last 750 000 years has been investigated by J. J. Morley and J. D. Hays.[53] They point out that there is ever-growing evidence that the timing and amplitude of variations in the ratio of $^{18}O/^{16}O$ in shells of calcareous benthic organisms are produced by global ice volume changes and so should be globally synchronous, limited solely by the mixing time of the ocean and the effects of bioturbation. In fact such characteristic variations have been utilised as the basis of a high resolution stratigraphy for the late Pleistocene by N. J. Shackleton.[54] Investigations have shown that the spectra of oxygen isotope records form distinct frequency peaks which have periods similar to those of the planetary orbital variations of eccentricity, obliquity and precession and this suggests that such astronomical variations play a significant role in determining the timing of major ice volume changes. This has led to attempts to convert this high resolution oxygen isotope stratigraphy into a precise chronology. Of course there is no *a priori* reason for believing that the frequency distribution of other geochemical or palaeontological parameters in widely separated deep sea cores should have a common frequency distribution. This would be the case if changes in northern hemisphere ice volume so dominated the global climatic system that all climatic changes harmonised with it on these time scales. This appears to be inherently unlikely. In order to compare in detail disparate geochemical and other records, it is necessary to have a common time scale applicable to all. J. D. Hays and his associates developed one for the last 450 000 years (TUNE-UP) based on the premise that frequency components of the oxygen isotope record having periods similar to Earth's orbital variations are phase locked with them.[55] Similar reasoning led M. A. Kominz and his associates to generate an age model for an equatorial Pacific core (V28–238) spanning the last 750 000 years; this was constructed by adjusting age estimates so as to phase lock the 41 000 year component of the oxygen isotope record with obliquity.[56] No attempt was made to phase lock the 23 000 year component of the oxygen isotope record with precession. Their time scale (TWEAQ) is identical (except for isotopic 1–2 boundary) with TUNE-UP through the last 350 000 years. Another time scale for the last 750 000 years can be constructed using data from C. Emiliani.[57] He calculated the arithmetic mean thickness of each oxygen isotope stage in a set of deep sea cores from the equatorial Atlantic, Caribbean and equatorial Pacific Oceans and assigned an age of 125 000 years to the isotopic sub-stage 5e and 700 000 years to the Brunhes–Matuyama magnetic reversal and determined the average duration of specific isotopic stages. Obviously a complete isotopic record is mandatory in order to improve the time scale for the past 750 000 years and also the astronomical parameters must be accurately known.

Eccentricity varies from 0 to 0·6 with an average period of 95 800 years during the last 750 000 years. Obliquity, the angle between the equatorial and ecliptic planes, varies between 22·1° and 24·5° with an average period of 41 000 years. Precession is a function of eccentricity and the longitude of perihelion based upon the moving equinox and is a quasi-periodic parameter with periods clustered about 23 000 and 19 000 years. Through careful correlation of oxygen isotope records in deep sea cores J. J. Morley and J. D. Hays made a composite isotopic section spanning the last 750 000 years with an average sedimentation rate of 2·3 cm/1000 years. A new chronology for the period was developed by adjustment of the ages of the oxygen isotope stage boundaries in this composite section so as to extend the consistent phase relationships existing between variations in oxygen isotope ratios and changes in the astronomical parameters during the last 300 000 years to the whole 750 000 year record. Previously identified difficulties in phase locking precession with the filtered isotopic signal between 365 000 and 465 000 years have been resolved with the recognition that precessional variations have an average period of 19 000 years and not 23 000 years during the interval. Since this new age model yields the best match between variations in obliquity and precession and their corresponding frequency components in the oxygen isotope record, the authors believed that it presents the most accurate chronology yet developed for deep sea sediments.

With the new age model providing the time control, power spectral analyses of South Atlantic and sub-Antarctic chemical and biotic indices show that there is a strong tendency for variance to be concentrated at frequencies corresponding to periods of ∼100 000, 41 000 and 23 000 years. Abundance variations of the radiolarian *Cycladophora davisiana* were used during this work and this species constitutes a stratigraphic tool of great importance for Pleistocene North Atlantic and interhemispheric correlations according to J. J. Morley and J. D. Hays.[58] The abundance changes of the species seem to be synchronous over $> 300\,000\,m^2$ of the late Pleistocene ($\simeq 300\,000$ years) and comparison with the oxygen isotope records in North Atlantic and sub-Antarctic cores suggests that *C. davisiana* fluctuations in the North Atlantic and Antarctica are also synchronous. This apparent synchronicity suggests a similarity of some related environmental factors.

The Brunhes time scale and interpretation of climatic change discussed by M. A. Kominz and his associates referred to the use of two new $\delta^{18}O$ time scales. The first is based on a constant accumulation rate of Al (acceptable for the past 360 000 years according to the authors) and it gives an age of 693 000 years for the Brunhes–Matuyama reversal. The second is derived from tuning the $\delta^{18}O$ record of core V28–238 to the record of the Earth's obliquity and this gave an age of 728 000 years for the age of this reversal.

Work has been done on Greenland ice cores with reference to past volcanism and climate by C. U. Hammer *et al.*[59] A new method was devised to measure annual injections of volcanic acids (mostly sulphuric) into the upper troposphere and stratosphere and the potentiality of it was demonstrated by data on some historically well known eruptions. Analyses of annual layers in a mid-Greenland ice core reveal a continuous year by year record of the volcanic activity north of 20°S back to 553 A.D. Comparison with various climatic records suggests that periods of frequent and violent eruptions usually coincide with cold climatic conditions. Thus, for instance, the highest volcanic activities since 553 A.D. occurred in 1250 A.D. to 1500 A.D. and 1550 A.D. to 1700 A.D., i.e. in the initial and culminating phases of the Little Ice Age.

Satellites are being used increasingly for study of the oceans. For instance, a comparison of radar altimetry with IR and *in situ* data for the detection of the surface boundaries of the Gulf Stream using data derived from the GEOS-3 satellite has been made by C. D. Leitao *et al.* in 1979.[60] The radar altimeter is capable of sensing these boundaries with as much precision as the IR-derived data analysis and both techniques provided excellent agreement with the *in situ* data.

Ridge studies progress and a recent investigation of ^3He indicated hydrothermal activity as probably occurring in the mid-Atlantic ridge. W. F. Jenkins and P. A. Rona with J. M. Edmond in 1980 indicated that significant patterns of excess ^3He in bottom waters over the mid-Atlantic ridge in the 'TAG Hydrothermal Field' occurred and the lateral regional gradients are comparable in magnitude to gradients observed in the above mentioned Galapagos rift where hydrothermal activity is known.[61] Hence it is inferred here. The site is at 26°N.

Recent work on the thorium isotope content of ocean water may be mentioned; this was done by W. S. Moore in 1981.[62] ^{232}Th concentrations of surface and deep Pacific Ocean waters are 0·01–0·02 dpm/1000 kg (60 pgm/kg). The ^{230}Th activity is given as 0·03 to 0·13 dpm/1000 kg in surface waters and 0·3 to 2·7 dpm/1000 kg in deep waters. Chemical residence times based upon *in situ* production from parent isotopes are approximately the same for ^{230}Th and ^{220}Th in surface waters (1–5 years) but are greater by a factor of ten for ^{230}Th in deep waters (10–100 years). Apparently there are additional sources of ^{230}Th into deep waters. At MANOP (manganese nodule project) site S manganese nodule tops are enriched in thorium isotopes by adsorption of thorium from sea water and not by incorporation of thorium-rich particulates. Interesting data on the growth rates of manganese nodules in Oneida Lake, New York, were given by W. S. Moore and his associates in 1980.[63] ^{226}Ra was used to provide information on discontinuous gradients in contents of this isotope resulting from periods of rapid growth (> 1 mm/100 years) separated by periods of no growth of erosion. The nodules' 'age' approximates the age of the lake, but the nodules are not sediment covered because they occur only in areas of the lake where fine grained sediments are not accumulating.

REFERENCES

1. TUREKIAN, K. K., 1972. *Chemistry of the Earth*, Holt, Rinehart and Winston, NY.
2. HESS, H. H., 1962. History of ocean basins. in: *Petrologic Studies: A Volume in Honour of A. F. Buddington*, ed. A. E. J. Engel *et al.*, Geol. Soc. Am., Boulder, Colorado.
3. HEEZEN, B. C., 1962. The deep sea floor. in: *Continental Drift*, ed. S. K. Runcorn, Academic Press, NY.
4. LEYDEN, R., SHERIDAN, R. and EWING, M., 1969. Symp. on continental drift emphasizing the history of the South Atlantic area, Montevideo, Uruguay, October 1967, quoted in *The Earth's Crust and Upper Mantle*. Geophys. Monograph 13, ed. P. J. Hart, Am. Geophys. Union, Washington DC.
5. CULKIN, 1960. In: *Chemical Oceanography*, ed. Riley and Skirrow, Academic Press, NY.
6. RICE, T. R. and WOLFE, D. A., 1971. Radioactivity—chemical and biological aspects. in: *Impingement of Man on the Oceans*, ed. D. W. Hood, John Wiley and Sons, London and New York, 328.

7. CORTECCI, G., NOTO, P. and MOLCARD, R., 1974. Tritium and sulfate oxygen profiles in the Mediterranean Sea: some profiles in the low Tyrrhenian Basin. *Boll. di Geofisica Teorica ed Applicata*, **XVI**, 64, 292–8.
8. JOHANNESSEN, O. M. and LEE, O. S., 1972. A deep thermohaline staircase in the Mediterranean Saclant (ASW Res. Centre), La Spezia, Italy, Sp. Rept M-74.
9. CORTECCI, G. and LONGINELLI, A., 1968. Oxygen isotope measurements of sulphate ions separated from diluted solutions. *Earth Planet. Sci. Letts*, **4**, 325–7.
10. LONGINELLI, A. and CORTECCI, G., 1970. Composizione isotopica dell' ossigeno nei solfati. Techniche di misura. *Rend. Soc. Ital. Min. Petrol.*, **XXVI**, 733–43.
11. CRAIG, H., 1961. Standard for reporting concentrations of deuterium and oxygen-18 in natural waters. *Science*, **133**, 1833–4.
12. OZTURGUT, E., 1976. The sources and spreading of the Levantine Intermediate Water in the eastern Mediterranean. Saclant (ASW Res. Centre), La Spezia, Italy, Rept SM-92.
13. CORTECCI, G., NOTO, P. and TONARELLI, B., 1979. Tritium and oxygen profiles in the eastern Mediterranean. *Tellus*, **31** (2), 179–83.
14. CAMERON, J. F., 1967. Survey of systems for concentration and low background counting of tritium in water. In: *Isotopes in Hydrology*, Proc, Symp. Vienna, 14–18 November 1966, IAEA, Vienna, 543–73.
15. KING, C. A. M., 1972. *Beaches and Coasts*, 2nd ed., Edward Arnold, London, 570 pp.
16. DEACON, G. E. R., 1949. Waves and swell. *O. J. Roy. Met. Soc.*, **75**, 227–38.
17. DAVIES, J. L., 1964. A morphogenetic approach to world coastlines. *Zeit. für Geom.*, Sp. No. 127–42.
18. KOMAR, P. D., 1971. The mechanism of sand transport on beaches. *J. Geophys. Res.*, **76**, 713–8.
19. EDEN, G. E. and BRIGGS, R., 1967. Radioisotope techniques developed in water pollution studies. In: *Isotopes in Hydrology*, Proc. Symp. Vienna, 14–18 November 1966, IAEA, Vienna, 190–206.
20. TUREKIAN, K. K., 1976. *Oceans*. Prentice-Hall Inc., NJ.
21. MERO, J., 1965. *The Mineral Resources of the Sea*. Elsevier, Amsterdam.
22. BOWEN, R. and GUNATILAKA, A., 1979. *Copper: Its Geology and Economics*. Applied Science Publishers Ltd, London.
23. VINE, F. J., 1966. Spreading of the ocean floor: new evidence. *Science*, **154**, 1405–15.
24. BULLARD, E. C., 1974. Minerals from the deep sea. *Endeavour*, **33**, 119, 80–5.
25. DEGENS, E. T., 1965. *Geochemistry of Sediments*. Prentice-Hall Inc., NJ.
26. TRUDINGER, P. A., LAMBERT, L. B. and SKYRING, G. W., 1972. Biogenic sulphide ores: a feasibility study. *Econ. Geol.*, **67**, 1114–27.
27. BOWEN, R., 1980. *Ground Water*. Applied Science Publishers Ltd, London.
28. LIBBY, W. F., 1955. *Radiocarbon Dating*. John Wiley and Sons, London and New York.
29. VINE, F. J. and MATTHEWS, D. H., 1963. Magnetic anomalies over oceanic ridges. *Nature*, **199**, 947–9.
30. HEIRTZLER, J. R., 1968. Marine magnetic anomalies, geomagnetic field reversals and motions of the ocean floor and continents. *J. Geophys. Res.*, **73**, 2119–36.

268 SURFACE WATER

31. Cox, A., Dalrymple, G. B. and Doell, R. R., 1967. Reversals of the Earth's magnetic field. *Sci. Amer.*, **216**, 44–54.
32. Bowen, R., 1966. Paleotemperature analysis. No. 2 in the series *Methods in Geochemistry and Geophysics*. Elsevier, Amsterdam.
33. Wilson, J. T., 1965. A new class of faults and their bearing on continental drift. *Nature*, **207**, 343–7.
34. Hallam, A., 1974. A revolution in the earth sciences. *From Continental Drift to Plate Tectonics*. Clarendon Press, Oxford.
35. Johnson, B. D., Powell, C. McA. and Veevers, J. J., 1980. Early spreading history of the Indian Ocean between India and Australia. *Earth Planet. Sci. Letts*, **47**, 131–43.
36. Norton, I. O. and Sclater, J. G., 1979. A model for the evolution of the Indian Ocean and the break-up of Gondwanaland. *J. Geophys. Res.*, **84**, 6803–30.
37. Burke, K., Fox, P. J. and Sengor, A. M. C., 1978. Buoyant ocean floor and the evolution of the Caribbean. *J. Geophys. Res.*, **83**, 3949–54.
38. Freeland, G. L. and Dietz, R. S., 1971. Plate tectonic evolution of the Caribbean–Gulf of Mexico region. *Nature*, **232**, 20–3.
39. Cochran, James R., 1981. The Gulf of Aden: structure and evolution of a young ocean basin and continental margin. *J. Geophys. Res.*, **86**, 263–87.
40. Green, K. E., von Herzen, R. P. and Williams, D. L., 1981. The Galapagos spreading centre at 86°W: a detailed geothermal field study. *J. Geophys. Res.*, **86**, 979–86.
41. Allmendinger, R. W. and Riis, F., 1979. The Galapagos rift at 86°W. 1. Regional morphological and structural analysis. *J. Geophys. Res.*, **84**, 5379–89.
42. Van Andel, T. H. and Ballard, R. D., 1979. The Galapagos rift at 86°W. 2. Volcanism, structure and evolution of the rift valley. *J. Geophys. Res.*, **84**, 5390–406.
43. Ballard, R. D., 1979. The Galapagos rift at 86°W. 3. Sheet flows, collapse pits and lava lakes of the rift valley. *J. Geophys. Res.*, **84**, 5407–22.
44. Crane, Kathleen and Ballard, R. D., 1980. Structure and morphology of hydrothermal fields and their relationship to the volcanic and tectonic processes of the rift valley (the Galapagos rift at 86°W). *J. Geophys. Res.*, **85**, 1443–54.
45. Hager, B. H. and O'Connell, R. J., 1981. A simple model of plate dynamics and mantle convection. *J. Geophys. Res.*, **86**, 4843–67.
46. Dickinson, W. R. and Snyder, W. S., 1979. Geometry of triple junctions related to San Andreas transform. *J. Geophys. Res.*, **84**, 561–72.
47. Zandt, George, 1981. Seismic images of the deep structure of the San Andreas fault system, central Coast Ranges, California. *J. Geophys. Res.*, **86**, 5039–52.
48. McKenzie, D., 1978. Active tectonics of the Alpine Himalayan belt: the Aegean sea and surrounding regions. *Geophys. J., Roy. Astron. Soc.*, **55**, 217–54.
49. Le Pichon, X. and Sibuet, J. C., 1981. Passive margins: a model of formation. *J. Geophys. Res.*, **86**, 3708–20.

50. BRULAND, K. W., 1980. Oceanographic distributions of Cd, Zn, Ni, and Cu in the north Pacific. *Earth Planet. Sci. Letts*, **47**, 176–98.
51. KRISHNAMURTI, S., SARIN, M. M. and SOMAYAJULU, B. L. K., 1981. Chemical and radiochemical investigations of surface and deep particles of the Indian Ocean. *Earth Planet. Sci. Letts*, **54**, 81–96.
52. THOMSON, J., TUREKIAN, K. K. and MCCAFFREY, R. J., 1975. in: *Estuarine Research*, ed. L. Cronin, 28–44.
53. MORLEY, J. J. and HAYS, J. D., 1981. Towards a high resolution global deep sea chronology for the last 750 000 years. *Earth Planet. Sci. Letts*, **53**, 279–95.
54. SHACKLETON, N. J., 1977. The oxygen isotope stratigraphic record of the late Pleistocene. *Phil. Trans. Roy. Soc., Lond., Ser. B*, **280**, 169–82.
55. HAYS, J. D., IMBRIE, J. and SHACKLETON, N. J., 1976. Variations in the Earth's orbit: pacemaker of the ice ages. *Science*, **194**, 1121–32.
56. KOMINZ, M. A., HEATH, G. R., KU, TI-L. and PISIAS, N. G., 1979. Brunhes time scales and the interpretation of climatic change. *Earth Planet. Sci. Letts*, **45**, 394–410.
57. EMILIANI, C., 1978. The cause of the ice ages. *Earth Planet. Sci. Letts*, **37**, 349–54.
58. MORLEY, J. J. and HAYS, J. D., 1979. *Cycladophora davisiana*: a stratigraphic tool for the Pleistocene North Atlantic and interhemispheric correlations. *Earth Planet. Sci. Letts*, **44**, 383–9.
59. HAMMER, C. U., CLAUSEN, H. B. and DANSGAARD, W., 1981. Past volcanism and climate revealed by Greenland ice cores. *J. Volcanol. and Geothermal Res.*, **11**, 3–10.
60. LEITAO, C. D., HUANG, N. E. and PARR, C. G., 1979. A note on the comparison of radar altimetry with IR and *in situ* data for the detection of the Gulf Stream surface boundaries. *J. Geophys. Res.*, **84**, 3969–73.
61. JENKINS, W. F., RONA, P. A. and EDMOND, J. M., 1980. Excess ^{3}He in the deep water over the mid-Atlantic ridge at 26°N: evidence of hydrothermal activity. *Earth Planet. Sci. Letts*, **49**, 39–44.
62. MOORE, W. S., 1981. The thorium isotope content of ocean water. *Earth Planet. Sci. Letts*, **53**, 419–26.
63. MOORE, W. S., DEAN, W. E., KRISHNASWAMI, S. and BOROLE, D. V., 1980. Growth rates of manganese nodules in Oneida Lake, N. Y. *Earth Planet. Sci. Letts*, **46**, 191–200.

Appendix

1. THE PROTO-ATLANTIC OCEAN

In this book detailed references have been made to the existing Atlantic Ocean and its comparative youth. Consequently, it is interesting to record the views of several geologists that, in order to apply the plate tectonic theory to the formation of the Caledonide–Appalachian fold belt now extending from Great Britain to the eastern USA, it is necessary to postulate a Proto-Atlantic Ocean opening in the Lower Palaeozoic era and closing during the late Palaeozoic era, thus existing within the time interval from approximately 570 million years to approximately 225 million years before the present.[1] This has been termed the Iapetus Ocean.[2] There is evidence favouring its existence along a region which now comprises the middle of the fold belt.[3,4]

As regards the opening phase of the Iapetus Ocean, the following observations may be made:

   (i)   Data of faunal provinces suggest increasing separation of the European and American species during the Cambrian and Lower Ordovician periods and only Ordovician and Silurian oceanic sediments are preserved since earlier (Cambrian) ones were probably destroyed during subduction.

  (ii)   Lata Precambrian and Lower Palaeozoic structural history on each side of the central (postulated) oceanic belt was very different.[5] There are slices of oceanic crust which were thrust locally on land as tectonic klippe (ophiolite complexes) and retain evidence of the types of early oceanic volcanics and sediments originally involved.

As regards the closing phase of the Iapetus Ocean, the following observations may be made:

(i) The initially distinctive European and American faunal provinces began to decline in the mid-Caradocian and the later Ordovician faunas provide evidence of mixing so that by the Silurian period the provinces became indistinguishable.

(ii) The formation of Benioff zones and therefore the contraction of the ocean is shown by the accumulation in the trench of oceanic sediments and volcanics, the formation of high pressure glaucophane-bearing assemblages and oceanic crust segments near the trench and the intrusion and extrusion of calc-alkaline plutonic and volcanic rocks on the continental margins.

(iii) The gradual elimination of the ocean yielded in certain localities to the onset of non-marine conditions in the Middle Silurian and by the Upper Silurian fish became restricted to brackish environments.[6] By the Devonian period Old Red Sandstone formed under desert (continental) conditions.

2. POLLUTION THREAT TO LAKE BAIKAL

This lake is believed to be about 20 million years old and supports 2681 known life types of which 84% are endemic including the Baikal seal and the golomyanka. The high oxygen level and relatively constant temperature from top to bottom have also sustained a microscopic shrimp (Epishura), a vital component of the life chain in the lake. At the end of the 1960s, a wood pulp mill was built at Baikalsk and pressure from environmentalists compelled subsequent installation of filters as an anti-pollution device. However, the Selenga river (the largest of the lake's 336 tributaries) still introduces pollution from the city of Ulan-Ude. Another problem arises from the Baikal–Amur mainline railway and of course the Trans-Siberian line has run peripherally to the southern shore since 1905. Finally oil tankers have been shipping oil through the lake to the BAM construction area and this could result in a spill. Conservationist measures have been made and a ban on fishing has restored stocks. It operated from 1969 to 1977. Also the seal population has grown to 70 000. This magnificent lake with winds capable of causing 15 foot waves remains endangered, however, and constant environmental controls remain necessary.

REFERENCES

1. WILSON, J. TUZO, 1966. Did the Atlantic close and then re-open? *Nature*, **211**, 676.
2. WINDLEY, BRIAN F., 1977. *The Evolving Continents.* John Wiley and Sons, London, p. 171.
3. DEWEY, J. F., 1969. Evolution of the Appalachian/Caledonian orogen. *Nature*, **222**, 124–9.
4. BIRD, J. M. and DEWEY, J. F., 1970. Lithosphere plate: continental margin tectonics and the evolution of the Appalachian orogen. *Bull. Geol. Soc. Am.*, **81**, 1031–59.
5. McKERROW, W. S. and ZIEGLER, A. M., 1972. Palaeozoic oceans. *Nature, Phys. Sci*, **240**, 92–4.
6. McKERROW, W. S. and ZIEGLER, A. M., 1972. Silurian palaeogeographic development of the Proto-Atlantic Ocean. *2nd International Geological Cong.*, Montreal, Sec. 6, 4–10.

Author Index

273

Subject Index

279

Places Index